Explorations in
CORE MATH
for Common Core Grade 6

© Houghton Mifflin Harcourt Publishing Company

 HOUGHTON MIFFLIN HARCOURT

Table of Contents Grade 6

COMMON CORE

Chapter 3 Decimals

Chapter 4 Number Theory and Fractions

► Chapter 5 Fraction Operations

► Chapter 6 Data Collection and Analysis

Chapter 7 Proportional Relationships

Chapter 8 Measurement and Geometry

Chapter 9 Integers and Coordinate Plane

Chapter 10 Functions

Learning the Standards for Mathematical Practice

The Common Core State Standards include eight Standards for Mathematical Practice. Here's how *Explorations in Core Math Grade 6* helps you learn those standards as you master the Standards for Mathematical Content.

① Make sense of problems and persevere in solving them.

In *Explorations in Core Math Grade 6*, you will work through Explores and Examples that present a solution pathway for you to follow. You are asked questions along the way so that you gain an understanding of the solution process, and then you will apply what you've learned in the Try This and Practice for the lesson.

> **2 EXAMPLE** Using Exponents to Write Expressions
>
> Use exponents to write each expression.
>
> A $6 \times 6 \times 6 \times 6 \times 6 \times 6 \times 6$
> What number is being multiplied? _____ This number is the base.
> How many times does the base appear in the product? _____ This number is the exponent.
> $6 \times 6 \times 6 \times 6 \times 6 \times 6 = $ _____
>
> B $\frac{2}{3} \times \frac{2}{3} \times \frac{2}{3}$
> What number is being multiplied? _____ This number is the base.
> How many times does the base appear in the product? _____ This number is the exponent.
> $\frac{2}{3} \times \frac{2}{3} \times \frac{2}{3} = $ _____

② Reason abstractly and quantitatively.

When you solve a real-world problem in *Explorations in Core Math Grade 6*, you will learn to represent the situation symbolically by translating the problem into a mathematical expression or equation. You will use these mathematical models to solve the problem and then state your answer in terms of the problem context. You will reflect on the solution process in order to check your answer for reasonableness and to draw conclusions.

> B Matthew throws a discus 58.7 meters. Zachary throws the discus 56.12 meters. How much farther did Matthew throw the discus?
>
> **Step 1** Align the decimal points.
> **Step 2** Add zeros as placeholders when necessary.
> **Step 3** Subtract from right to left, regrouping when necessary.
>
> | | 5 | 8 | . | 7 | |
> |---|---|---|---|---|---|
> | − | 5 | 6 | . | 1 | 2 |
> | | | | . | | |
>
> Matthew threw the discus _____ meters farther than Zachary.
>
> To check that your answer is reasonable, you can estimate. Round each decimal to the nearest whole number.
>
> 58.7 ⟶ _____
> − 56.12 ⟶ _____
>
> Check that your answer is close to your estimate.

> **2 EXAMPLE** Writing an Equation
>
> Mark scored 17 points in a basketball game. His teammates scored a total of *p* points, and the team as a whole scored 46 points. Write an equation to represent this situation.
>
>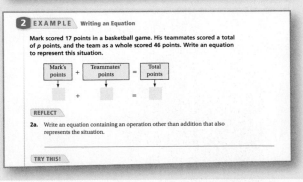
>
> **REFLECT**
>
> **2a.** Write an equation containing an operation other than addition that also represents the situation.
>
> _____
>
> **TRY THIS!**

③ Construct viable arguments and critique the reasoning of others.

Throughout *Explorations in Core Math Grade 6*, you will be asked to make conjectures, construct a mathematical argument, explain your reasoning, and justify your conclusions. Reflect questions offer opportunities for cooperative learning and class discussion. You will have additional opportunities to critique reasoning in Error Analysis problems.

3b. Error Analysis Marisol said, "Bailey's lemonade is stronger because it has more lemon juice. Bailey's lemonade has 3 cups of lemon juice, and Anna's lemonade has only 2 cups of lemon juice." Explain why Marisol is incorrect.

_____

_____

19. Reasoning The length of a particular object is x inches.

a. Will this object's length in centimeters be greater than x or less than x? Explain.

_____

_____

b. Will this object's length in meters be greater than x or less than x? Explain.

_____

_____

④ Model with mathematics.

Explorations in Core Math Grade 6 presents problems in a variety of contexts such as science, business, and everyday life. You will use mathematical models such as expressions, equations, tables, and graphs to represent the information in the problem and to solve the problem. Then you will interpret your results in the problem context.

Essential question: *How can you use equations, tables, and graphs to represent relationships between two variables?*

CC.6.EE.9

1 EXPLORE Equations in Two Variables

Tina is buying DVDs from an online store. Each DVD costs $8, and there is a flat fee of $6 for shipping.

Let x represent the number of DVDs that Tina buys. Let y represent Tina's total cost. An equation in two variables can represent the relationship between x and y.

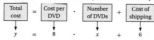

Total cost	=	Cost per DVD	·	Number of DVDs	+	Cost of shipping
y	=	8	·	x	+	6

Complete the table.

DVDs Bought x	$8x + 6$	Total Cost y ($)
1	8(1) + 6	14
2	8( ) + 6	
3	8( ) + 6	
4	8( ) + 6	
5	8( ) + 6	
6	8( ) + 6	
7	8( ) + 6	

REFLECT

1a. Look at the y-values in the right column of the table. What pattern do you see? What does this pattern mean in the problem?

_____

1b. A **solution of an equation in two variables** is an ordered pair (x, y) that makes the equation true. The ordered pair (1, 14) is a solution of $y = 8x + 6$. Write the other solutions from the table as ordered pairs.

_____

⑤ Use appropriate tools strategically.

You will use a variety of tools in *Explorations in Core Math Grade 6,* including manipulatives, paper and pencil, and technology. You might use manipulatives to develop concepts, paper and pencil to practice skills, and technology (such as graphing calculators, spreadsheets, or geometry software) to investigate more complicated mathematical ideas.

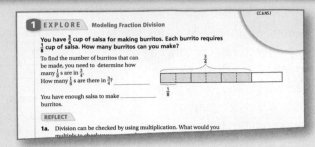

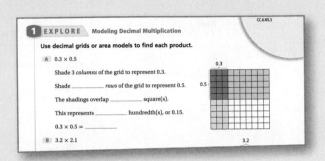

⑥ Attend to precision.

Precision refers not only to the correctness of arithmetic calculations, algebraic manipulations, and geometric reasoning but also to the proper use of mathematical language, symbols, and units to communicate mathematical ideas. Throughout *Explorations in Core Math Grade 6* you will demonstrate your skills in these areas when you are asked to calculate, describe, show, explain, prove, and predict.

REFLECT

2a. The answers to A and B are not the same, even though the expressions are very similar. Why?

_____

_____

TRY THIS!

Evaluate each expression for $n = 5$.

2b. $3(n + 1)$ _____   **2c.** $3n + 1$ _____   **2d.** $(4n - 4) + 14$ _____

2e. $4n - (4 + 14)$ _____   **2f.** $4(n - 4) + 14$ _____   **2g.** $6n + n^2$ _____

REFLECT

1a. Lisa evaluated the expressions $2x$ and x^2 for $x = 2$ and found that both expressions were equal to 4. Lisa concluded that $2x$ and x^2 are equivalent expressions. How could you show Lisa that she is incorrect?

_____

_____

1b. What does **1a** demonstrate about expressions?

_____

_____

In *Explorations in Core Math Grade 6,* you will look for patterns or regularity in mathematical structures such as expressions, equations, operations, geometric figures, and diagrams. You will use these patterns to generalize beyond a specific case and to make connections between related problems.

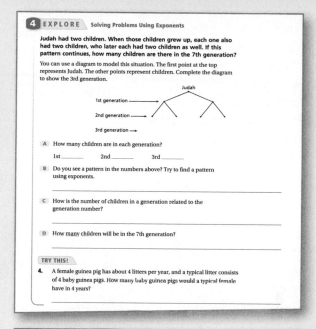

4 EXPLORE Solving Problems Using Exponents

Judah had two children. When those children grew up, each one also had two children, who later each had two children as well. If this pattern continues, how many children are there in the 7th generation?

You can use a diagram to model this situation. The first point at the top represents Judah. The other points represent children. Complete the diagram to show the 3rd generation.

A How many children are in each generation?

1st _____   2nd _____   3rd _____

B Do you see a pattern in the numbers above? Try to find a pattern using exponents.

_____

C How is the number of children in a generation related to the generation number?

_____

D How many children will be in the 7th generation?

_____

TRY THIS!

4. A female guinea pig has about 4 litters per year, and a typical litter consists of 4 baby guinea pigs. How many baby guinea pigs would a typical female have in 4 years?

1 EXPLORE Using Variables to Describe Patterns

Look at the pattern of squares below.

Stage 1   Stage 2   Stage 3

A What is the pattern? _____

How many squares will be in stage 4? _____

B What is the relationship between the stage number and the number of squares?

_____

Use this relationship to complete the table below.

Stage	1	2	3	4	5	6	7	8	
Squares	3	6	9						

C Let *n* represent any stage number. How many squares are in stage *n*?

_____

Add a column to the end of the table in **B** for stage *n*.

REFLECT

1. When might it be useful to know how many squares are in stage *n*?

Operations and Properties

Chapter Focus

You will continue improving your estimation skills as you learn to estimate quotients. You will divide multi-digit numbers using long division and check the reasonableness of your answers by estimating the quotients. Exponents are used to show repeated multiplication. You will use exponents to rewrite expressions and find the value of powers. The order of operations is a rule for simplifying expressions. You will write and simplify expressions using the order of operations including expressions with exponents. Properties of operations can be used to write equivalent expressions that make mental math easier. You will solve problems using the properties of operations and mental math.

Chapter at a Glance

Lesson		Standards for Mathematical Content
1-1	Estimating with Whole Numbers	CC.6.NS.2
1-2	Divide Multi-Digit Whole Numbers	CC.6.NS.2
1-3	Exponents	CC.6.EE.1
1-4	Order of Operations	CC.6.EE.2a, CC.6.EE.2c
1-5	Properties and Mental Math	CC.6.EE.3
	Problem Solving Connections	
	Performance Task	
	Assessment Readiness	

Unpacking the Standards

Understanding the standards and the vocabulary terms in the standards will help you know exactly what you are expected to learn in this chapter.

COMMON CORE **CC.6.NS.2**

Fluently divide multi-digit numbers using the standard algorithm.

Key Vocabulary

algorithm *(algoritmo)* A set of rules or procedure for solving a mathematical problem in a finite number of steps.

What It Means to You

You will learn how to divide multi-digit numbers by using long division.

EXAMPLE

A school wants to separate 364 students into equal-sized homeroom classes. There are 13 classrooms in the school that can be used for a homeroom. How many students will be in each homeroom?

Divide.

$$
\begin{array}{r}
28 \\
13\overline{)364} \\
-26\downarrow \\
\hline
104 \\
-104 \\
\hline
0
\end{array}
$$

So, each homeroom will have 28 students.

COMMON CORE **CC.6.EE.1**

Write and evaluate numerical expressions involving whole-number exponents.

Key Vocabulary

evaluate *(evaluar)* To find the value of a numerical or algebraic expression.

numerical expression *(expresión numérica)* An expression that contains only numbers and operations.

exponent *(exponente)* The number that indicates how many times the base is used as a factor.

What It Means to You

You will use exponents to show repeated multiplication.

EXAMPLE

Find the value of 6^4.

$$6^4$$
$$= 6 \times 6 \times 6 \times 6$$
$$= 1,296$$

COMMON CORE **CC.6.EE.2c**

Evaluate expressions at specific values of their variables. Include expressions that arise from formulas used in real-world problems. Perform arithmetic operations, including those involving whole number exponents, in the conventional order when there are no parentheses to specify a particular order (Order of Operations).

Key Vocabulary

expression *(expresión)* A mathematical phrase that contains operations, numbers, and/or variables.

formula *(fórmula)* A rule showing relationships among quantities.

What It Means to You

You will evaluate expressions, including expressions that represent real-world problems.

EXAMPLE

Regina bought 5 carved wooden beads for $3 each and 8 glass beads for $2 each. Simplify $5 \times 3 + 8 \times 2$ to find the amount Regina spent for beads.

$$5 \times 3 + 8 \times 2$$
$$= \quad 15 \quad + \quad 16$$
$$= \qquad 31$$

Regina spent $31 for beads.

COMMON CORE **CC.6.EE.3**

Apply the properties of operations to generate equivalent expressions.

Key Vocabulary

equivalent expression *(expresión equivalente)* Equivalent expressions have the same value for all values of the variables.

What It Means to You

Given an expression, you will write equivalent expressions.

EXAMPLE

Use the Distributive Property to find the product.

4 × 23

$4 \times 23 = 4 \times (20 + 3)$ *"Break apart" 23 into 20 + 3.*

$= (4 \times 20) + (4 \times 3)$ *Use the Distributive Property.*

$= \quad 80 \quad + \quad 12$ *Use mental math to multiply.*

$= \qquad 92$ *Use mental math to add.*

Key Vocabulary

base *(base)* When a number is raised to a power, the number that is used as a factor is the base.

equivalent expression *(expresión equivalente)* Equivalent expressions have the same value for all values of the variables.

exponent *(exponente)* The number that indicates how many times the base is used as a factor.

order of operations *(orden de las operaciones)* A rule for evaluating expressions: first perform the operations in parentheses, then compute powers and roots, then perform all multiplication and division from left to right, and then perform all addition and subtraction from left to right.

power *(potencia)* A number produced by raising a base to an exponent.

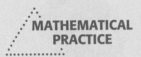

MATHEMATICAL PRACTICE

The Common Core Standards for Mathematical Practice describe varieties of expertise that mathematics educators at all levels should seek to develop in their students. Opportunities to develop these practices are integrated throughout this program.

1. Make sense of problems and persevere in solving them.
2. Reason abstractly and quantitatively.
3. Construct viable arguments and critique the reasoning of others.
4. Model with mathematics.
5. Use appropriate tools strategically.
6. Attend to precision.
7. Look for and make use of structure.
8. Look for and express regularity in repeated reasoning.

CHAPTER 1

Estimating with Whole Numbers
Going Deeper: Estimating Quotients

Essential question: *How do you estimate quotients?*

CC.6.NS.2

1 EXPLORE Estimating Quotients

A local petting zoo had a total of 98,464 visitors last year. The zoo was open every day except Thanksgiving, Christmas, and New Year's Day. Estimate the average number of visitors per day.

A To find the average number of visitors per day, you need to divide. To estimate the quotient, first estimate the dividend by rounding the number of visitors to the nearest ten thousand.

$$\text{divisor}\overline{)\text{dividend}}^{\text{quotient}}$$

98,464 rounded to the nearest ten thousand is _____.

B There were 365 days last year. How many days was the petting

zoo open? _____

C Estimate the divisor by rounding the number of days that the zoo was open to the nearest hundred.

_____ rounded to the nearest hundred is _____.

D Estimate the quotient. _____ ÷ _____ = _____

The average number of visitors per day last year was about _____.

REFLECT

1a. How can you check that your quotient is correct?

_____

_____

1b. Do you think that your estimate is greater than or less than the actual answer? Explain.

_____

_____

1c. **Error Analysis** A student said there were 250 visitors at the zoo each day last year. Explain why this is incorrect.

_____

_____

Estimate each quotient by rounding to the greatest place value.

1. 4,172 ÷ 53

_____

2. 7,890 ÷ 96

_____

3. 20,904 ÷ 490

_____

4. 63,011 ÷ 319

_____

5. 187)‾5‾2‾,‾1‾4‾7

_____

6. 87)‾9‾3‾,‾6‾0‾7

_____

The table shows the total number of text messages sent last month by the subscribers of four small cellular service companies.

Company	Subscribers	Text Messages
A	1,834	131,761
B	4,302	392,807
C	790	36,299
D	5,044	377,008

7. Estimate the average number of messages sent per subscriber for each company by rounding to the greatest place value.

Company A

_____ messages

Company B

_____ messages

Company C

_____ messages

Company D

_____ messages

8. Which company transmitted the most text messages per subscriber last month?

_____

9. Which two companies transmitted about the same number of text messages per subscriber last month?

_____

10. Reflect Why might you use estimation when solving a problem involving division?

_____

_____

_____

Additional Practice

Estimate each quotient.

1. $59 \div 6$

_____

2. $83 \div 4$

_____

3. $147 \div 5$

_____

4. $1,118 \div 9$

_____

5. $4,921 \div 6$

_____

6. $8,617 \div 32$

_____

7. $48\overline{)10,109}$

_____

8. $204\overline{)31,910}$

_____

9. $96\overline{)20,895}$

_____

10. $1,334 \div 29$

_____

11. $7,870 \div 52$

_____

12. $11,023 \div 15$

_____

13. $2,920 \div 18$

_____

14. $15,800 \div 40$

_____

15. $2,503 \div 53$

_____

16. $55,242 \div 617$

_____

17. $42,525 \div 173$

_____

18. $395 \div 39$

_____

19. Natalie is driving to see her aunt who lives 1,530 miles from Natalie's house. If Natalie drives 55 miles per hour, about how long will it take her to drive to her aunts house?

_____

20. The managers at an electronics store want to sell all 1,236 computers in the store's warehouse in 48 days. About home many computers does the staff need to sell each day to meet the goal?

_____

21. Ali, a gardener, is preparing to fertilize a lawn. The lawn is 30 yards by 25 yards. One bag of fertilizer will cover an area of 100 square yards. How many bags of fertilizer does Ali need to buy?

_____

Problem Solving

Write the correct answer.

1. At the school book fair, 2,786 books were displayed on 28 tables. If each table held the same number of books, about how many books were on each table?

_____

2. The book fair made $6,216 on the first day and $5,721 on the second day with books selling for an average price of $12 each. About how many books were sold during the first two days of the book fair?

_____

3. A caterer is setting up tables for an event. 263 guests plan to attend and the caterer wants no more than 18 people at each table. About how many tables should the caterer set up?

_____

4. Clara made $1,878 babysitting last summer. If she made $12 per hour, about how many hours did she babysit?

_____

Choose the letter for the best answer.

5. The Pacific Ocean is 35,837 feet deep at its greatest depth. There are 5,280 feet in a mile. About how many miles deep is the deepest point in the Pacific Ocean?

   A about 0.7 mile

   B about 7 miles

   C about 70 miles

   D about 700 miles

6. An airplane with 403 seats carried 8,045 passengers from Houston to Chicago last week. If all of the flights were close to full, about how many flights did the plane make last week?

   F about 10 flights

   G about 20 flights

   H about 32 flights

   J about 200 flights

7. A monorail train carries people from the parking lot of an airport to any terminal. A round-trip on the train takes 18 minutes. About how many round-trips does the train make in 9 hours?

   A about 2 round-trips

   B about 25 round-trips

   C about 50 round-trips

   D about 200 round-trips

8. If a monorail train can carry 78 people and makes 96 trips during the day, about how many people can it carry in one day?

   F about 8 people

   G about 800 people

   H about 8,000 people

   J about 80,000 people

1-2

Divide Multi-Digit Whole Numbers
Going Deeper

Essential question: *How do you divide multi-digit numbers?*

Use long division to find the quotient of two multi-digit numbers.

video tutor

CC.6.NS.2

1 EXAMPLE Long Division

Antwon has 3,234 songs in the music library on his computer. He wants to burn the songs onto CDs so that he has backup copies of them. Each CD will hold 21 songs. How many CDs will he need?

Divide 3,234 by 21.

First, estimate the quotient _____ ÷ _____ = _____

Now find the exact quotient.

Step 1 21 is greater than 3, so divide 32 by 21. Place the first digit in the quotient in the hundreds place. Multiply 1 by 21 and place the product under 32. Subtract.

$$
\begin{array}{r}
1 \\
21\overline{)3{,}234} \\
-2\,1 \\
\hline
1\,1
\end{array}
$$

Step 2 Bring down the tens digit. Divide 113 by 21. Multiply 5 by 21 and place the product under 113. Subtract.

$$
\begin{array}{r}
15 \\
21\overline{)3{,}234} \\
-2\,1\downarrow \\
\hline
1\,13 \\
-1\,05 \\
\hline
8
\end{array}
$$

Step 3 Bring down the ones digit. Divide the ones.

$$
\begin{array}{r}
15 \\
21\overline{)3{,}234} \\
-2\,1 \\
\hline
1\,13 \\
-1\,05\downarrow \\
\hline
8 \\
-
\end{array}
$$

So Antwon needs a total of _____ CDs to copy his songs.

REFLECT

1a. How could the estimate in **1** be used to place the first digit of the quotient?

_____

_____

1b. How can you check that your quotient is correct?

_____

_____

2 EXAMPLE   Long Division with a Remainder

Callie has 1,850 books. She must pack them into boxes to ship to a bookstore. Each box holds 12 books. How many boxes will she need to pack all of the books?

First, estimate the quotient _____ ÷ _____ = _____

Divide 1,850 by 12.

```
        15   R
   12)1,850
   −
        6
      −6 0

     −
        2
```

Notice that the numbers do not divide evenly. There is a remainder. What does the remainder mean in this situation?

_____

_____

How many boxes does Callie need to pack the books? _____ boxes Explain.

_____

_____

TRY THIS!

2a. Divide 5,796 by 28. _____

2b. 67)3,098

REFLECT

2c. Explain how you know your answer in ❷ is reasonable.

_____

2d. How can you check that your quotient in ❷ is correct?

_____

_____

_____

3 EXAMPLE Writing the Remainder as a Fraction

The employees at a company's 12 offices volunteer their time for community projects throughout the year. Last year, the company's employees volunteered a total of 2,249 hours. What is the average number of volunteer hours at each of the 12 offices?

First, estimate the quotient.

_____

Now find the exact quotient. Write the remainder as a fraction.

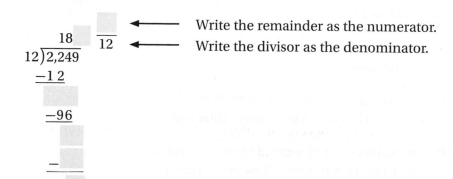

The average number of volunteer hours per office is _____ hours.

REFLECT

3a. The remainder was expressed as a fraction. What does the fraction mean in this situation?

_____

_____

3b. **What If…?** Suppose one of the offices was opened in December last year and its employees were unable to volunteer that month. How would this change the average number of hours for the other offices? Find the new average.

_____

_____

TRY THIS!

Divide. Write each remainder as a fraction in simplest form.

3c. $5,164 \div 24$ _____

3d. $1,448 \div 16 =$ _____

Divide. Write each remainder with an R.

1. 1,643 ÷ 53 _____

2. Divide 578 by 34. _____

3. 134⟌3,685

4. 423 ÷ 12 _____

Divide. Write each remainder as a fraction.

5. 10,626 ÷ 21 _____

6. 24⟌6,339

7. A theater has 1,120 seats in 35 equal rows. How many seats are in each row?

_____ seats

8. At a wedding reception, there will be 1,012 guests. A round table will seat 12 guests. How many tables will be needed?

_____ tables

9. Emilio has 8,450 trees to plant in rows on his tree farm. He will plant 115 trees per row. How many rows of trees will he have?

_____ rows

10. Camila has 1,296 beads to make bracelets. Each bracelet will contain 24 beads. How many bracelets can she make?

_____ bracelets

11. The table shows the number of miles that Awan drove over six months. Find the average number of miles per day for each month.

January: _____ miles

February: _____ miles

March: _____ miles

April: _____ miles

May: _____ miles

June: _____ miles

Month	Number of Days	Miles Traveled
January	31	1,922
February	28	2,940
March	31	3,565
April	30	3,630
May	31	2,418
June	30	3,510

12. Reasoning How is the quotient 80,000 ÷ 2,000 different from the quotient 80,000 ÷ 200 or 80,000 ÷ 20?

_____

_____

13. Reasoning Given that 9,554 ÷ 562 = 17, how can you find the quotient 95,540 ÷ 562?

_____

_____

Additional Practice

Write the correct answer.

1. A scientist has 1,050 samples to observe. She has 14 assistants for the job. If she splits the samples evenly among the assistants, how many samples will each assistant observe?

   _____

2. At the outdoor stadium, 15 summer concerts were completely sold out. A total of 9,375 people attended the concerts. How many people, on average, attended each concert?

   _____

3. Jerry has 25 weeks left to save $2,320 for a trip. If he saves an equal amount each week, how much money does he save each week to meet his goal?

   _____

4. The managers at an electronics store want to sell all 1,536 computers in the store's warehouse in 48 days. How many computers do the staff need to sell each day to meet the goal?

   _____

5. The Appalachian Trail is about 2,175 miles long. If Sharon hikes 12 miles each day, how many days will it take her to hike the Appalachian Trail?

   _____

6. The art teacher bought 3,200 pounds of clay. He has 84 students. He wants to divide the clay evenly so each student gets the same amount of clay. How many pounds will each student get?

   _____

Find each quotient.

7. $1,334 \div 29$	8. $7,890 \div 52$	9. $2,902 \div 18$	10. $8,765 \div 88$
_____	_____	_____	_____

11. $11,023 \div 45$	12. $15,812 \div 40$	13. $20,884 \div 92$	14. $34,680 \div 64$
_____	_____	_____	_____

Problem Solving

Write the correct answer.

1. The Bank of America Tower in New York is 1,200 feet tall and has 54 stories. What is the average number of feet per story?

   _____

2. A hybrid car gets an average of 41 miles per gallon. How many gallons will it take the car to travel the 2,595 miles between Boston and Los Angeles?

   _____

3. In May 2009, 20,336 tent campers stayed at Grand Canyon National Park. What was the average number of campers per day in May? (May has 31 days.)

   _____

4. Last year, Mariska saved $4,893 in her bank account. She put the same amount in the account each month. How much did she save each month?

   _____

Choose the letter for the best answer.

5. Janine paid $1,170 for a carpenter to build her new deck, not including the cost of materials. The carpenter earns $65 per hour. How many hours did the carpenter spend building the deck?

   A   10 hours

   B $11\frac{1}{13}$ hours

   C   18 hours

   D $55\frac{11}{20}$ hours

6. Colin has 978 seedlings to sell. He wants to package a dozen plants per container. How many full containers will he have to sell once he is done packaging them?

   F   80 containers

   G   81 containers

   H   82 containers

   J   85 containers

7. A peanut vendor at the football stadium puts an average of 34 peanuts in each bag. If he has 1,725 peanuts, how many whole bags can he make?

   A   50 bags

   B   51 bags

   C   55 bags

   D   57 bags

8. A baseball team pitched a total of 1,905 pitches in 13 games. What was the average number of pitches thrown per game?

   F   145 pitches

   G $146\frac{7}{13}$ pitches

   H   147 pitches

   J $147\frac{4}{13}$ pitches

Exponents
Going Deeper

Essential question: *How do you use exponents to represent numbers?*

CC.6.EE.1

1 EXPLORE Exponents

video tutor

Ricardo observed the hourly growth of bacteria in a test tube and recorded his observations in a table.

Time (h)	Total Bacteria
0	1
1	2
2	$2 \times 2 =$
3	$2 \times 2 \times 2 =$
4	$2 \times 2 \times 2 \times 2 =$

A Complete the table. What pattern(s) do you see in the Total Bacteria column?

_____

B At 2 hours, the total is equal to the product of two 2's.

At 3 hours, the total is equal to the product of _____ 2's.

At 4 hours, the total is equal to the product of _____ 2's.

To show a number multiplied by itself, you can write a *power*. A **power** is an expression with an *exponent* and a *base*. For example, 7^3 means the product of three 7's:

$$7^3 = 7 \times 7 \times 7 = 343$$

The **base** is the number that is multiplied.

The **exponent** tells how many times the base appears in the product.

TRY THIS!

Circle the base.

1a. 4^7 **1b.** 3^5 **1c.** 2^5 **1d.** $\left(\frac{1}{5}\right)^3$

Circle the exponent.

1e. 6^2 **1f.** 10^6 **1g.** $\left(\frac{7}{10}\right)^8$ **1h.** 9^4

1i. **Conjecture** What do you think it means to have an exponent of 1? For example, what is the value of 8^1?

_____

Reading Powers

7^2 "the 2nd power of 7" 7^3 "the 3rd power of 7"

7^4 "the 4th power of 7" 7^5 "the 5th power of 7" and so on...

CC.6.EE.1

2 E X A M P L E   Using Exponents to Write Expressions

Use exponents to write each expression.

A $6 \times 6 \times 6 \times 6 \times 6 \times 6 \times 6$

What number is being multiplied? _____ This number is the base.

How many times does the base appear in the product? _____ This number is the exponent.

$6 \times 6 \times 6 \times 6 \times 6 \times 6 \times 6 =$ _____

B $\frac{2}{3} \times \frac{2}{3} \times \frac{2}{3}$

What number is being multiplied? _____ This number is the base.

How many times does the base appear in the product? _____ This number is the exponent.

$\frac{2}{3} \times \frac{2}{3} \times \frac{2}{3} =$ _____

TRY THIS!

Use exponents to write each expression.

2a. $3 \times 3 \times 3 \times 3 \times 3 \times 3 \times 3 \times 3$ _____

2b. $4 \times 4 \times 4$ _____

2c. 6 _____

2d. $\frac{1}{8} \times \frac{1}{8}$ _____

2e. $5 \times 5 \times 5 \times 5 \times 5 \times 5$ _____

CC.6.EE.1

3 E X A M P L E   Finding the Value of a Power

Find the value of each power.

A 9^3

What is the base? _____

The exponent is 3, so the base will appear in the product 3 times.

$9^3 =$ _____ $\times$ _____ $\times$ _____ $=$ _____

B $\left(\frac{1}{2}\right)^2$

What is the base? _____ What is the exponent? _____

$\left(\frac{1}{2}\right)^2 =$ _____

TRY THIS!

Find the value of each power.

3a. 3^4 _____ **3b.** 1^9 _____ **3c.** $\left(\frac{2}{5}\right)^3$ _____ **3d.** 12^2 _____

CC.6.EE.1

4 **E X P L O R E** **Solving Problems Using Exponents**

Judah had two children. When those children grew up, each one also had two children, who later each had two children as well. If this pattern continues, how many children are there in the 7th generation?

You can use a diagram to model this situation. The first point at the top represents Judah. The other points represent children. Complete the diagram to show the 3rd generation.

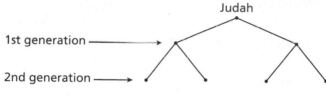

1st generation ⟶

2nd generation ⟶

3rd generation ⟶

A How many children are in each generation?

1st _____ 2nd _____ 3rd _____

B Do you see a pattern in the numbers above? Try to find a pattern using exponents.

_____

C How is the number of children in a generation related to the generation number?

_____

D How many children will be in the 7th generation?

_____

TRY THIS!

4. A female guinea pig has about 4 litters per year, and a typical litter consists of 4 baby guinea pigs. How many baby guinea pigs would a typical female have in 4 years?

_____

PRACTICE

Write each power.

1. the 10th power of 8 _____

2. the 8th power of 10 _____

3. the 11th power of $\frac{1}{2}$ _____

4. the 6th power of $\frac{2}{3}$ _____

Use exponents to write each expression.

5. $6 \times 6 \times 6$ _____

6. $10 \times 10 \times 10 \times 10 \times 10 \times 10 \times 10$ _____

7. $\frac{3}{4} \times \frac{3}{4} \times \frac{3}{4} \times \frac{3}{4} \times \frac{3}{4}$ _____

8. $\frac{7}{9} \times \frac{7}{9} \times \frac{7}{9} \times \frac{7}{9} \times \frac{7}{9} \times \frac{7}{9} \times \frac{7}{9} \times \frac{7}{9}$ _____

Find the value of each power.

9. 8^3 _____

10. 7^4 _____

11. 5^3 _____

12. 4^2 _____

13. $\left(\frac{1}{4}\right)^2$ _____

14. $\left(\frac{1}{3}\right)^3$ _____

15. $\left(\frac{6}{7}\right)^2$ _____

16. $\left(\frac{9}{10}\right)^1$ _____

Write the missing exponent.

17. $100 = 10^{\square}$

18. $8 = 2^{\square}$

19. $25 = 5^{\square}$

20. $27 = 3^{\square}$

21. $\frac{1}{169} = \left(\frac{1}{13}\right)^{\square}$

22. $14 = 14^{\square}$

23. $32 = 2^{\square}$

24. $\frac{64}{81} = \left(\frac{8}{9}\right)^{\square}$

Write the missing base.

25. $1,000 = \square^3$

26. $256 = \square^4$

27. $16 = \square^4$

28. $9 = \square^2$

29. $\frac{1}{9} = \left(\square\right)^2$

30. $64 = \square^2$

31. $\frac{9}{16} = \left(\square\right)^2$

32. $729 = \square^3$

33. Hadley's softball team has a phone tree in case a game is cancelled. The coach calls 3 players. Then each of those players calls 3 players, and so on. How many players will be notified during the 3rd round of calls? _____

34. Reasoning What is the value of all powers of 1? Explain.

_____

_____

Additional Practice

Write each expression in exponential form.

1. 9×9

2. $7 \times 7 \times 7$

3. $1 \times 1 \times 1 \times 1 \times 1$

_____

4. $5 \times 5 \times 5 \times 5$

5. $2 \times 2 \times 2 \times 2 \times 2 \times 2$

6. $10 \times 10 \times 10 \times 10$

_____

Find each value.

7. 6^2

8. 5^3

9. 10^3

10. 7^2

_____

11. 2^5

12. 3^4

13. 25^1

14. 16^0

_____

Compare. Write <, >, or =.

15. 8^0 ___ 7^1

16. 10^2 ___ 11^2

17. 8^2 ___ 4^3

18. 3^4 ___ 5^2

19. 2^5 ___ 9^2

20. 6^2 ___ 3^3

21. What whole number equals 25 when it is squared and 125 when it is cubed?

_____

22. Use exponents to write the number 81 three different ways.

_____

Problem Solving

1. The Sun is the center of our solar system. The Sun is the star closest to our planet. The surface temperature of the Sun is close to 10,000°F. Write 10,000 using exponents.

_____

2. Patty Berg has won 4^2 major women's titles in golf. Write 4^2 in standard form.

_____

3. William has 3^3 baseball cards and 4^3 football cards. Write the number of baseball cards and footballs cards that William has.

_____

4. Michelle recorded the number of miles she ran each day last year. She used the following expression to represent the total number of miles: $3 \times 3 \times 3 \times 3 \times 3 \times 3 \times 3$. Write this expression using exponents. How many miles did Michelle run last year?

_____

Choose the letter for the best answer.

5. In Tyrone's science class he is studying cells. Cell A divides every 30 minutes. If Tyrone starts with two cells, how many cells will he have in 3 hours?

   A 6 cells

   B 32 cells

   C 128 cells

   D 512 cells

6. Tanisha's soccer team has a phone tree in case a soccer game is postponed or cancelled. The coach calls 2 families. Then each family calls 2 other families. How many families will be notified during the 4th round of calls?

   F 2 families

   G 4 families

   H 8 families

   J 16 families

7. The Akashi-Kaiko Bridge is the longest suspension bridge in the world. It is located in Kobe-Naruto, Japan and was completed in 1998. It is about 3^8 feet long. Write the approximate length of the Akashi-Kaiko Bridge in standard form.

   A 6,561 feet

   B 2,187 feet

   C 512 feet

   D 24 feet

8. The Strahov Stadium is the largest sports stadium in the world. It is located in Prague, Czech Republic. Its capacity is about 12^5 people. Write the capacity of the Strahov Stadium in standard form.

   F 60 people

   G 144 people

   H 20,736 people

   J 248,832 people

video tutor

Order of Operations
Going Deeper

Essential question: *How do you use the order of operations to simplify expressions?*

The **order of operations** is a rule for simplifying expressions.

Order of Operations

1. Perform operations in parentheses.
2. Find the value of numbers with exponents.
3. Multiply or divide from left to right as ordered in the expression.
4. Add or subtract from left to right as ordered in the expression.

CC.6.EE.2a

1 EXAMPLE **Writing and Simplifying an Expression**

Cole, Joachim, and Austin play on the same soccer team. So far this season, Cole has scored 3 times as many goals as Austin and Joachim combined. If Austin has scored 2 goals and Joachim has scored 4 goals, how many goals has Cole scored?

Step 1 Write an expression for the number of goals that Cole scored.

Austin scored _____ goals and Joachim scored _____ goals.

Cole scored _____ times Austin's and Joachim's goals combined.

_____ × (_____ + _____)

Step 2 Simplify the expression.

Which operation should be performed first? _____

The value of the expression is 3 × _____ = _____.

Cole has scored _____ goals so far this season.

REFLECT

1. **What if...?** If the parentheses are not included in the expression in **1**, which operation is performed first? What is the value of the new expression? Does this value make sense? Explain.

_____

_____

2 EXPLORE Simplifying an Expression with Exponents

Amy, Chantrea, Kenji, and Sonjay have just launched a new web site. Each of them will e-mail the site's web address to three friends. They will ask their friends to forward the web address to three of their own friends. If no one receives the e-mail more than once, how many people will receive the web address in the second wave of e-mails?

A Use a diagram to model the situation for Amy. Each dot represents one e-mail. Complete the diagram to show the 2nd wave.

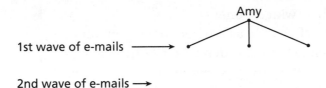

How many e-mails are sent in each wave of Amy's diagram?

1st _____   2nd _____

Write these two values as powers of 3. _____

Amy is just one of four people initiating the 1st wave of e-mails. Write an expression for the total number of e-mails sent in the 2nd wave.

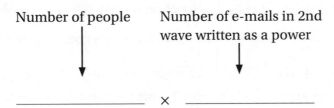

Number of people   Number of e-mails in 2nd
                          wave written as a power

_____ × _____

B Now simplify the expression.

Circle the computation that should be done first.

multiply 4 and 3   find the value of 3^2

The value of the expression is $4 \times$ _____ = _____.

_____ people will receive e-mails in the 2nd wave.

REFLECT

2. **Error Analysis** Mariah says that the value of the expression 3×4^2 is 144. Explain what Mariah did incorrectly when simplifying the expression. What is the correct value of the expression?

_____

_____

3 EXAMPLE Solving Problems Using the Order of Operations

During a family reunion last summer, 7 adults and 17 children from the Nakai family went to a water park. Admissions were $16 per adult and $9 per child. What was the total cost of the admissions?

The total cost of the admissions is the sum of the cost for the adults and the cost for the children. Complete the expression for the total cost.

$$7 \times \underline{\hspace{2cm}} + \underline{\hspace{2cm}} \times 9$$

Now find the value of the expression using the order of operations.

$$7 \times \underline{\hspace{2cm}} + \underline{\hspace{2cm}} \times 9$$

$$\underline{\hspace{2cm}} + \underline{\hspace{2cm}} \times 9$$

$$\underline{\hspace{2cm}} + \underline{\hspace{2cm}}$$

$$\underline{\hspace{2cm}}$$

The total cost of the admissions was $ \underline{\hspace{2cm}}.

REFLECT

3a. What is represented by the first product in the expression in ③?

_____

3b. What is represented by the second product in the expression in ③?

_____

3c. Use the order of operations to find the value of $(7 \times 16) + (17 \times 9)$. How does this value compare to the value found in ③? Explain using the order of operations.

_____

_____

_____

_____

TRY THIS!

Simplify each expression using the order of operations.

3d. $4 \times 9 \div 3^2$ **3e.** $4 \times (9 \div 3)^2$ **3f.** $(7 + 17) \div 6 - 2^2$

_____   _____   _____

Simplify each expression using the order of operations.

1. $(12 - 7) \times 6$

2. $36 - 4 \times 8$

3. 8×3^2

_____

_____

_____

4. $2^4 \times 3$

5. $5^2 \times (4 \div 2)$

6. $(16 - 7) \div 3^2$

_____

_____

_____

7. $14 \times 5 + 3 \times 11$

8. $21 + 9 \div 3 - 2^3$

9. $(21 + 9) \div 3 - 2^3$

_____

_____

_____

10. During the basketball season, Morgan made 3 times as many 2-point baskets as she made 3-point baskets and free throws combined. If she made 14 free throws and eight 3-point baskets, how many 2-point baskets did she make?

Write and simplify an expression to solve the problem.

_____

_____

The table shows the grams of protein for several food items.

Food (single serving size)	Protein (g)
Lowfat Yogurt (8 oz)	4
Lowfat Pudding (8 oz)	6
Lowfat Cottage Cheese (8 oz)	4
Hard Cheese (1.5 oz)	12
Calcium-Fortified Soy Milk (8 oz)	4

11. Write and simplify an expression that gives the total grams of protein in 2 servings of hard cheese and 2 servings of yogurt.

_____

12. Write and simplify an expression that gives the total grams of protein in 1 serving of pudding, 2 servings of soy milk, and 1 serving of cottage cheese.

_____

13. Place one pair of parentheses in the expression so that its value is 25. Show the steps for simplifying the expression.

$40 \div 2^3 \times 8 - 3$

_____

Additional Practice

Simplify each expression.

1. $10 + 6 \times 2$

2. $(15 + 39) \div 6$

3. $(20 - 15) \times 2 + 1$

4. $(4^2 + 6) \div 11$

5. $9 + (7 - 1) \times 2$

6. $(2 \times 4) + 8 - (5 \times 3)$

7. $5 + 18 \div 3^2 - 1$

8. $8 + 5 \times 10 - 12$

9. $14 + (50 - 7^2) \times 3$

Add parentheses so that each equation is correct.

10. $7 + 9 \times 3 - 1 = 25$

11. $2^3 - 7 \times 4 = 4$

12. $5 + 6 \times 9 \div 3 = 23$

13. $12 \div 3 \times 2 = 2$

14. $8 + 3 \times 6 - 4 - 1 = 13$

15. $4 \times 3^2 + 1 = 40$

16. $9 \times 0 + 5 - 3 = 42$

17. $15 \times 3^2 - 2^3 = 15$

18. $14 \div 2 + 5 \times 5 = 10$

19. Tyler walked 2 miles a day for the first week of his exercise plan. Then he walked 3 miles a day for the next 9 days. How many miles did Tyler walk in all?

_____

20. Paulo's father bought 8 pizzas and 12 bottles of juice for the class party. Each pizza cost $9 and each bottle of juice cost $2. Paulo's father paid with a $100-bill. How much change did he get back?

_____

Problem Solving

Evaluate each expression to complete the table.

Mammals with the Longest Tails

	Mammal	Expression	Tail Length
1.	Asian elephant	$2 + 3^2 \times 7 - (10 - 4)$	
2.	Leopard	$5 \times 6 + 5^2$	
3.	African elephant	$6 \times (72 \div 8) - 3$	
4.	African buffalo	$51 + 6^2 \div 9 - 12$	
5.	Giraffe	$4^3 - 3 \times 7$	
6.	Red kangaroo	$11 + 48 \div 6 \times 4$	

Choose the letter for the best answer.

7. Adam and his two brothers went to the zoo. Each ticket to enter the zoo costs $7. Adam bought two bags of peanuts for $4 each, and one of his brothers bought a lion poster for $12. Which expression shows how much money they spent at the zoo in all?

   A $7 + 4 + 12$

   B $7 \times 3 + 4 + 12$

   C $7 \times 3 + 4 \times 2 + 12$

   D $(7 \times 3) + (4 \times 12)$

8. An elephant eats about 500 pounds of grass and leaves every day. There are 2 Africa elephants and 3 Asian elephants living in the City Zoo. How many pounds of grass and leaves do the zookeepers need to order each week to feed all the elephants?

   F 2,500 pounds

   G 17,500 pounds

   H 3,000 pounds

   J 21,000 pounds

9. The average giraffe is 18 feet tall. Which of these expressions shows the height of a giraffe?

   A $4^2 - 2$

   B $3 \times 12 \div 4 + 2$

   C $3^3 \div 9 \times 6$

   D $20 \div 5 + 5 - 6$

10. Some kangaroos can cover 30 feet in a single jump! If a kangaroo could jump like that 150 times in a row, how much farther would it need to go to cover a mile? (1 mile = 5,280 feet)

   F 780 feet   H 176 feet

   G 26 feet   J 5,100 feet

Properties and Mental Math
Going Deeper

Essential question: *How can you use properties to solve problems?*

Expressions that have the same value are called **equivalent expressions**. You can use properties of operations to write equivalent expressions that can be simplified using mental math.

video tutor

Properties of Operations	Examples
Commutative Property of Addition: When adding, changing the order of the numbers does not change the sum.	$5 + 7 = 7 + 5$
Commutative Property of Multiplication: When multiplying, changing the order of the numbers does not change the product.	$3 \times 8 = 8 \times 3$
Associative Property of Addition: When adding more than two numbers, the grouping of the numbers does not change the sum.	$(4 + 6) + 9 = 4 + (6 + 9)$
Associative Property of Multiplication: When multiplying more than two numbers, the grouping of the numbers does not change the product.	$(2 \times 9) \times 5 = 2 \times (9 \times 5)$

CC.6.EE.3

1 EXPLORE   Using Properties to Add Whole Numbers

**Use the properties of operations and mental math to find the sum
14 + 21 + 16 + 17 + 9.**

A Which pairs of numbers have sums that are easy to compute with using mental math? Explain.

_____

_____

B Which property can be used to reorder the addends? _____

Use the property to write an equivalent expression.

$14 + 21 + 16 + 17 + 9 = 14 + \underline{\hspace{1cm}} + \underline{\hspace{1cm}} + \underline{\hspace{1cm}} + 17$

C Which property can be used to regroup the addends? _____

Use the property to group the addends. Then use mental math to add.

$(14 + 16) + (21 + 9) + 17 = \underline{\hspace{1cm}} + \underline{\hspace{1cm}} + 17$

$= \underline{\hspace{1cm}} + 17$

$= \underline{\hspace{1cm}}$

1a. Show how you could use the properties of operations to find $8 \times 9 \times 5$.

_____

REFLECT

1b. Explain how you used properties of operations in **1a**.

_____

_____

_____

1c. Use the Commutative and Associative Properties to write two expressions equivalent to $8 \times 3 \times 5$ that would be easy to solve using mental math. Explain why the three expressions are equivalent.

_____

_____

CC.6.EE.3

2 EXAMPLE Using Properties and Mental Math to Solve Problems

For the past six weeks, Kyra has been keeping a record of the number of hours she spent volunteering at a local animal shelter. The chart shows her recordkeeping. How many total hours did she volunteer during these six weeks?

Week	Number of Hours
1	6
2	8
3	5
4	14
5	5
6	12

Find the sum using mental math.

$6 + 8 + 5 + 14 + 5 + 12$

$6 + \boxed{} + 8 + \boxed{} + \boxed{} + \boxed{}$ *Use the Commutative Property.*

$\left(6 + \boxed{}\right) + \left(8 + \boxed{}\right) + \left(\boxed{} + \boxed{}\right)$ *Use the Associative Property.*

$\boxed{} + \boxed{} + \boxed{}$ *Use mental math to add.*

$\boxed{}$

Kyra volunteered a total of _____ hours during these six weeks.

TRY THIS!

2a. $22 + 34 + 13 + 6 + 27$ _____

2b. $18 + 25 + 19 + 32 + 15$ _____

2c. $5 \times 7 \times 4$ _____

2d. $6 \times 11 \times 5$ _____

The Distributive Property involves two different operations, either multiplication and addition or multiplication and subtraction.

Distributive Property	Examples
Multiplying a number by a sum or difference is the same as multiplying by each number in the sum or difference and then adding or subtracting.	$6(5 + 7) = 6(5) + 6(7)$ $3(8 - 4) = 3(8) - 3(4)$

CC.6.EE.3

3 EXAMPLE Using the Distributive Property

The owner of a toy store buys small remote control cars in cartons that each contain 36 cars. She just ordered 7 cartons. How many remote control cars did she order?

Use the Distributive Property and mental math to multiply 7×36.

A Use multiplication and addition.

$$7 \times 36 \quad = 7 \times \left(\boxed{} + 6 \right) \qquad \textit{Rewrite 36 as a sum.}$$

$$= \left(7 \times \boxed{} \right) + \left(7 \times \boxed{} \right) \qquad \textit{Use the Distributive Property.}$$

$$= \boxed{} + \boxed{} \qquad \textit{Use mental math to multiply.}$$

$$= \underline{} \qquad \textit{Use mental math to add.}$$

B Use multiplication and subtraction.

$$7 \times 36 \quad = 7 \times \left(\boxed{} - 4 \right) \qquad \textit{Rewrite 36 as a difference.}$$

$$= \left(7 \times \boxed{} \right) - \left(7 \times \boxed{} \right) \qquad \textit{Use the Distributive Property.}$$

$$= \boxed{} - \boxed{} \qquad \textit{Use mental math to multiply.}$$

$$= \underline{} \qquad \textit{Use mental math to subtract.}$$

The owner ordered a total of _____ remote control cars.

REFLECT

3a. The product 7×36 was rewritten in two ways, as $7 \times (30 + 6)$ and as $7 \times (40 - 4)$. Rewite the products 8×53 and 6×29 each in two ways.

_____

3b. **Conjecture** How might the product 7×136 be rewritten so that the Distributive Property could be used to multiply using mental math? Simplify your expression.

_____

Show how to use properties of operations and mental math to simplify each expression.

1. $5 + 13 + 15 + 11 + 7 + 9$

2. $5 \times 7 \times 8$

3. $(6 + 28) + (12 + 7)$

4. 6×57

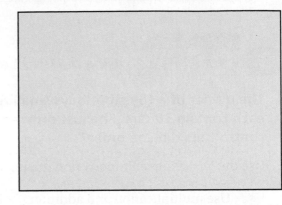

5. Mika has five framed pieces of art that she wants to arrange in a group on her wall. Each piece has an area of (8×12) square inches. Simplify the expression $5 \times (8 \times 12)$ to find the total area of the wall covered by the art.

_____

6. The table shows the number of new shows appearing on a television network in the past five years. What is the total number of new shows that have appeared over this time?

Year	2007	2008	2009	2010	2011
New Shows	8	21	5	9	12

_____

7. How are the Commutative and Associative Properties of Addition and Multiplication used to help simplify expressions?

_____

_____

_____

Additional Practice

Simplify.

1. $17 + 4 \times 5$

2. $25 \times 3 \times 4$

3. $28 + 39 + 11 + 22$

_____

4. $12 + 7 + 8 + 13$

5. $10 + 3 \times 2$

6. $9 \times 8 \times 5$

_____

7. $97 + 4 + 3 + 26$

8. $2 \times 6 \times 5$

9. $28 + 2 \times 6$

_____

Use the Distributive Property to find each product.

10. 4×16

11. 8×31

12. 3×62

13. 2×46

_____

14. 5×29

15. 7×22

16. 9×21

17. 6×15

_____

18. 8×44

19. 4×29

20. 7×31

21. 5×57

_____

22. Each ticket to a play costs \$27. How much will it cost to buy 4 tickets? Which property did you use to solve this problem with mental math?

_____

23. Mr. Stanley bought two cases of pencils. Each case has 20 boxes. In each box there is 10 pencils. Use mental math to find how many pencils Mr. Stanley bought.

_____

24. When you consider that cows eat grass and the water needed to grow the grass that cows eat, it takes 65 gallons of water to produce one serving of milk! Use mental math to find how many gallons of water are needed to produce 5 servings of milk.

_____

Problem Solving

Write the correct answer.

1. Each DVD costs $21. How much will it cost to buy 5 DVDs?

   _____

   _____

2. Emily rode a 27-mile trail once a week for 6 weeks. How many miles did she ride altogether?

   _____

   _____

3. The expression $23 + 16 + 17 + 24$ represents the total number of miles Connor rode his bike on four Saturdays one month. Simplify the expression to find the total number of miles he rode his bike on those four Saturdays.

   _____

   _____

4. Charlotte bought new clothes to wear on her vacation. She bought two pairs of shoes that cost $27 and $35 and two shirts that cost $33 and $15. How much did Charlotte spend in all?

   _____

   _____

Circle the letter of the correct answer.

5. Shaun won first place in a fishing contest last weekend. He caught four fish weighing 17 pounds, 12 pounds, 13 pounds, and 8 pounds. What was the total weight of the fish Shaun caught?

   A 25 pounds

   B 30 pounds

   C 49 pounds

   D 50 pounds

6. Jenn is planting vegetables in six garden plots in her yard. Each plot has an area of (4×8) square feet. Simplify the expression $6 \times (4 \times 8)$ to find the total area covered by the garden plots.

   F 32 square feet

   G 72 square feet

   H 192 square feet

   J 1,152 square feet

Problem Solving Connections

It Pays to Advertise The manager of a new frozen yogurt shop, Yo To Go, wants to advertise the shop in three ways: printed materials, t-shirts, and radio advertisements. The manager has a budget of $10,000. What is the best way for the manager to spend this money on the three types of advertisements?

COMMON CORE

CC.6.NS.2
CC.6.EE.1
CC.6.EE.2a
CC.6.EE.2c
CC.6.EE.3

1 Printed Materials

The manager contacts a printer to find out how much it costs to print brochures, flyers, and postcards. The printer shares the costs for some recent jobs, as shown in the table. (Note: A box contains 100 brochures, flyers, or postcards.)

Printing Costs		
Type of Printed Material	Number of Boxes Ordered	Total Cost
Color Brochure	192	$6,336
Black & White Brochure	66	$1,848
Flyer	325	$5,850
Postcard	88	$1,320

A The manager wants to know the cost per box for each type of printed material. What arithmetic operation should the manager use to find the cost per box? Explain.

B How can the manager estimate the cost per box for color brochures?

C Find the cost per box for each type of printed material.

D The printer also makes posters. In a previous job, the printer made 100 posters for $325. What is the cost per poster? What is the remainder written as a fraction? What does the fraction mean in this situation?

2 T-Shirts

The manager wants to use word of mouth to get people to visit the yogurt shop. People who hear about the shop from a friend can visit the shop and receive a free t-shirt.

A The shop's 5 employees each tell 2 friends to visit the shop and receive a free t-shirt. The manager assumes that each friend will tell 2 new people, and then each of these people will tell 2 new people, and so on.

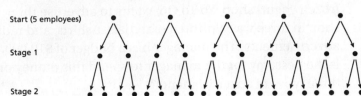

Complete the table to show the number of people who hear about the shop at each stage of the process.

Stage	Number of People at this Stage	Expression with an Exponent
1	5 × 2	5 × 2^1
2	5 × 2 × 2	
3		
4		
5		
6		
7		

B Write an expression for the total number of people who hear about the shop. Be sure to include all the people in stages 1 through 7, and assume different people hear about the shop at each stage.

C Simplify the expression to find the total number of people who hear about the shop. This is the total number of t-shirts the manager plans to order.

Total number of t-shirts to order: _____

D The manager claims that more than 10,000 people would hear about the shop in stage 10 alone if the process continued. Do you agree? Explain.

© Houghton Mifflin Harcourt Publishing Company

3 Radio Advertisements

The manager plans to buy 20 advertisements on a local radio station. The table shows the rates for running a single advertisement at 4 different radio stations. Note that the cost depends on the time of day that the advertisement airs.

Rates for One Radio Advertisement			
Station	Morning	Afternoon	Evening
WGKH	$60	$50	$60
Rock 101	$55	$20	$70
WPQR	$40	$45	$50
Mega 92.5	$80	$40	$45

A The manager decides to buy 5 morning advertisements, 8 afternoon advertisements, and 7 evening advertisements. Write and simplify an expression to find the cost of these advertisements at WGKH.

B Find the cost of the advertisements at the other stations.

C Radio station WUVW offers a flat rate of $52 per advertisement no matter when the advertisement airs. Show how the manager can use mental math to find the cost of 20 advertisements on WUVW. Which property did you use?

D The table shows the fees for buying advertisements at WUVW. The fees do not depend upon the number of advertisements purchased. Write an expression for the total cost of the fees. Then show how the manager can use mental math to find this cost.

Fees at WUVW	
Fee	Cost($)
DJ Fee	27
Prep Work	6
Administration	18
Legal Fee	44
Accounting	13

E Taking the fees into account, how does advertising at WUVW compare to advertising at the stations in the table at the top of the page?

4 Answer the Question

Recall that the manager has a budget of $10,000 for printed materials, t-shirts, and radio advertisements. Make a proposal for how this money should be spent.

A The manager decides that the shop needs 100 boxes of printed materials. Also, the manager learns that t-shirts cost $5 each. Look back over your work to find a combination of printed materials, t-shirts, and radio advertisements that fits the budget. Fill in the empty cells of the table to help organize your work.

Printed Materials			
Type of Printed Material	Number of Boxes	Cost per Box	Total Cost of Printed Materials
	100		
T-Shirts			
	Number of T-Shirts	Cost per T-Shirt	Total Cost of T-Shirts
		$5	
Radio Advertisements			
Station	Number of Advertisements		Total Cost of Radio Advertisements
	5 morning, 8 afternoon 7 evening		

B What is the total cost of your proposal? Does it fit the manager's budget?

C The manager asks for an alternate proposal. Describe a different combination of printed materials, t-shirts, and radio advertisements that fits the budget.

D Is it possible for the manager to get color brochures, the t-shirts, and the radio advertisements and stay within the budget? Explain.

Performance Task

CHAPTER 1

COMMON CORE

CC.6.NS.2
CC.6.EE.1
CC.6.EE.2c
CC.6.EE.3

★ **1.** Yolanda puts 18-inch square athletic tiles down to create a space to do yoga. She puts down 4 rows of 5 tiles each. Write and simplify an expression to find the total area in square feet of the space.

★ **2.** One day, a grocery store sells 150 gallons of milk and makes a profit of $300.

   a. Write and simplify an expression to find the profit made on each gallon of milk.

   b. The next day, it sells 125 gallons of milk. Write and simplify an expression to find the store's profit on the next day.

★ **3.** Four friends each buy a movie ticket for $9 at the theater. They also each buy a small popcorn for $3.75 and a medium drink for $3.50.

   a. Write and simplify an expression for the amount, in dollars, that each friend spends at the movie theater.

b. Write an expression for the total amount the friends spend at the movie theater. Explain how you can use the Distributive Property to help simplify the expression. (*Hint:* Try rewriting a decimal number as the sum of a whole number and a decimal less than one.)

4. A bowling alley charges each bowler $2 to rent shoes and $1.50 per game. Each bowler must rent a pair of shoes. A team of 3 bowlers goes to practice, and each bowls 3 games.

a. Seamus writes the expression $3 \cdot 2 + 3 \cdot 1.5$ to represent the total amount the team spends. Is he correct? Explain.

b. Write an expression to represent the total amount the team spends. Then simplify.

c. The bowling alley offers a "rent a lane" option. For $15, a group of 3 to 5 bowlers can play as many games as they wish. The $15 does not include shoe rental. Should the three friends have used this option? Explain your reasoning.

Name _____ Class _____ Date _____

SELECTED RESPONSE

1. Find the quotient $1{,}430 \div 75$.

   A. 1,505   **C.** $19\frac{1}{15}$

   B. $19\frac{5}{19}$ **D.** 1,355

2. One hundred thirty four sixth-grade students sit together in the auditorium. Each row has 12 seats. How many rows do the sixth graders need?

   F. $10\frac{5}{6}$ **H.** $11\frac{1}{6}$

   G. 132   **J.** 146

3. Brigetta's car will hold 25 cartons of books. What is the fewest number of trips that she must make in order to deliver 250 cartons?

   A. 5   **C.** 15

   B. 10   **D.** 20

4. Mr. Gonzalez's sixth-grade class is putting on a play. He reserved the first 6 rows of the auditorium for family members and friends of the 24 students in his class. If each row contains 17 seats and each student can invite the same number of guests, how many guests can each student invite?

   F. 8 guests   **H.** 4 guests

   G. 5 guests   **J.** 9 guests

5. Dora plants 414 flower seeds in 18 equal rows. How many seeds does she plant in each row?

   A. 23   **C.** 18

   B. 81   **D.** 32

6. Members of a high school club sold hamburgers at a baseball game to raise money. They sold 278 hamburgers. If the buns come in packages of 16, how many packages of buns did the club members open?

   F. 17.42 packages

   G. 17.38 packages

   H. 17 packages

   J. 18 packages

7. A city ordinance in River City requires that there be a police officer for every 470 residents. If the population of River City is 410,300, what is the minimum number of police officers needed?

   A. 874.63 police officers

   B. 872.98 police officers

   C. 873 police officers

   D. 874 police officers

8. Helen earns $30 per week on her paper route. So far she has earned $3,360. For how many weeks has she had the paper route?

   F. 112   **H.** 11

   G. 60   **J.** 3,330

9. Write the expression $7 \times 7 \times 7 \times 7 \times 7$ in exponential form.

   A. 7^4 **C.** 5^7

   B. 16,807   **D.** 7^5

10. What is $8 \cdot 8 \cdot 8 \cdot 8$ written in exponential form?

    F. 32   **H.** 4,096

    G. 8^4 **J.** 4^8

11. Find the value of 3^5.

    A. 25   **C.** 81

    B. 125   **D.** 243

12. Simplify $12 + 3(18 - 4^2) + 9$.

    F. 39   **H.** 27

    G. 217   **J.** 59

13. Simplify $(25 + 20) \div 5 + 2^2$.

    A. 13   **C.** 33

    B. 5   **D.** 121

14. Which is an example of the Distributive Property?

    F. $7(34) = 7(3) + 7(4)$

    G. $7 + (3 + 4) = (7 + 3) + 4$

    H. $7(34) = 7(30) + 7(4)$

    J. $7 + (3 + 4) = 7 + (4 + 3)$

15. $(18 + 13) + 7 = 18 + (13 + 7)$ is an example of which property?

    A. Commutative

    B. Associative

    C. Distributive

    D. Identity

CONSTRUCTED RESPONSE

16. Tim's grandfather lends him $105 to buy a new cell phone. Each week Tim pays his grandfather $15. How many weeks will it take Tim to pay back all the money?

_____

_____

17. Layne sends an email to 7 people and those 7 people send the email to 7 more people, and so on. Write an expression to show the number of people who will receive the email after the fifth round.

_____

18. Consider the expression:

$(28 \div 4) \cdot 5 - 6 + 4^2$.

Explain the order of operations you would use to simplify this expression. Then simplify it.

_____

_____

_____

_____

_____

_____

_____

_____

_____

_____

_____

Introduction to Algebra

Chapter Focus

You will learn how to evaluate algebraic expressions involving the order of operations, more than one variable, and formulas. Translating words into algebraic expressions and equations is another valuable skill you will learn in this chapter. You will look for patterns and use tables to write expressions for sequences and find missing values in tables. You will determine if a given value is a solution of an equation. Finally, you will solve equations involving addition, subtraction, multiplication, and division.

Chapter at a Glance

COMMON CORE

Lesson		Standards for Mathematical Content
2-1	Variables and Expressions	**CC.6.EE.2c**
2-2	Translating Between Words and Math	**CC.6.EE.2a**
2-3	Translating Between Tables and Expressions	**CC.6.EE.2a**
2-4	Equations and Their Solutions	**CC.6.EE.5, CC.6.EE.6**
2-5	Addition Equations	**CC.6.EE.7, CC.6.EE.6**
2-6	Subtraction Equations	**CC.6.EE.7, CC.6.EE.6**
2-7	Multiplication Equations	**CC.6.EE.7, CC.6.EE.6**
2-8	Division Equations	**CC.6.EE.7, CC.6.EE.6**
	Problem Solving Connections	
	Performance Task	
	Assessment Readiness	

Unpacking the Standards

Understanding the standards and the vocabulary terms in the standards will help you know exactly what you are expected to learn in this chapter.

COMMON CORE CC.6.EE.2a

Write expressions that record operations with numbers and with letters standing for numbers.

Key Vocabulary

expression *(expresión)* A mathematical phrase that contains operations, numbers, and/or variables.

What It Means to You

You will write algebraic expressions containing variables to stand for numbers that are not yet known.

EXAMPLE

Let *s* represent the number of senators that each of the 50 states has in the U.S. Senate. Write an expression for the total number of senators.

To put together 50 equal groups of s, multiply 50 times *s*.

$$50s$$

There are 50*s* senators in the U.S. Senate.

COMMON CORE CC.6.EE.5

Understand solving an equation or inequality as a process of answering a question: which values from a specified set, if any, make the equation or inequality true? Use substitution to determine whether a given number in a specified set makes an equation or inequality true.

Key Vocabulary

equation *(ecuación)* A mathematical sentence that shows that two expressions are equivalent.
inequality *(desigualdad)* A mathematical sentence that shows the relationship between quantities that are not equal.
substitute *(sustituir)* To replace a variable with a number or another expression in an algebraic expression.

What It Means to You

You will use substitution to determine whether a number is a solution of an equation or inequality.

EXAMPLE

Determine whether the given value of the variable is a solution.

6   **6**

$$60 \div c = 6 \text{ for } c = 10$$

$$60 \div c = 6$$

$$60 \div 10 \stackrel{?}{=} 6 \qquad \textit{Substitute 10 for c.}$$

$$6 \stackrel{?}{=} 6 \qquad \textit{Divide.}$$

NON-EXAMPLE

Determine whether the given value of the variable is a solution.

84   **82**

$$a + 23 = 82 \text{ for } a = 61$$

$$a + 23 = 82$$

$$61 + 23 \stackrel{?}{=} 82 \qquad \textit{Substitute 61 for a.}$$

$$84 \stackrel{?}{=} 82 \qquad \textit{Add.}$$

COMMON CORE CC.6.EE.7

Solve real-world and mathematical problems by writing and solving equations of the form $x + p = q$ and $px = q$ for cases in which p, q and x are all nonnegative rational numbers.

Key Vocabulary

rational number *(número racional)*
A number that can be written in the form $\frac{a}{b}$, where a and b are integers and $b \neq 0$.

What It Means to You

You will use your knowledge of operations to solve equations.

EXAMPLE

When Theodore Roosevelt became president of the United States, he was 42 years old. He was 27 years younger than Ronald Reagan was when Reagan became president. How old was Reagan when he became president?

Let *a* represent Ronald Reagan's age.

Ronald Reagan's age	−	27	=	Theodore Roosevelt's age
a	−	27	=	42

$$a - 27 = 42$$
$$\underline{+ 27 \quad + 27}$$
$$a \quad = 69$$

Ronald Reagan was 69 years old when he became president.

COMMON CORE CC.6.EE.7

Solve real-world and mathematical problems by writing and solving equations of the form $x + p = q$ and $px = q$ for cases in which p, q and x are all nonnegative rational numbers.

What It Means to You

You will use your knowledge of operations to solve equations.

EXAMPLE

Nine banded armadillos are always born in groups of 4. If you count 32 babies, what is the number of mother armadillos?

Let *m* represent the number of mother armadillos.

$$4m = 32$$
$$\frac{4m}{4} = \frac{32}{4}$$
$$m = 8$$

There are 8 mother armadillos.

CHAPTER 2

Key Vocabulary

algebraic expression *(expresión algebraica)* An expression that contains at least one variable.

constant *(constante)* A value that does not change.

equation *(ecuación)* A mathematical sentence that shows that two expressions are equivalent.

evaluate *(evaluar)* To find the value of a numerical or algebraic expression.

solution of an equation *(solución de una ecuación)* A value or values that make an equation true.

variable *(variable)* A symbol used to represent a quantity that can change.

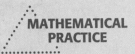

MATHEMATICAL PRACTICE

The Common Core Standards for Mathematical Practice describe varieties of expertise that mathematics educators at all levels should seek to develop in their students. Opportunities to develop these practices are integrated throughout this program.

1. Make sense of problems and persevere in solving them.
2. Reason abstractly and quantitatively.
3. Construct viable arguments and critique the reasoning of others.
4. Model with mathematics.
5. Use appropriate tools strategically.
6. Attend to precision.
7. Look for and make use of structure.
8. Look for and express regularity in repeated reasoning.

Variables and Expressions
Going Deeper: Evaluating Expressions

Essential question: *How do you evaluate expressions?*

A **variable** is a letter or symbol used to represent an unknown or unspecified number. The value of a variable may change. A **constant** is a number that does not change.

An **algebraic expression** contains one or more variables. You can substitute a number for that variable and then find the value of the expression. This is called **evaluating** the expression.

CC.6.EE.2c

1 EXAMPLE Evaluating Expressions

Evaluate each expression for the given value of the variable.

A $x - 9; x = 15$

☐ $- 9$ *Substitute 15 for x.*

☐   *Subtract.*

When $x = 15$, $x - 9 = $ ☐ .

B $n + 19; n = 8$

☐ $+ 19$ *Substitute 8 for n.*

☐   *Add.*

When $n = 8$, $n + 19 = $ ☐ .

C $0.5y; y = 1.4$

$0.5\left(\boxed{}\right)$ *Substitute 1.4 for y.*

☐   *Multiply.*

When $y = 1.4$, $0.5y = $ ☐ .

D $6k; k = \frac{1}{3}$

          Substitute $\frac{1}{3}$ for k.

☐   *Multiply.*

When $k = \frac{1}{3}$, $6k = $ ☐ .

Evaluate each expression for the given value of the variable.

1a. $4x$; $x = 8$ _____   **1b.** $6.5 - n$; $n = 1.8$ _____   **1c.** $\frac{m}{6}$; $m = 18$ _____

To evaluate expressions with more than one operation, use the order of operations.

CC.6.EE.2c

2 EXAMPLE   **Using the Order of Operations**

Evaluate each expression for $x = 7$.

A $4(x - 4)$

$$4\left(\boxed{} - 4\right)$$ *Substitute 7 for x.*

$$4\left(\boxed{}\right)$$ *Subtract inside the parentheses.*

$$\boxed{}$$ *Multiply.*

B $4x - 4$

$$4\left(\boxed{}\right) - 4$$ *Substitute 7 for x.*

$$\boxed{} - 4$$ *Multiply.*

$$\boxed{}$$ *Subtract.*

C $x^2 + x$

$$\left(\boxed{}\right)^2 + \boxed{}$$ *Substitute 7 for x.*

$$\boxed{} + 7$$ *Find the values of numbers with exponents.*

$$\boxed{}$$ *Add.*

REFLECT

2a. The answers to **A** and **B** are not the same, even though the expressions are very similar. Why?

_____

_____

Evaluate each expression for $n = 5$.

2b. $3(n + 1)$ _____   **2c.** $3n + 1$ _____   **2d.** $(4n - 4) + 14$ _____

2e. $4n - (4 + 14)$ _____   **2f.** $4(n - 4) + 14$ _____   **2g.** $6n + n^2$ _____

3 EXAMPLE Expressions with More than One Variable

Evaluate $w - x + y$ for $w = 6$, $x = 5$, and $y = 3$.

☐ − ☐ + ☐   *Substitute* ☐ *for w,* ☐ *for x, and* ☐ *for y.*

☐ + 3   *Subtract.*

☐   *Add.*

REFLECT

3a. In this example, why do you subtract before adding?

_____

_____

TRY THIS!

Evaluate each expression for $a = 3$, $b = 4$, and $c = 5$.

3b. $ab - c$ _____

3c. $bc + 5a$ _____

4 EXAMPLE Using Formulas

The expression $2(\ell w + \ell h + hw)$ gives the surface area of a rectangular prism with length ℓ, width w, and height h. Find the surface area of the rectangular prism shown.

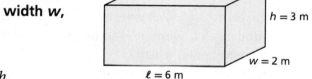

$h = 3$ m
$w = 2$ m
$\ell = 6$ m

Use the diagram to find the values of ℓ, w, and h.

$\ell = $ ☐ $w = $ ☐ $h = $ ☐

Substitute these values into the expression $2(\ell w + \ell h + hw)$.

$2\left[(\ \ )(\ \ ) + (\ \ )(\ \ ) + (\ \ )(\ \ )\right]$

$= 2\left(\ \ + \ \ + \ \ \right)$ *Multiply inside the parentheses.*

$= 2\left(\ \ \right)$ *Add inside the parentheses.*

$= $ ☐   *Multiply.*

The surface area of the rectangular prism is ☐ m².

TRY THIS!

4a. The expression $6x^2$ gives the surface area of a cube, and the expression x^3 gives the volume of a cube, where x is the length of one side of the cube. Find the surface area and the volume of a cube with a side length of 2 m.
$S = $ _____ m²; $V = $ _____ m³

4b. The expression $60m$ gives the number of seconds in m minutes. How many seconds are there in 7 minutes? _____ seconds

© Houghton Mifflin Harcourt Publishing Company

Evaluate each expression for the given value(s) of the variable(s).

1. $x - 7$; $x = 23$ _____

2. $3r$; $r = 6$ _____

3. $\frac{8}{t}$; $t = 4$ _____

4. $9 + m$; $m = 1.5$ _____

5. $p - 2$; $p = 19$ _____

6. $3h$; $h = \frac{1}{6}$ _____

7. $2.5 - n$; $n = 1.8$ _____

8. k^2; $k = 4$ _____

9. $4(b - 4)$; $b = 5$ _____

10. $38 - \frac{x}{2}$; $x = 12$ _____

11. $\frac{30}{d} - 2$; $d = 6$ _____

12. $x^2 - 34$; $x = 10$ _____

13. $\frac{1}{2}w + 2$; $w = \frac{1}{9}$ _____

14. $5(6.2 + z)$; $z = 3.8$ _____

15. $2a^2 + a$; $a = 8$ _____

16. $7y + 32$; $y = 9$ _____

17. xy; $x = 8$ and $y = 6$

_____

18. $x + y - 1$; $x = 12$ and $y = 4$

_____

19. $3x + 4y$; $x = 4$ and $y = 5$

_____

20. $4x + 1 + 3y$; $x = 6$ and $y = 8$

_____

21. The expression ℓwh gives the volume of a rectangular prism with length ℓ, width w, and height h. Find the volume of the rectangular prism.

_____ in^3

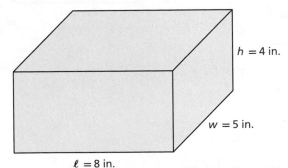

$h = 4$ in.

$w = 5$ in.

$\ell = 8$ in.

22. The expression $1.8c + 32$ gives the temperature in degrees Fahrenheit for a given temperature in degrees Celsius c. Find the temperature in degrees Fahrenheit that is equivalent to 30 °C.

_____°F

23. Error Analysis Marjorie evaluated the expression $3x + 2$ for $x = 5$ as shown:

$$3x + 2 = 35 + 2 = 37$$

What was Marjorie's mistake? What is the correct value of $3x + 2$ for $x = 5$?

_____

Additional Practice

Evaluate each expression to find the missing values in the tables.

1.

n	$n + 8^2$
7	71
9	
22	
35	

2.

n	$25 - n$
20	5
5	
18	
9	

3.

n	$n \cdot 7$
8	56
9	
11	
12	

4.

n	$24 \div n$
2	12
6	
4	
8	

5.

n	$n + 15$
35	
5	
20	
85	

6.

n	$n \cdot 2^3$
7	
4	
10	
13	

7. A car is traveling at a speed of 55 miles per hour. You want to write an algebraic expression to show how far the car will travel in a certain number of hours. What will be your constant? your variable?

_____

_____

_____

8. Shawn evaluated the algebraic expression $x \div 4$ for $x = 12$ and gave an answer of 8. What was his error? What is the correct answer?

_____

_____

_____

Problem Solving

Write the correct answer.

1. To cook 4 cups of rice, you use 8 cups of water. To cook 10 cups of rice, you use 20 cups of water. Write an expression to show how many cups of water you should use if you want to cook c cups of rice. How many cups of water should you use to cook 5 cups of rice?

2. Sue earns the same amount of money for each hour that she tutors students in math. In 3 hours, she earns $27. In 8 hours, she earns $72. Write an expression to show how much money Sue earns working h hours. At this rate, how much money will Sue earn if she works 12 hours?

3. Bees are one of the fastest insects on Earth. They can fly 22 miles in 2 hours, and 55 miles in 5 hours. Write an expression to show how many miles a bee can fly in h hours. If a bee flies 4 hours at this speed, how many miles will it travel?

4. A friend asks you to think of a number, triple it, and then subtract 2. Write an algebraic expression using the variable x to describe your friend's directions. Then find the value of the expression if the number you think of is 5.

Circle the letter of the correct answer.

5. The ruble is the currency in Russia. In 2005, 1 United States dollar was worth 28 rubles. How many rubles were equivalent to 10 United States dollars?

   A 28

   B 38

   C 280

   D 2,800

6. The peso is the currency in Mexico. In 2005, 1 United States dollar was worth 10 pesos. How many pesos were equivalent to 5 United States dollars?

   F 1

   G 10

   H 15

   J 50

Translating Between Words and Math
Going Deeper

Essential question: *How do you write algebraic expressions?*

CC.6.EE.2a

1 EXPLORE Writing Expressions from Models

video tutor

Write a description in words for each situation. Then write an algebraic expression from the description. Use *x* as the variable.

A Andrew has a bag containing an unknown number of counters. He reaches in and removes 5 counters.

Description in Words	Algebraic Expression

B Mercedes folds a piece of paper in half.

Description in Words	Algebraic Expression

REFLECT

1a. What are some words that can describe addition and subtraction?

_____

_____

1b. What are some words that can describe multiplication and division?

_____

1c. Write three algebraic expressions that represent the phrase "5 times *y*."

_____

TRY THIS!

Write each phrase as an algebraic expression.

1d. 8 fewer than m _____

1e. the product of 10 and c _____

Expressions can be written with constants and variables, or they may be described in words. When given an expression in words, it is important to be able to translate the words into algebra.

There are several different ways to describe expressions with words.

Operation	Addition	Subtraction	Multiplication	Division
Words	• added to • plus • sum • more than	• subtracted from • minus • difference • less than • take away • taken from	• times • multiplied by • product • groups of	• divided by • divided into • quotient

CC.6.EE.2a

2 EXAMPLE   Writing Algebraic Expressions

Write each phrase as an algebraic expression.

A   **5 subtracted from y**

The operation is _____.

The algebraic expression is y 5.

B   **The product of 9 and p**

The operation is _____.

The algebraic expression is _____.

TRY THIS!

Write each phrase as an algebraic expression.

2a. n times 7 _____

2b. 4 minus y _____

2c. 13 added to x _____

2d. x divided by 9 _____

2e. 9 divided by x _____

2f. c plus 3 _____

REFLECT

2g. **Error Analysis** Erica wrote "5 added to y" as $5 + y$ and "5 subtracted from y" as $5 - y$. Why is the first expression correct but the second incorrect? When is order important in writing an expression?

_____

_____

_____

When solving real-world problems, you may need to identify the action taking place to know which operation to use.

Action	Operation
Put parts together	Addition
Put equal parts together	Multiplication
Find how much more or less	Subtraction
Separate into equal parts	Division

CC.6.EE.2

3 EXAMPLE Translating Words into Algebraic Expressions

Center City is 10 miles farther from Sam's house than Westonville is. Write an algebraic expression to represent the distance from Sam's house to Center City.

Let w represent the distance from Sam's house to Westonville.

The distance from Sam's house to Center City is 10 miles more / less than w.

So, to find the distance from Sam's house to Center City, put together
_____ and _____.

Which operation represents this action? _____

The distance from Sam's house to Center City can be represented by the
expression _____.

TRY THIS!

3a. Sonia worked 25 hours last week. She was paid the same amount of money
per hour that she worked. Let h represent Sonia's hourly pay. Write an algebraic
expression that represents Sonia's total pay last week.

_____

3b. Noah is saving to buy a new laptop computer. He has saved $119 so far.
Let c represent the cost of the laptop. Write an algebraic expression that
represents the amount of money Noah still needs to save.

_____

REFLECT

3c. **What If…?** Suppose Center City was 10 miles *closer* to Sam's house than
Westerville. How would the expression you wrote in **3** change?

_____

_____

3d. Are the expressions $w - 10$ and $10 - w$ equivalent expressions? Explain.

_____

PRACTICE

Write each phrase as an algebraic expression.

1. n divided by 8 _____

2. p multiplied by 4 _____

3. 3 groups of w _____

4. the sum of 1 and q _____

5. the quotient of 13 and z _____

6. c added to 45 _____

7. h less than 30 _____

8. 47 subtracted from m _____

Write a phrase in words for each algebraic expression.

9. $m + 8$ _____

10. $42s$ _____

11. $\dfrac{v}{12}$ _____

12. $t - 29$ _____

13. $32 - r$ _____

14. $9b$ _____

15. $\dfrac{20}{d}$ _____

16. $k + 32$ _____

17. Kai's score on a test was 12 points greater than Julia's score. Let k represent Kai's score. Write an algebraic expression to represent Julia's score. _____

18. The town of Rayburn received 6 more inches of snow than the town of Greenville. Let g represent the amount of snow in Greenville. Write an algebraic expression to represent the amount of snow in Rayburn. _____

19. Abby baked 48 cookies and divided them evenly into bags. Let b represent the number of bags. Write an algebraic expression to represent the number of cookies in each bag. _____

20. Eli is driving at a speed of 55 miles per hour. Let h represent the number of hours that Eli drives at this speed. Write an algebraic expression to represent the number of miles that Eli travels during this time. _____

21. Explain the difference between "b divided by 10" and "b divided into 10."

_____

_____

_____

Translating Between Tables and Expressions

Modeling

Essential question: *How do you write an expression for a sequence?*

video tutor

CC.6.EE.2a

1 EXPLORE **Using Variables to Describe Patterns**

Look at the pattern of squares below.

Stage 1   Stage 2   Stage 3

A What is the pattern? _____

How many squares will be in stage 4? _____

B What is the relationship between the stage number and the number of squares?

_____

Use this relationship to complete the table below.

Stage	1	2	3	4	5	6	7	8	
Squares	3	6	9						

C Let *n* represent any stage number. How many squares are in stage *n*?

_____

Add a column to the end of the table in **B** for stage *n*.

REFLECT

1a. When might it be useful to know how many squares are in stage *n*?

_____

_____

_____

1b. **What If...?** Suppose there are 3 squares in Stage 1 and one more square is added at each stage. What is the relationship between the stage number and the number of squares? If *n* represents the stage number, how many squares are in stage *n*?

_____

Fill in the missing values or expressions in each table.

1.

PE Classes	4	8	12	
Weeks	2		6	w

2.

Movie Tickets	1	2	3	t
Cost (dollars)	7	14		

3.

Pies		2	3	p
Slices	6		18	

The table at the right shows data from Mrs. Petersen's last science test. Use the table for Exercises 4–7.

Correct	Incorrect	Score
21	4	84
20	5	80
23	2	92
17	8	68
c		

4. What is the relationship between the first two columns?

_____

_____

5. What is the relationship between the first and last columns?

_____

_____

6. Fill in the missing expressions for the last row of the table.

7. Suppose you answered x questions incorrectly on the quiz. Write an expression for your score. _____

8. Look at the pattern of circles at the right. What is the relationship between the stage number and the number of circles? If n represents the stage number, how many circles are in stage n?

Stage 1   Stage 2   Stage 3

_____

_____

Additional Practice

Write an expression for the missing value in each table.

1.
Bicycles	Wheels
1	2
2	4
3	6
b	

2.
Ryan's Age	Mia's Age
14	7
16	9
18	11
r	

3.
Minutes	Hours
60	1
120	2
180	3
m	

4.
Bags	Potatoes
3	21
4	28
5	35
b	

Write an expression for the sequence in each table.

5.
Position	1	2	3	4	5	n
Value of Term	3	4	5	6	7	

6.
Position	1	2	3	4	5	n
Value of Term	5	9	13	17	21	

7. A rectangle has a width of 6 inches. The table shows the area of the rectangle for different widths. Write an expression that can be used to find the area of the rectangle when its length is l inches.

Width (in.)	Length (in.)	Area (in.^{2})
6	8	48
6	10	60
6	12	72
6	l	

Problem Solving

Use the table to write an expression for the missing value. Then use your expression to answer the questions.

1. How many cars are produced on average each year?

   _____

2. How many cars will be produced in 6 years?

   _____

3. After how many years will there be an average production of 3,750 cars?

   _____

Cars Produced By Company X

Numbers of Years	Average Number of Cars Produced
2	2,500
5	6,250
7	8,750
10	12,500
12	15,000
14	17,500
n	

Circle the letter of the correct answer.

Company Y produces twice as many cars as Company X.

4. How many cars does Company Y produce on average in 8 years?

   A 1,250

   B 10,000

   C 11,250

   D 20,000

5. How many more cars on average does Company Y produce in 4 years than Company X?

   F 2,500

   G 5,000

   H 6,125

   J 7,500

6. Which company produces an average of 11,250 cars in 9 years?

   A Company X

   B Company Y

   C both companies

   D neither company

7. How many cars are produced on average by both companies in 10 years?

   F 3,750

   G 12,500

   H 25,000

   J 37,500

2-4

Equations and Their Solutions
Going Deeper

Essential question: *How do you determine whether a number is a solution of an equation?*

An **equation** is a mathematical statement that two expressions are equal. An equation may or may not contain variables. For an equation that has a variable, a **solution** of the equation is a value of the variable that makes the equation true.

CC.6.EE.5

1 EXAMPLE Checking Solutions

Determine whether the given value is a solution of the equation.

A $x + 9 = 15; x = 6$

$$\boxed{} + 9 \overset{?}{=} 15 \qquad\qquad \textit{Substitute 6 for x.}$$

$$\boxed{} \overset{?}{=} 15 \qquad\qquad \textit{Add.}$$

6 is / is not a solution of $x + 9 = 15$.

B $5 = t - 4; t = 11$

$$5 \overset{?}{=} \boxed{} - 4 \qquad\qquad \textit{Substitute 11 for t.}$$

$$5 \overset{?}{=} \boxed{} \qquad\qquad \textit{Subtract.}$$

11 is / is not a solution of $5 = t - 4$.

C $8x = 72; x = 9$

$$8\left(\boxed{}\right) \overset{?}{=} 72 \qquad\qquad \textit{Substitute 9 for x.}$$

$$\boxed{} \overset{?}{=} 72 \qquad\qquad \textit{Multiply.}$$

9 is / is not a solution of $8x = 72$.

D $\frac{y}{4} = 32; y = 8$

$$\frac{\boxed{}}{4} \overset{?}{=} 32 \qquad\qquad \textit{Substitute 8 for y.}$$

$$\boxed{} \overset{?}{=} 32 \qquad\qquad \textit{Divide.}$$

8 is / is not a solution of $\frac{y}{4} = 32$.

Determine whether the given value is a solution of the equation.

1a. $11 = n + 6; n = 5$ **1b.** $y - 6 = 24; y = 18$ **1c.** $\frac{36}{x} = 9; x = 4$

_____   _____   _____

REFLECT

1d. Write an equation containing a variable that has a solution of 16.

_____

CC.6.EE.6

2 EXAMPLE Writing an Equation

Mark scored 17 points in a basketball game. His teammates scored a total of _p_ points, and the team as a whole scored 46 points. Write an equation to represent this situation.

Mark's points	+	Teammates' points	=	Total points

☐ + ☐ = ☐

REFLECT

2a. Write an equation containing an operation other than addition that also represents the situation.

_____

TRY THIS!

Write an equation to represent each situation.

2b. Marilyn has a fish tank that contains 38 fish. There are 9 goldfish and f other fish.

_____

2c. Juanita has 102 beads to make n necklaces. Each necklace will have 17 beads.

_____

2d. Craig is c years old. His 12-year-old sister Caitlin is 3 years younger than Craig.

_____

2e. Sonia rented ice skates for h hours. The rental fee was $2 per hour and she paid a total of $8.

_____

3 EXAMPLE Writing an Equation and Checking Solutions

Sarah used a gift card to buy $47 worth of groceries. Now she has $18 left on her gift card. Write an equation to determine whether Sarah had $65 or $59 on the gift card before buying groceries.

A The boxes below represent the three quantities given in the problem. Write an equation to show the relationship between these quantities by writing mathematical symbols between the boxes.

| Amount on card | | Amount spent | | Amount left on card |

Which two quantities in the equation are known?

_____

Rewrite the equation, substituting numbers from the problem for the two known quantities. Substitute the variable x for the unknown quantity.

_____

B How can you use the equation from **A** to check whether Sarah had $65 or $59 on the gift card before buying groceries?

_____

Use the space below to check whether Sarah had $65 or $59 before buying groceries.

The amount on Sarah's gift card before she bought groceries was $_____.

TRY THIS!

3a. Pedro bought 8 tickets to a basketball game. He paid a total of $208. Write an equation to determine whether each ticket cost $26 or $28.

_____

3b. On Saturday morning, Owen earned $24 raking leaves. By the end of the afternoon he had earned a total of $62. Write an equation to determine whether Owen earned $38 or $31 on Saturday afternoon.

_____

Determine whether the given value is a solution of the equation.

1. $23 = x - 9$; $x = 14$ _____

2. $\frac{n}{13} = 4$; $n = 52$ _____

3. $14 + x = 46$; $x = 32$ _____

4. $17y = 85$; $y = 5$ _____

5. $25 = \frac{k}{5}$; $k = 5$ _____

6. $2.5n = 45$; $n = 18$ _____

7. $21 = m + 9$; $m = 11$ _____

8. $21 - h = 15$; $h = 6$ _____

9. $d - 4 = 19$; $d = 15$ _____

10. $5 + x = 47$; $x = 52$ _____

11. $w - 9 = 0$; $w = 9$ _____

12. $5q = 31$; $q = 13$ _____

13. $7a = 126$; $a = 18$ _____

14. $3.6 = 3c$; $c = 1.2$ _____

15. $\frac{1}{2}r = 8$; $r = 4$ _____

16. $9x = 117$; $x = 12$ _____

For 17–19, write an equation to represent the situation.

17. Each floor of a hotel has r rooms. On 8 floors, there are a total of 256 rooms.

_____

18. Mario had b books. After receiving 5 new books for his birthday, he had 18 books.

_____

19. In the school band, there are 5 trumpet players and f flute players. There are twice as many flute players as there are trumpet players.

_____

20. Halfway through a bus route, 48 students remain on the bus, and 23 students have already been dropped off. Write an equation to determine whether there are 61 or 71 students on the bus at the beginning of the route.

_____

21. The high temperature was 92 °F. This was 24 °F higher than the overnight low temperature. Write an equation to determine whether the low temperature was 62 °F or 68 °F.

_____

22. Andy is one-fourth as old as his grandfather, who is 76 years old. Write an equation to determine whether Andy is 19 or 22 years old.

_____

Additional Practice

Determine whether the given value of the variable is a solution.

1. $9 + x = 21$ for $x = 11$ _____

2. $n - 12 = 5$ for $n = 17$ _____

3. $25 \cdot r = 75$ for $r = 3$ _____

4. $72 \div q = 8$ for $q = 9$ _____

5. $28 + c = 43$ for $c = 15$ _____

6. $u \div 11 = 10$ for $u = 111$ _____

7. $\dfrac{k}{8} = 4$ for $k = 24$ _____

8. $16x = 48$ for $x = 3$ _____

9. $73 - f = 29$ for $f = 54$ _____

10. $67 - j = 25$ for $j = 42$ _____

11. $39 \div v = 13$ for $v = 3$ _____

12. $88 + d = 100$ for $d = 2$ _____

13. $14p = 20$ for $p = 5$ _____

14. $6w = 30$ for $w = 5$ _____

15. $7 + x = 70$ for $x = 10$ _____

16. $6 \cdot n = 174$ for $n = 29$ _____

Replace each ? with a number that makes the equation correct.

17. $5 + 1 = 2 + \boxed{?}$ _____

18. $10 - \boxed{?} = 12 - 7$ _____

19. $\boxed{?} \cdot 3 = 2 \cdot 9$ _____

20. $28 \div 4 = 14 \div \boxed{?}$ _____

21. $\boxed{?} + 8 = 6 + 3$ _____

22. $12 \cdot 0 = \boxed{?} \cdot 15$ _____

23. Carla had $15. After she bought lunch, she had $8 left. Write an equation using the variable x to model this situation. What does your variable represent?

_____

_____

24. Seventy-two people signed up for the soccer league. After the players were evenly divided into teams, there were 6 teams in the league. Write an equation to model this situation using the variable x.

_____

_____

Problem Solving

Use the table to write and solve an equation to answer each question. Then use your answers to complete the table.

1. A hippopotamus can stay underwater 3 times as long as a sea otter can. How long can a sea otter stay underwater?

   _____

   _____

How Many Minutes Can Mammals Stay Underwater?	
Hippopotamus	15
Human	
Muskrat	
Platypus	10
Polar bear	
Sea cow	16
Sea otter	
Seal	22
Sperm whale	

2. A seal can stay underwater 10 minutes longer than a muskrat can. How long can a muskrat stay underwater?

   _____

   _____

3. A sperm whale can stay underwater 7 times longer than a sea cow can. How long can a sperm whale stay underwater?

   _____

   _____

Circle the letter of the correct answer.

4. The difference between the time a platypus and a polar bear can stay underwater is 8 minutes. How long can a polar bear stay underwater?

   A   1 minute

   B   2 minutes

   C   3 minutes

   D   5 minutes

5. When you divide the amount of time any of the animals in the table can stay underwater by itself, the answer is always the amount of time the average human can stay underwater. How long can the average human stay underwater?

   F   6 minutes

   G   4 minutes

   H   2 minutes

   J   1 minute

Addition Equations
Modeling

Essential question: *How do you solve whole-number equations that contain addition?*

2-5

CC.6.EE.7

1 **E X P L O R E** Addition Equations

A puppy weighed 6 ounces at birth. After two weeks, the puppy weighed 14 ounces. How much weight did the puppy gain?

Let x represent the number of ounces gained.

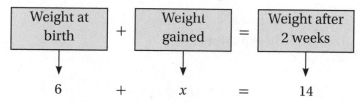

$$6 + x = 14$$

To answer this question, you can solve the equation $6 + x = 14$.

Algebra tiles can model some equations. An equation mat represents the two sides of an equation. To solve the equation, remove the same number of tiles from both sides of the mat until the x-tile is by itself on one side.

A Model $6 + x = 14$.

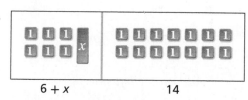

$6 + x$ \qquad 14

B How many unit tiles must you remove on the left side so that the x-tile is by itself? _____ Cross out these tiles on the equation mat.

C Whenever you remove tiles from one side of the mat, you must remove the same number of tiles from the other side of the mat. Cross out the tiles that should be removed on the right side of the mat.

D How many tiles remain on the right side of the mat? _____ This is the solution of the equation.

The puppy gained _____ ounces.

TRY THIS!

Solve each equation.

1a. $x + 2 = 7$ \qquad **1b.** $x + 9 = 12$ \qquad **1c.** $6 + x = 11$

$x =$ _____ \qquad $x =$ _____ \qquad $x =$ _____

Removing the same number of tiles from each side of an equation mat models subtracting the same number from both sides of an equation.

> ## Subtraction Property of Equality
>
> You can subtract the same number from both sides of an equation, and the two sides will remain equal.

When an equation contains addition, solve by subtracting the same number from both sides.

CC.6.EE.7

2 EXAMPLE Using the Subtraction Property of Equality

Solve each equation.

A $a + 15 = 26$

What number is added to a? _____

Subtract this number from both sides of the equation.

$$a + \quad 15 \quad = \quad 26$$

$$-\boxed{} \quad -\boxed{}$$

$$a \qquad = \boxed{} \qquad \textit{Subtract.}$$

Check: $a + 15 = 26$

$$\boxed{} + 15 \stackrel{?}{=} 26 \qquad \textit{Substitute} \boxed{} \textit{for a.}$$

$$\boxed{} \stackrel{?}{=} 26 \qquad \textit{Add on the left side.}$$

B $23 = d + 17$

What number is added to d? _____

Subtract this number from both sides of the equation.

$$23 \quad = d \ + \ 17$$

$$-\boxed{} \quad -\boxed{}$$

$$\boxed{} = d \qquad \textit{Subtract.}$$

TRY THIS!

Solve each equation.

2a. $n + 34 = 56$

$n =$ _____

2b. $w + 31 = 72$

$w =$ _____

2c. $z + 54 = 712$

$z =$ _____

3 EXAMPLE   Solving Problems with Addition Equations

The towns of Pocahontas, Humboldt, and Clarion are located in that order in a straight line along a portion of Highway 3 in western Iowa. It is 24 miles from Pocahontas to Humboldt and 47 miles from Pocahontas to Clarion. Find the distance *d* from Humboldt to Clarion.

Complete the model using information from the problem.

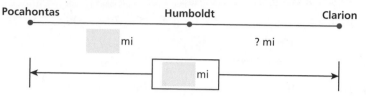

Now write and solve an equation.

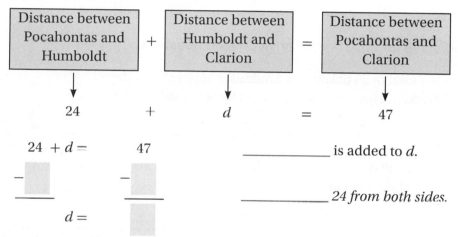

$$24 + d = 47$$

_____ is added to *d*.

_____ 24 *from both sides.*

$$d =$$

The distance between Humboldt and Clarion is _____ miles.

REFLECT

3a. How did the model help you solve the problem?

_____

_____

3b. Explain how to check your answer.

_____

TRY THIS!

3c. At a large city park, a slide, a carousel, and a set of swings are located in that order along a straight walkway. It is 42 feet from the carousel to the swings and 75 from the slide to the swings. Write an equation to find the distance *d* from the slide to the carousel.

_____

_____

Solve each equation.

1. $t + 6 = 10$

$t =$ _____

2. $a + 7 = 15$

$a =$ _____

3. $w + 57 = 102$

$w =$ _____

4. $k + 13 = 61$

$k =$ _____

5. $m + 49 = 82$

$m =$ _____

6. $b + 79 = 106$

$b =$ _____

7. $19 + d = 29$

$d =$ _____

8. $26 + h = 96$

$h =$ _____

9. $82 + p = 122$

$p =$ _____

For 10–15, write and solve an equation to answer each question.

10. Marcus needs to sell a total of 25 tickets to a fundraiser supper by Friday. So far, he has sold 9 tickets. How many tickets does he still need to sell?

_____

11. Taylor has read 125 pages in a novel. The novel has a total of 262 pages. How many pages does she have left to read to finish the novel?

_____

12. The Acme Car Company sold 37 vehicles in June. How many compact cars were sold in June?

_____

Acme Car Company – June Sales	
Type of Car	Number Sold
SUV	8
Compact	?

_____

13. Cari has 91 songs on her MP3 player. Of these songs, 55 are pop songs and the rest are rock songs. How many rock songs are on her MP3 player?

_____

14. The gas tank on Mr. Chang's car holds 22 gallons. He filled the tank at a gas station by buying 13 gallons of gas. How many gallons of gas were in the tank before he made his purchase?

_____

15. A library has 108 movies available for checkout. The movies are in VHS format or DVD format. If there are 65 VHS tapes, how many DVDs are there?

_____

Additional Practice

Solve each equation. Check your answers.

1. $s + 3 = 23$

_____

2. $v + 10 = 49$

_____

3. $q + 9 = 16$

_____

4. $81 + m = 90$

_____

5. $38 + x = 44$

_____

6. $28 + n = 65$

_____

7. $t + 31 = 50$

_____

8. $25 + p = 39$

_____

9. $19 + v = 24$

_____

Solve each equation. Check your answers.

10. $m + 8 = 17$

_____

11. $r + 14 = 20$

_____

12. $25 + x = 32$

_____

13. $47 + p = 55$

_____

14. $19 + d = 27$

_____

15. $13 + n = 26$

_____

16. $q + 12 = 19$

_____

17. $34 + f = 43$

_____

18. $52 + w = 68$

_____

19. Kenya bought 28 beads, and Nancy bought 25 beads. It takes 35 beads to make a necklace. Write and solve two addition equations to find how many more beads they each need to make a necklace.

_____

_____

_____

20. During a sales trip, Mr. Jones drove 15 miles east from Brownsville to Carlton. Then he drove several more miles east from Carlton to Sun City. The distance from Brownsville to Sun City is 35 miles. Write and solve an addition equation to find how many miles it is from Carlton to Sun City.

_____

_____

_____

Problem Solving

Use the bar graph and addition equations to answer the questions.

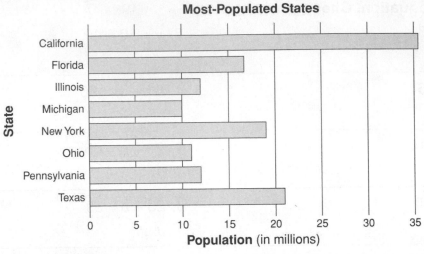

Most-Populated States

1. How many more people live in California than in New York?

_____

2. How many more people live in Ohio than in Michigan?

_____

3. How many more people live in Florida than in Illinois?

_____

4. How many more people live in Texas than in Pennsylvania?

_____

Circle the letter of the correct answer.

5. Which two states' populations are used in the equation $12 + x = 12$?

   A   Pennsylvania and Texas

   B   Ohio and Florida

   C   Michigan and Illinois

   D   Illinois and Pennsylvania

6. What is the value of x in the equation in Exercise 5?

   F   0   H   12

   G   1   J   24

7. In 2003, the total population of the United States was 292 million. How many of those people did not live in one of the states shown on the graph?

   A   416 million   C   154 million

   B   73 million   D   292 million

8. The combined population of Ohio and one other state is the same as the population of Texas. What is that state?

   F   California

   G   Florida

   H   Michigan

   J   Pennsylvania

Subtraction Equations
Modeling

Essential question: *How do you solve whole-number equations that contain subtraction?*

video tutor

CC.6.EE.7

1 EXPLORE Subtraction Equations

Luke's teacher placed some counters in a box. After removing 6 counters from the box, his teacher said that there were 9 counters left in the box. How many counters were in the box to begin with?

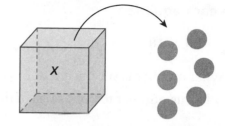

Use the diagram to help you solve the problem.

A What operation is modeled by the action of taking away counters? _____

B Write the subtraction equation in the table. Let x represent the number of counters in the box to begin with.

Counters taken out of the box	Counters left in the box	Subtraction Equation	Value of x
6	9		

C Why is a variable used to represent the number of counters in the box to begin with?

_____

D What operation "undoes" subtraction? _____

E Explain how the diagram can help you solve the equation.

_____

_____

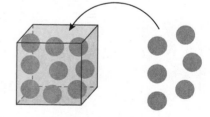

F Record the solution in the table.

There were _____ counters in the box to begin with.

TRY THIS!

Solve each equation.

1a. $v - 10 = 25$ **1b.** $w - 22 = 34$ **1c.** $17 = z - 13$

$v =$ _____ $w =$ _____ $z =$ _____

When an equation contains subtraction, solve by adding the same number to both sides.

Addition Property of Equality

You can add the same number to both sides of an equation, and the two sides will remain equal.

CC.6.EE.7

2 EXAMPLE Using the Addition Property of Equality

Solve each equation.

A $y - 21 = 18$

What number is subtracted from y? _____

Add this number to both sides of the equation.

$$y - 21 = 18$$

$+$ ☐ $+$ ☐
_____   _____

y $=$ ☐   *Add.*

B $31 = g - 16$

What number is subtracted from g? _____

Add this number to both sides of the equation.

$$31 = g - 16$$

$+$ ☐ $+$ ☐
_____   _____

☐ $= g$ *Add.*

Check: $31 = g - 16$

$31 \overset{?}{=} $ ☐ $- 16$ *Substitute* ☐ *for g.*

$31 \overset{?}{=} $ ☐   *Subtract on the right side.*

TRY THIS!

Solve each equation.

2a. $x - 16 = 72$

$x = $ _____

2b. $h - 24 = 31$

$h = $ _____

2c. $t - 17 = 84$

$t = $ _____

3 EXAMPLE Solving Problems with Subtraction Equations

To reach a California condor's nest, a scientist rappels 44 feet down from the top of a sea cliff. If the nest is estimated to be 90 feet above the base of the cliff, what is the approximate height of the sea cliff?

Write and solve an equation.

Let h represent the overall height of the sea cliff.

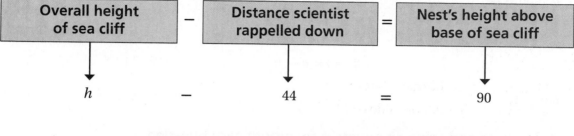

| Overall height of sea cliff | − | Distance scientist rappelled down | = | Nest's height above base of sea cliff |

h − 44 = 90

$h - 44 = 90$ _____ is subtracted from h.

$+ \quad \quad +$ _____ 44 to both sides.

$h \quad = \quad$

The approximate height of the sea cliff is _____ feet.

REFLECT

3a. How do you know what number to add to both sides of an equation containing subtraction?

_____

_____

3b. Describe how solving an addition equation is similar to solving a subtraction equation.

_____

_____

TRY THIS!

Write and solve a subtraction equation to answer the question.

3c. While staying at a large hotel in the city, you get in an elevator and ride it down 15 floors, getting out on the 28th floor. On what floor did you get into the elevator?

_____

Solve each equation.

1. $r - 8 = 56$

$r =$ _____

2. $x - 61 = 37$

$x =$ _____

3. $d - 25 = 55$

$d =$ _____

4. $p - 36 = 29$

$p =$ _____

5. $f - 41 = 106$

$f =$ _____

6. $h - 57 = 88$

$h =$ _____

7. $16 = a - 28$

$a =$ _____

8. $46 = c - 49$

$c =$ _____

9. $112 = k - 77$

$k =$ _____

For 10–14, write and solve an equation to answer each question.

10. Lindsey finished a race in 58 seconds. This was 4 seconds faster than her best practice time. What was Lindsey's best practice time?

_____

11. Jackson needed new pencils for school today. He took 6 pencils from a new box of pencils. If there are 18 pencils left in the box, how many pencils were in the brand new box?

_____

12. At the end of the sales day, the manager at The Shirt Store checked the shirt inventory. There were 82 short sleeve shirts still in stock. How many short sleeve shirts were in stock before today's sales?

_____

_____

The Shirt Store — Today's Sales	
Shirt Type	**Number Sold**
Short Sleeve	24
Long Sleeve	17

13. The manager at The Shirt Store found that there were 76 long sleeve shirts still in stock at the end of the sales day. How many long sleeve shirts were in stock before today's sales?

_____

14. Kimiko has been working on her math assignment. So far she has completed 18 of the assigned homework problems. She counts and finds that she has 14 problems left to do. How many problems were assigned for this homework?

_____

Additional Practice

Solve each equation. Check your answers.

1. $s - 8 = 12$

_____

2. $v - 11 = 7$

_____

3. $9 = q - 5$

_____

4. $m - 21 = 5$

_____

5. $34 = x - 12$

_____

6. $n - 45 = 45$

_____

7. $t - 19 = 9$

_____

8. $p - 6 = 27$

_____

9. $15 = v - 68$

_____

Solve each equation. Check your answers.

10. $7 = m - 5$

_____

11. $r - 10 = 22$

_____

12. $16 = x - 4$

_____

13. $40 = p - 11$

_____

14. $28 = d - 6$

_____

15. $n - 9 = 42$

_____

16. $q - 85 = 8$

_____

17. $f - 13 = 18$

_____

18. $47 = w - 38$

_____

19. Ted took 17 pictures at the aquarium. He now has 7 pictures left on the roll. Write and solve a subtraction equation to find out how many photos Ted had when he went to the aquarium.

_____

20. Ted bought a dolphin poster for $12. He now has $5. Write and solve a subtraction equation to find out how much money Ted took to the aquarium.

_____

Problem Solving

Write and solve subtraction equations to answer the questions.

1. Dr. Felix Hoffman invented aspirin in 1899. That was 29 years before Alexander Fleming invented penicillin. When was penicillin invented?

_____

_____

2. Kimberly was born on February 2. That is 10 days earlier than Kent's birthday. When is Kent's birthday?

_____

_____

3. Kansas and North Dakota are the top wheat-producing states. In 2000, North Dakota produced 314 million bushels of wheat, which was 34 million bushels less than Kansas produced. How much wheat did Kansas farmers grow in 2000?

_____

_____

4. Scientists assign every element an atomic number, which is the number of protons in the nucleus of that element. The atomic number of silver is 47, which is 32 less than the atomic number of gold. How many protons are in the nucleus of gold?

_____

_____

Circle the letter of the correct answer.

5. The spine-tailed swift and the frigate bird are the two fastest birds on earth. A frigate bird can fly 95 miles per hour, which is 11 miles per hour slower than a spine-tailed swift. How fast can a spine-tailed swift fly?

   A 84 miles per hour

   B 101 miles per hour

   C 106 miles per hour

   D 116 miles per hour

6. The Green Bay Packers and the Kansas City Chiefs played in the first Super Bowl in 1967. The Chiefs lost by 25 points, with a final score of 10. How many points did the Packers score in the first Super Bowl?

   F 35

   G 25

   H 15

   J 0

7. The Rocky Mountains extend 3,750 miles across North America. That is 750 miles shorter than the Andes Mountains in South America. How long are the Andes Mountains?

   A 3,000 miles   C 180 miles

   B 5 miles   D 4,500 miles

8. When the United States took its first census in 1790, only 4 million people lived here. That was 288 million fewer people than the population in 2003. What was the population of the United States in 2003?

   F 292 million   H 69 million

   G 284 million   J 1,108 million

2-7

Multiplication Equations
Modeling

Essential question: *How do you solve whole-number equations that contain multiplication?*

CC.6.EE.7

1 EXPLORE Multiplication Equations

Deanna has a cookie recipe that requires 12 eggs to make 3 batches of cookies. How many eggs are needed per batch of cookies?

Let x represent the number of eggs needed.

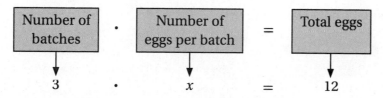

$$3 \cdot x = 12$$

To answer this question, you can use algebra tiles to solve $3x = 12$.

A Model $3x = 12$.

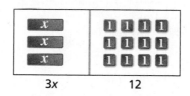

$3x$ 12

B There are 3 variable tiles, so draw circles to separate the tiles into 3 equal groups. One group has been circled for you.

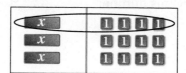

C How many unit tiles are in each group? _____ This is the solution of the equation.

_____ eggs are needed per batch of cookies.

TRY THIS!

1. Caroline ran 15 miles in 5 days. She ran the same distance each day. Write and solve an equation to determine the number of miles she ran each day.

_____

Separating the tiles on both sides of an equation mat into an equal number of groups models dividing both sides of an equation by the same number.

> ### Division Property of Equality
>
> You can divide both sides of an equation by the same nonzero number, and the two sides will remain equal.

When an equation contains multiplication, solve by dividing both sides of the equation by the same number.

CC.6.EE.7

2 EXAMPLE Using the Division Property of Equality

Solve each equation.

A $9a = 54$

What number is multiplied by a? _____

Divide both sides of the equation by this number.

$$\frac{9a}{\boxed{}} = \frac{54}{\boxed{}}$$

$a = \boxed{}$ *Divide.*

Check: $9a = 54$

$9\left(\boxed{}\right) \overset{?}{=} 54$ *Substitute* $\boxed{}$ *for a.*

$\boxed{} \overset{?}{=} 54$ *Multiply on the left side.*

B $72 = 3d$

What number is multiplied by d? _____

Divide both sides of the equation by this number.

$$\frac{72}{\boxed{}} = \frac{3d}{\boxed{}}$$

$\boxed{} = d$ *Divide.*

Check: $72 = 3d$

$72 \overset{?}{=} 3\left(\boxed{}\right)$ *Substitute* $\boxed{}$ *for d.*

$72 \overset{?}{=} \boxed{}$ *Multiply on the right side.*

TRY THIS!

Solve each equation.

2a. $3x = 21$

$x =$ _____

2b. $18h = 216$

$h =$ _____

2c. $143 = 11y$

$y =$ _____

3 EXAMPLE · Solving Problems with Multiplication Equations

Mr. Nguyen is planting a new rectangular garden. The garden will be 8 feet wide and he needs 200 square feet for the vegetables he wants to plant. How long should he make the garden?

Draw a diagram.

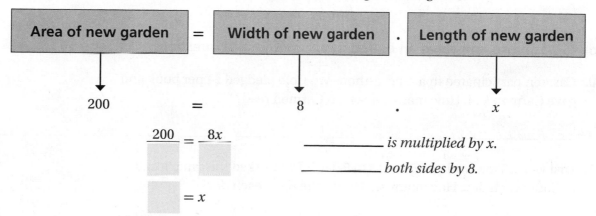

Area = ⬜ square feet ⬜ ft

? ft

Now write and solve an equation. Let x represent the length of the garden.

Area of new garden	=	Width of new garden	·	Length of new garden
200	=	8	·	x

$$\frac{200}{} = \frac{8x}{}$$ _____ *is multiplied by x.*

_____ *both sides by 8.*

$$\boxed{} = x$$

Mr. Nyugen should make his new garden _____ feet long.

REFLECT

3a. Explain how to check your answer in ③.

_____

3b. Describe how solving an addition equation is different than solving a multiplication equation.

_____

_____

_____

TRY THIS!

3c. At a garden center, 180 containers of small bushes are separated into groups of 12. Write and solve an equation to find how many groups of containers there will be.

_____

Solve each equation.

1. $6c = 18$

$c =$ _____

2. $2a = 14$

$a =$ _____

3. $75 = 15x$

$x =$ _____

4. $9y = 81$

$y =$ _____

5. $7h = 805$

$h =$ _____

6. $25d = 350$

$d =$ _____

7. $96 = 24f$

$f =$ _____

8. $594 = 6k$

$k =$ _____

9. $32v = 672$

$v =$ _____

For 10–15, write and solve an equation to answer each question.

10. Carmen participated in a read-a-thon. Mr. Cole pledged $4 per book and gave Carmen $44. How many books did Carmen read?

_____

11. Last week, Tina worked 35 hours in 5 days. She worked the same number of hours each day. How many hours did she work each day?

_____

12. Lee drove his car 476 miles and used 17 gallons of gasoline. How many miles did Lee's car travel per gallon of gasoline?

_____

13. A large rectangular area rug for a living room covers an area of 135 square feet. If the length of the rug is 15 feet, how wide is it?

_____

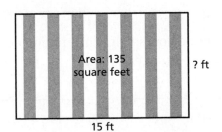

Area: 135 square feet   ? ft

15 ft

14. On some days, Mercedes commutes 4 hours per day to the city for business meetings. Last month she commuted for a total of 36 hours. How many days did she commute to the city last month?

_____

15. A volunteer group collected 384 cans of food. The food will be divided evenly among 6 local charities. How many cans of food will each charity receive?

_____

Additional Practice

Solve each equation. Check your answers.

1. $8s = 72$

2. $4v = 28$

_____

3. $27 = 9q$

4. $12m = 60$

_____

5. $48 = 6x$

6. $7n = 63$

_____

7. $10t = 130$

8. $15p = 450$

_____

9. $84 = 6v$

_____

Solve each equation. Check your answers.

10. $49 = 7m$

11. $20r = 80$

12. $64 = 8x$

_____

13. $36 = 4p$

14. $147 = 7d$

15. $11n = 110$

_____

16. $12q = 144$

17. $25f = 125$

18. $128 = 16w$

_____

19. A hot-air balloon flew at 10 miles per hour. Using the variable h, write and solve a multiplication equation to find how many hours the balloon traveled if it covered a distance of 70 miles.

_____

20. A passenger helicopter can travel 300 miles in the same time it takes a hot-air balloon to travel 20 miles. Using the variable s, write and solve a multiplication equation to find how many times faster the helicopter can travel than the hot air balloon.

_____

Problem Solving

Write and solve a multiplication equation to answer each question.

1. In 1975, a person earning minimum wage made $80 for a 40-hour work week. What was the minimum wage per hour in 1975?

   _____

   _____

2. If an ostrich could maintain its maximum speed for 5 hours, it could run 225 miles. How fast can an ostrich run?

   _____

   _____

3. About 2,000,000 people live in Paris, the capital of France. That is 80 times larger than the population of Paris, Texas. How many people live in Paris, Texas?

   _____

   _____

4. The average person in China goes to the movies 12 times per year. That is 3 times more than the average American goes to the movies. How many times per year does the average American go to the movies?

   _____

   _____

Circle the letter of the correct answer.

5. Recycling just 1 ton of paper saves 17 trees! If a city recycled enough paper to save 136 trees, how many tons of paper did it recycle?

   A 7 tons

   B 8 tons

   C 9 tons

   D 119 tons

6. Seaweed found along the coast of California, called giant kelp, grows up to 18 inches per day. If a giant kelp plant has grown 162 inches at this rate, for how many days has it been growing?

   F 180 days   H 9 days

   G 144 days   J 8 days

7. The distance between Atlanta, Georgia, and Denver, Colorado, is 1,398 miles. That is twice the distance between Atlanta and Detroit, Michigan. How many miles would you have to drive to get from Atlanta to Detroit?

   A 2,796 miles

   B 349.5 miles

   C 699 miles

8. Jupiter has 2 times more moons than Neptune has, and 8 times more moons than Mars has. Jupiter has 16 moons. How many moons do Neptune and Mars each have?

   F 8 moons, 2 moons

   G 2 moons, 8 moons

   H 128 moons, 32 moons

   J 32 moons, 128 moons

2-8

Division Equations
Modeling

Essential question: *How do you solve whole-number equations that contain division?*

video tutor

CC.6.EE.7

1 EXPLORE Division Equations

Nolan and his two friends ate an entire pizza. Each person ate 4 pieces. How many pieces were in the pizza to start with?

A Let *x* represent the number of pieces in the pizza to start with.

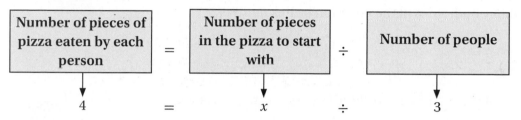

Number of pieces of pizza eaten by each person	=	Number of pieces in the pizza to start with	÷	Number of people
4	=	*x*	÷	3

To answer this question, you can solve the equation $4 = \frac{x}{3}$.

B The number of pieces in the pizza to start with is divided into _____ equal groups.

Each person ate _____ of the total number of pieces.

C $\frac{1}{3}$ of the total number of pieces is _____ so $\frac{1}{3}x = $ _____.

D Fraction pieces and counters can be used to model the equation. Use a $\frac{1}{3}$ fraction piece to represent $\frac{1}{3}x$ or $\frac{x}{3}$. Use 4 counters to represent 4.

E How many $\frac{1}{3}$ pieces do you need to model the entire pizza? _____

Complete the model by drawing more fraction pieces and counters.

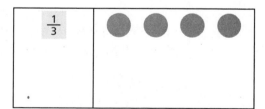

F Explain how the model shows the answer.

_____

_____

There were _____ pieces of pizza to start with.

When an equation contains division, solve by multiplying both sides of the equation by the same number.

Multiplication Property of Equality

You can multiply both sides of an equation by the same number, and the two sides will remain equal.

CC.6.EE.7

2 EXAMPLE Using the Multiplication Property of Equality

Solve each equation.

A $\frac{x}{5} = 20$

What number is x divided by? _____

Multiply both sides of the equation by this number.

$$\boxed{} \cdot \frac{x}{5} = \boxed{} \cdot 20$$

$$x = \boxed{} \qquad \textit{Multiply.}$$

Check: $\frac{x}{5} = 20$

$$\frac{\boxed{}}{5} \overset{?}{=} 20 \qquad \textit{Substitute} \boxed{} \textit{ for x.}$$

$$\boxed{} \overset{?}{=} 20 \qquad \textit{Divide on the left side.}$$

B $15 = \frac{r}{2}$

What number is r divided by? _____

Multiply both sides of the equation by this number.

$$\boxed{} \cdot 15 = \boxed{} \cdot \frac{r}{2}$$

$$\boxed{} = r \qquad \textit{Multiply.}$$

Check: $15 = \frac{r}{2}$

$$15 \overset{?}{=} \frac{\boxed{}}{2} \qquad \textit{Substitute} \boxed{} \textit{ for r.}$$

$$15 \overset{?}{=} \boxed{} \qquad \textit{Divide on the right side.}$$

3 EXAMPLE Solving Problems with Division Equations

For a music concert, Mrs. DeSoe has chosen 12 students to hand out programs as people enter the auditorium. She has divided the programs evenly into 12 bundles, one for each student. Each bundle contains 55 programs. How many programs did Mrs. DeSoe have printed for the concert?

Write and solve an equation.

Let x represent the total number of programs.

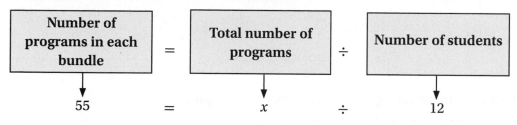

Number of programs in each bundle	=	Total number of programs	÷	Number of students

$$55 \qquad = \qquad x \qquad ÷ \qquad 12$$

To answer the question, you can solve the equation $55 = \frac{x}{12}$.

$$55 \quad = \quad \frac{x}{12} \qquad\qquad x \text{ is divided by } \underline{\hspace{3cm}}.$$

$$\boxed{} \cdot 55 \quad = \quad \boxed{} \cdot \frac{x}{12} \qquad \underline{\hspace{3cm}} \text{ both sides by 12.}$$

$$\boxed{} \quad = \quad x$$

Mrs. DeSoe had a total of _____ programs printed.

REFLECT

3a. Explain how this figure models the equation $\frac{x}{4} = 8$.

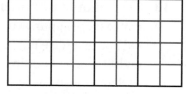

_____

_____

_____

_____

TRY THIS!

Solve each equation.

3b. $\frac{y}{9} = 12$

$y =$ _____

3c. $\frac{x}{4} = 24$

$x =$ _____

3d. $9 = \frac{w}{9}$

$w =$ _____

Solve each equation.

1. $\frac{n}{4} = 68$

$n = \underline{\hspace{3cm}}$

2. $\frac{a}{6} = 27$

$a = \underline{\hspace{3cm}}$

3. $\frac{b}{7} = 19$

$b = \underline{\hspace{3cm}}$

4. $\frac{h}{10} = 15$

$h = \underline{\hspace{3cm}}$

5. $29 = \frac{w}{8}$

$w = \underline{\hspace{3cm}}$

6. $7 = \frac{t}{24}$

$t = \underline{\hspace{3cm}}$

7. $\frac{s}{11} = 33$

$s = \underline{\hspace{3cm}}$

8. $12 = \frac{m}{9}$

$m = \underline{\hspace{3cm}}$

9. $\frac{z}{64} = 8$

$z = \underline{\hspace{3cm}}$

For 10–15, write and solve an equation to answer each question.

10. The total cost of tickets to a professional basketball game was divided equally among 5 friends. If each person paid \$32, what was the total cost of the tickets?

11. Students trying out for cheerleader at a school were divided into 6 equal groups to learn the routine. There were 8 people in each group. How many students tried out for cheerleader?

12. What division equation is modeled by the figure at the right? Find the solution of the equation.

13. The children who attended a youth fitness camp were separated into groups to use the various exercise equipment. Since there were eight pieces of equipment, they were placed in 8 groups. If there were 14 children in each of the groups, how many children attended the fitness camp?

14. During a radio promotion, identical prize packages each included 4 concert tickets. How many tickets were given away if there were 15 prize packages?

15. At Baker Middle School, there are 5 Spanish classes with 24 students in each class. There are 4 French classes with 26 students in each class. How many students altogether are in the Spanish and French classes?

Additional Practice

Solve each equation. Check your answers.

1. $\dfrac{s}{6} = 7$

_____

2. $\dfrac{v}{5} = 9$

_____

3. $12 = \dfrac{q}{7}$

_____

4. $\dfrac{m}{2} = 16$

_____

5. $26 = \dfrac{x}{3}$

_____

6. $\dfrac{n}{8} = 4$

_____

7. $\dfrac{t}{11} = 11$

_____

8. $\dfrac{p}{7} = 10$

_____

9. $7 = \dfrac{v}{8}$

_____

Solve each equation. Check your answers.

10. $10 = \dfrac{m}{9}$

_____

11. $\dfrac{r}{5} = 8$

_____

12. $11 = \dfrac{x}{7}$

_____

13. $9 = \dfrac{p}{12}$

_____

14. $15 = \dfrac{d}{5}$

_____

15. $\dfrac{n}{4} = 28$

_____

16. $\dfrac{q}{2} = 134$

_____

17. $\dfrac{u}{16} = 1$

_____

18. $2 = \dfrac{w}{25}$

_____

19. All the seats in the theater are divided into 6 groups. There are 35 seats in each group. Using the variable s, write and solve a division equation to find how many seats there are in the theater.

_____

20. There are 16 ounces in one pound. A box of nails weighs 4 pounds. Using the variable w, write and solve a division equation to find how many ounces the box weighs.

_____

Problem Solving

Use the table to write and solve a division equation to answer each question.

1. How many total people signed up to play soccer in Bakersville this year?

_____

2. How many people signed up to play lacrosse this year?

_____

3. What was the total number of people who signed up to play baseball this year?

_____

4. Which two sports in the league have the same number of people signed up to play this year? How many people are signed up to play each of those sports?

_____

Bakersville Sports League

Sport	Number of Teams	Players on Each Team
Baseball	7	20
Soccer	11	15
Football	8	24
Volleyball	12	9
Lacrosse	6	17
Basketball	10	10
Tennis	18	6

Circle the letter of the correct answer.

5. Which sport has a higher total number of players, football or tennis? How many more players?

   A football; 10 players

   B tennis; 144 players

   C football; 84 players

   D tennis; 18 players

6. Only one sport this year has the same number of players on each team as its number of teams. Which sport is that?

   F basketball

   G football

   H soccer

   J tennis

CHAPTER 2

Problem Solving Connections

How Much Paint? Jody's family has moved into a new house, and Jody is going to repaint her new bedroom. Jody's dad says that she first has to calculate how much paint to buy. How can Jody use algebraic expressions to find the amount of paint she will need?

COMMON CORE

CC.6.EE.1
CC.6.EE.2a, b, c
CC.6.EE.3
CC.6.EE.4
CC.6.EE.6

1 Write Expressions

A Jody's bedroom is rectangular. Let a represent the width (shorter side) of the room, and let b represent the length (longer side). Let c represent the height of each wall.

The rectangular prism below can be used to model Jody's bedroom. Label a, b, and c on the prism.

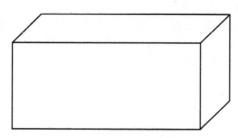

B Write an algebraic expression to represent the combined area of the two larger walls of the room. Explain your thinking.

_____

_____

C Write an algebraic expression to represent the combined area of the two smaller walls. Explain your thinking.

_____

_____

D Write an algebraic expression to represent the area of the ceiling.

_____

E Use your answers above to write an algebraic expression to represent the total area of all four walls and the ceiling.

_____

2 Evaluate Expressions

A Now Jody must measure her bedroom so she can substitute the measurements into the algebraic expressions. First Jody measures the height c of the walls and the length b of the longer wall. She finds that $c = 12$ feet and $b = 20$ feet.

Rewrite the expression that represents the combined area of the two larger walls. Then evaluate this expression using the values of b and c that Jody found. What is the total area of these two walls?

B Jody cannot reach high enough to measure the ceiling, so she measures the floor instead. She already knows that the longer side of the floor b measures 20 feet. She finds that the shorter side a measures 8 feet.

Rewrite the expression that represents the area of the ceiling. Then evaluate this expression using the values of a and b that Jody found. What is the area of the ceiling?

C Does Jody need to measure anything else to find the area of the two smaller walls? Why or why not?

_____

_____

D Rewrite the expression that represents the combined area of the two smaller walls. Then evaluate this expression using the appropriate values. What is the total area of these two walls?

E Find the total area of the four walls and the ceiling. Explain how you found your answer.

F "Now we can go to the paint store and buy the paint," Jody says. "Wait!" says Dad. "Some of the walls are not really rectangles. Your room has a door and two square windows. You can paint the door if you want, but you are definitely not going to paint the windows!" After thinking about it, Jody decides that she will paint her door.

Both windows are the same size. Let *s* represent the side length of one of the windows. Write an algebraic expression with an exponent to represent the combined area of both windows. Explain your thinking.

G Jody returns to her room to measure one of the windows. She measures the window's length as 4 feet.

Rewrite the expression that represents the combined area of the two windows. Then evaluate that expression using Jody's measurement. What is the total area of the two windows?

H Explain how you used the order of operations to evaluate the expression for the windows' area.

I What operation should Jody use to find the total area of the surfaces she is going to paint?

Find the total area that Jody will paint.

A Jody and her dad arrive at the paint store, where Jody chooses two paint colors—light blue for the walls and white for the ceiling.

Look back to find the area of the ceiling and write it here: _____ ft²

How can Jody find the total area of just the four walls (not including the ceiling)?

_____

Find the area of only the four walls.

B The label on each paint can reads "Covers 300 square feet." Jody reasons that the area of the four walls is about 600 ft², so she will need $\frac{600}{300} = 2$ cans of blue paint. Do you agree with Jody? Why or why not? If not, how many cans of blue paint do you think Jody should buy?

_____

_____

C How many cans of white paint does Jody need? Explain your thinking.

_____

_____

D The paint store associate recommends that Jody put two coats on each surface to completely cover the existing color. Does one can of white paint contain enough paint for two coats on the ceiling? Explain.

_____

_____

Jody and her dad agree with the paint store associate and decide to apply two coats. Jody says, "Then we need twice as much paint, two cans of white paint and six cans of blue paint." Is Jody correct? Explain.

_____

_____

_____

_____

Name _____ Class _____ Date _____

Performance Task

COMMON
CORE

CC.6.EE.2, 2a
CC.6.EE.5
CC.6.EE.6
CC.6.EE.7

⭐ **1.** Jasper runs 5 laps around the school track. Then Kelly joins him, and they run some laps together.

a. Define a variable for the number of laps Jasper and Kelly run together. Use the variable to write an expression for the total number of laps Jasper runs.

b. Jasper and Kelly ran 12 laps together. Use your expression from part **a** to find the total number of laps Jasper ran.

⭐ **2.** The table shows the cost for different amounts of grapes.

Grapes (pounds)	Cost ($)
3	9
4	12
5	15

a. Write an expression to represent the cost of p pounds of grapes.

b. Marty wants to buy 6 pounds of grapes. He has $20. Does he have enough money? Explain.

© Houghton Mifflin Harcourt Publishing Company

3. A gym has an enrollment fee of $80. There is also a $25 fee per month of membership.

a. Write an expression to represent the total cost of *m* months of membership.

b. Caryn wants to get into shape for an upcoming backpacking trip. She will work out in a gym for 6 months. How much would the gym cost for 6 months?

c. A new gym offers no enrollment fee and costs $40 per month of membership. Should she join this gym, or the one described in part **a**? Explain.

4. Mr. Rollins has a rectangular garden that is 14 feet wide and 20 feet long. He decides to extend the length of the garden. His plan would add another 70 square feet to the area of the garden.

a. How many feet does Mr. Rollins plan to extend the length of the garden? Explain how you know.

b. Mr. Rollins's wife asks him to instead extend the *width* of the garden by 4 feet. Does this give a greater total area for the garden? Explain.

Name _____ Class _____ Date _____

SELECTED RESPONSE

1. Miguel and his team must answer the following question correctly in order to win a quiz bowl contest.

A sunflower grows 5 inches every month. How many months will it take for the sunflower to reach a height of 60 inches?

Which equation can be used to solve this problem?

A. $m + 5 = 60$ **C.** $5m = 60$

B. $m - 5 = 60$ **D.** $\frac{m}{5} = 60$

2. Look at the model.

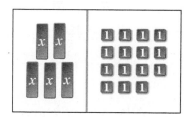

What is the value of x?

F. 3   **H.** 10

G. 7   **J.** 13

3. Erik made a model train that was 25 feet shorter in length than an actual train. Let m represent the length of Erik's model. Which expression represents the length of the actual train?

A. $25 - m$ **C.** $m + 25$

B. $25m$ **D.** $m - 25$

4. Last week Randy worked 42 hours in 5 days. Which equation could Randy use to find the average number of hours he worked each day?

F. $\frac{h}{5} = 42$ **H.** $\frac{h}{42} = 5$

G. $5h = 42$ **J.** $42h = 5$

5. Eight batches of pancakes can be made with 16 eggs. How many eggs are needed for one batch of pancakes?

A. 2 eggs   **C.** 8 eggs

B. 4 eggs   **D.** 24 eggs

6. Mark has been asked to find the value of $4(9 + 24) + 7$. What should he do first?

F. Add 4 and 7.

G. Multiply 4 and 9.

H. Multiply 4 and 24.

J. Add 9 and 24.

7. The new county park has an area that is 3.5 times the area of the old park. Let p represent the area of the old park. Which expression represents the area of the new park?

A. $3.5p$ **C.** $p + 3.5$

B. $p - 3.5$ **D.** $\frac{p}{3.5}$

8. Look at the model.

What is the value of x?

F. 3   **H.** 10

G. 5   **J.** 15

9. Evaluate the expression $24x - 13y$ for $x = 3$ and $y = 2$.

A. 11   **C.** 37

B. 33   **D.** 46

10. Which expression does **not** equal 15?

F. $3k$ for $k = 5$

G. $3 + k$ for $k = 12$

H. $\frac{k}{3}$ for $k = 60$

J. $k - 10$ for $k = 25$

11. The new building in City Center is 345 feet taller than the Jefferson Building. Let h represent the height of the Jefferson Building. Which expression represents the height of the new building?

A. $h + 345$ **C.** $h - 345$

B. $345 - h$ **D.** $345h$

12. Jenna's basketball team scored 54 points in its last game. Jenna scored 18 of the points. Which equation could be used to determine the number of points p scored by Jenna's teammates?

F. $18p = 54$ **H.** $p - 18 = 54$

G. $\frac{54}{p} = 18$ **J.** $p + 18 = 54$

13. Lucinda is arranging 150 patio blocks to build a patio. Let p represent the number of patio blocks Lucinda arranged in one hour. Which equation describes the relationship between p and h, the total number of hours Lucinda needed to arrange all 150 patio blocks?

A. $h = 150 + p$ **C.** $h = 150p$

B. $h = \frac{150}{p}$ **D.** $h = 150 - p$

14. Which expression has a value of 74 when $a = 10$, $b = 8$, and $c = 12$?

F. $4abc$ **H.** $2ac - 3b$

G. $a + 5b + 2c$ **J.** $6abc + 8$

15. Which quantity **cannot** be represented by the expression $0.20x$?

A. The total cost of x text messages, where each text message costs $0.20

B. The total amount of calcium in x servings of a cereal that contains 0.2 gram of calcium per serving

C. The area of a rectangle with length x and width 0.2

D. The amount of change due when an item that costs $0.20 is paid for with x dollars

CONSTRUCTED RESPONSE

16. Write two different phrases in words that describe the expression $7z$.

_____

_____

17. Write an algebraic expression...

a. that has three terms. _____

b. in which one term is the product of two variables. _____

c. that is the sum of a product and a constant. _____

18. The distance from Ray's house to the shopping center is 3.5 miles more than the distance from Ray's house to the city park.

a. Let c equal the distance from Ray's house to the city park. Write an expression to represent the distance from Ray's house to the shopping center.

_____

b. The distance from Ray's house to the city park is 2 miles. How can you use this information and your answer to part **a** to find the distance from Ray's house to the shopping center?

_____

c. What is the distance from Ray's house to the shopping center?

_____

19. The table shows the time Sue spent tutoring two of her students and how much she was paid.

Sue's Tutoring		
	Hours	Pay
Will	3	$27
Hector	8	$72

Write an expression to show how much Sue will earn in h hours. How many hours must Sue tutor to earn $45? Justify your answer.

_____

Decimals

Chapter Focus

You will compare and order decimals. You will build on your estimation skills by estimating decimal sums, differences, products, and quotients. You will also add, subtract, multiply, and divide decimal numbers. Real-world problems will give you the opportunity to interpret the quotient in terms of the given situation. This will help you decide if your answer makes sense or if you should round your answer up or down. Finally, you will combine skills learned in the chapter to solve decimal equations.

Chapter at a Glance

Lesson		Standards for Mathematical Content
3-1	Representing, Comparing, and Ordering Decimals	PREP FOR **CC.6.NS.7b**
3-2	Estimating Decimals	**CC.6.NS.3**
3-3	Adding and Subtracting Decimals	**CC.6.NS.3**
3-4	Multiplying Decimals	**CC.6.NS.3**
3-5	Dividing Decimals by Whole Numbers	**CC.6.NS.3**
3-6	Dividing by Decimals	**CC.6.NS.3**
3-7	Interpreting the Quotient	**CC.6.NS.3**
3-8	Solving Decimal Equations	**CC.6.EE.7**
	Problem Solving Connections	
	Performance Task	
	Assessment Readiness	

Unpacking the Standards

Understanding the standards and the vocabulary terms in the standards will help you know exactly what you are expected to learn in this chapter.

COMMON CORE CC.6.NS.3

Fluently add, subtract, multiply, and divide multi-digit decimals using the standard algorithm for each operation.

Key Vocabulary

algorithm *(algoritmo)* A set of rules or procedure for solving a mathematical problem in a finite number of steps.

What It Means to You

You will use your knowledge of operations with whole numbers to perform the same operations with decimals.

EXAMPLE

Find the product.

$$3.25 \times 4.8$$

$$3 \times 5 = 15$$

$$
\begin{array}{r}
3.25 \\
\times\ 4.8 \\
\hline
2600 \\
13000 \\
\hline
15.600
\end{array}
$$

COMMON CORE CC.6.EE.7

Solve real-world and mathematical problems by writing and solving equations of the form $x + p = q$ and $px = q$ for cases in which p, q and x are all nonnegative rational numbers.

Key Vocabulary

equation *(ecuación)* A mathematical sentence that shows that two expressions are equivalent.

rational number *(número racional)* A number that can be written in the form $\frac{a}{b}$, where a and b are integers and $b \neq 0$.

What It Means to You

You will use your knowledge of operations to solve equations.

EXAMPLE

Felipe has earned $45.20 by mowing lawns for his neighbors. He wants to buy inline skates that cost $69.95. Write and solve an equation to find how much more money Felipe must earn to buy the skates.

Let m be the amount of money Felipe needs.

$$
\begin{array}{r}
\$45.20\ + m = \$69.95 \\
-\$45.20 \qquad\quad -\$45.20 \\
\hline
m = \$24.75
\end{array}
$$

Felipe needs $24.75 more to buy the inline skates.

COMMON CORE CC.6.EE.2c

Evaluate expressions at specific values of their variables. Include expressions that arise from formulas used in real-world problems. Perform arithmetic operations, including those involving whole number exponents, in the conventional order when there are no parentheses to specify a particular order (Order of Operations).

Key Vocabulary

evaluate *(evaluar)* To find the value of a numerical or algebraic expression.

expression *(expresión)* A mathematical phrase that contains operations, numbers, and/or variables.

exponent *(exponente)* The number that indicates how many times the base is used as a factor.

What It Means to You

You will identify variables in expressions. You will learn the order in which to perform arithmetic operations.

EXAMPLE

Evaluate $7.52 - s$ for $s = 2.9$.

$$7.52 - s$$
$$7.52 - 2.9$$

$$\begin{array}{r} 7.52 \\ -\ 2.90 \\ \hline 4.62 \end{array}$$

COMMON CORE CC.6.EE.6

Use variables to represent numbers and write expressions when solving a real-world or mathematical problem; understand that a variable can represent an unknown number, or, depending on the purpose at hand, any number in a specified set.

Key Vocabulary

variable *(variable)* A symbol used to represent a quantity that can change.

What It Means to You

You will learn to write algebraic expressions to represent real-world and mathematical problems.

EXAMPLE

The area of the floor in Jonah's bedroom is 28 square meters. If its length is 3.5 meters, what is the width of the bedroom?

$$\text{area} = \text{length} \cdot \text{width}$$
$$28 = 3.5 \cdot w$$

$$28 = 3.5w$$

$$\frac{28}{3.5} = \frac{3.5w}{3.5}$$

$$8 = w$$

The width of Jonah's bedroom is 8 meters.

Key Vocabulary

front-end estimation *(estimación por partes)* An estimating technique in which the front digits of the addends are added.

MATHEMATICAL PRACTICE

The Common Core Standards for Mathematical Practice describe varieties of expertise that mathematics educators at all levels should seek to develop in their students. Opportunities to develop these practices are integrated throughout this program.

1. Make sense of problems and persevere in solving them.
2. Reason abstractly and quantitatively.
3. Construct viable arguments and critique the reasoning of others.
4. Model with mathematics.
5. Use appropriate tools strategically.
6. Attend to precision.
7. Look for and make use of structure.
8. Look for and express regularity in repeated reasoning.

CHAPTER 3

3-1

Representing, Comparing, and Ordering Decimals
Going Deeper

Essential question: *How do you compare and order decimals?*

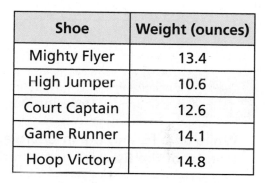

video tutor

PREP FOR **CC.6.NS.7b**

1 EXPLORE   Comparing Decimals

Before buying new basketball shoes, Colin wants to compare the weights of the most popular shoes. The table shows the weights of some shoes he is considering.

Shoe	Weight (ounces)
Mighty Flyer	13.4
High Jumper	10.6
Court Captain	12.6
Game Runner	14.1
Hoop Victory	14.8

A   Which shoe is the heaviest? _____

B   Which shoe is the lightest? _____

C   Graph the shoe weights on a number line.

D   How can you use the number line to compare decimals?

_____

_____

E   Which shoe is lighter than the Court Captain? How do you know?

_____

F   Which shoe has the second greatest weight? _____

You can use the symbols < and > to compare decimals.

• The symbol < means "is less than."
• The symbol > means "is greater than."

G   Compare the weight of Game Runner to the weight of Hoop Victory. _____

H   Colin read about a new shoe that was heavier than Game Runner and lighter than Hoop Victory. Which could be the weight of the new shoe?

14.09   14.14

1a. Quickness on the court is an important part of Colin's game. Which of the shoes do you think he should buy? Justify your answer.

_____

_____

1b. Colin read about another basketball shoe, the Swift Dunker, that weighs 10.65 ounces. Compare the weight of the Swift Dunker to the weight of the High Jumper. Where would you graph the weight of the Swift Dunker on the number line?

_____

_____

PREP FOR **CC.6.NS.7b**

2 EXPLORE Ordering Decimals

While on a fishing trip in Georgia, Beth caught five fish. The weights and lengths of the fish are shown in the table.

Fish Species	Spotted Bass	Brook Trout	Walleye	White Bass	Channel Catfish
Weight (lb)	7.8	5.06	10.38	4.625	9.5
Length (in.)	18.25	18.125	20.5	14.125	22.75

A Graph the lengths of the fish on a number line.

B Order the fish from _longest to shortest_.

_____

C How do you read the lengths from longest to shortest on a number line?

_____

D List the three longest fish in order from _heaviest to lightest_.

_____

E Is the longest fish also the heaviest fish? Explain.

_____

Additional Practice

Write each decimal in standard form, expanded form, and words.

1. 2.07 _____

2. 5 + 0.007 _____

3. four and six tenths _____

4. sixteen and five tenths _____

5. 9 + 0.6 + 0.08 _____

6. 1.037 _____

7. 2 + 0.1 + 0.003 _____

8. eighteen hundredths _____

9. 6.11 _____

Order the decimals from least to greatest.

10. 3.578, 3.758, 3.875

_____

11. 0.0943, 0.9403, 0.9043

_____

12. 12.97, 12.957, 12.75

_____

13. 1.09, 1.901, 1.9, 1.19

_____

14. Your seventh and eighth ribs are two of the longest bones in your body. The average seventh rib is nine and forty-five hundredths inches long, and the average eighth rib is 9.06 inches long. Which bone is longer?

_____

15. The average female human heart weighs nine and three tenths ounces, while the average male heart weighs eleven and one tenth ounces. Which human heart weighs less, the male or the female?

_____

16. The state has $42.3 million for a new theater. The theater that an architect designed would cost $42.25 million. Can the theater be built for the amount the state can pay?

_____

17. Lyn traveled 79.47 miles on Saturday, 54.28 miles on Sunday, 65.5 miles on Monday, and 98.43 miles on Tuesday. Which day did she travel the greatest number of miles?

_____

Problem Solving

Use the table to answer the questions.

1. What is the heaviest marine mammal on Earth?

   _____

2. Which mammal in the table has the shortest length?

   _____

3. Which mammal in the table is longer than a humpback whale, but shorter than a sperm whale?

   _____

Largest Marine Mammals

Mammal	Length (ft)	Weight (T)
Blue whale	110.0	127.95
Fin whale	82.0	44.29
Gray whale	46.0	32.18
Humpback whale	49.2	26.08
Right whale	57.4	39.37
Sperm whale	59.0	35.43

Circle the letter of the correct answer.

4. Which mammal measures forty-nine and two tenths feet long?

   A blue whale

   B gray whale

   C sperm whale

   D humpback whale

5. Which mammal weighs thirty-five and forty-three hundredths tons?

   F right whale

   G sperm whale

   H gray whale

   J fin whale

6. Which of the following lists shows mammals in order from the least weight to the greatest weight?

   A sperm whale, right whale, fin whale, gray whale

   B fin whale, sperm whale, gray whale, blue whale

   C fin whale, right whale, sperm whale, gray whale

   D gray whale, sperm whale, right whale, fin whale

7. Which of the following lists shows mammals in order from the greatest length to the least length?

   F sperm whale, right whale, humpback whale, gray whale

   G gray whale, humpback whale, right whale, sperm whale

   H right whale, sperm whale, gray whale, humpback whale

   J humpback whale, gray whale, sperm whale, right whale

Estimating Decimals
Modeling

Essential question: *How can you estimate decimal sums, differences, products, and quotients?*

You can estimate decimal sums and differences using *rounding*. You can also use **front-end estimation** which means to use only the whole number part of the decimal.

video tutor

CC.6.NS.3

1 EXPLORE   Using a Model to Estimate Sums

Use base-ten models to estimate the sum 1.6 + 3.2.

A   Use front-end estimation.

Estimate

1.6

+ 3.2

Front-end estimate of 1.6 + 3.2: _____

B   Round to the nearest whole number.

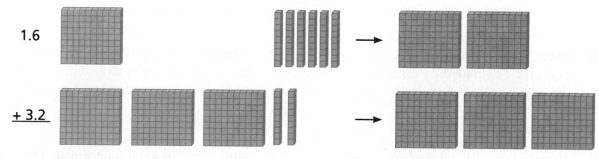

Estimate

1.6

+ 3.2

Rounding estimate of 1.6 + 3.2: _____

REFLECT

1. Which estimate do you think is closer to the actual answer? Why?

_____

_____

2 E X A M P L E Estimating Products and Quotients

A The manager of a store orders a shipment of 48 sweatshirts. Each sweatshirt costs $21.45. Estimate the total cost of the order.

Estimate the product by rounding to the nearest 10.

48   × $21.45

_____ × _____ = _____

The total cost of the sweatshirt order is about _____.

B Henrik's aunt brought him a road map from her trip to Europe. The map shows a distance of 37.6 kilometers between two cities. Henrik knows that 1 mile is equal to about 1.61 kilometers. Estimate the number of miles between the two cities.

Estimate the quotient using compatible numbers.

37.6   ÷   1.61

_____ ÷ _____ = _____

The distance between the two cities is about _____ miles.

P R A C T I C E

Estimate each sum, difference, product, or quotient.

1. $6.72 + 8.31$ _____

2. $19.48 - 6.27$ _____

3. 31.55×18.88 _____

4. $82.1 \div 8.94$ _____

5. At top speed, a hornet can fly 13.39 miles per hour. Estimate the number of hours it would take a hornet to fly 65 miles.

_____

6. Jeremy bought 2 small bottles of water for $1.90 each and a large lemonade for $3.85. Estimate the total cost of his items.

_____

7. Morgan is paid $8.90 per hour at her job. She worked a total of 39.25 hours this week. Estimate her total pay for the week.

_____

8. The winner of a triathlon finished in 54.67 minutes. The average time for all the runners was 73.88 minutes. Estimate the difference between these times.

_____

Additional Practice

Estimate by rounding to the indicated place value.

1. 7.462 + 1.809; tenths

2. 15.3614 – 2.0573; hundredths

3. 56.4059 – 4.837; ones

4. 0.60871 + 1.2103; hundredths

Estimate each product or quotient.

5. 42.1 ÷ 5.97

6. 11.8 • 6.125

7. 63.78 ÷ 8.204

8. 7.539 • 3.0642

9. 80.794 ÷ 8.61

10. 19.801 • 2.78

Estimate a range for each sum.

11. 6.8 + 4.3 + 5.6

12. 12.63 + 9.86 + 20.30

13. Two sixth-grade classes are collecting money to buy a present for one of their teachers. One class collected $24.68 and the other class collected $30.25. About how much money did they collect in all? The gift they want to buy costs $69.75. About how much more money do they need?

14. On the highway, Anita drove an average speed of 60.2 miles per hour. At that speed, about how far can she travel in three and a half hours? At that same speed, about how many hours will it take Anita to drive 400 miles?

Problem Solving

Write the correct answer.

1. Men in Iceland have the highest average life expectancy in the world—76.8 years. The average life expectancy for a man in the United States is 73.1 years. About how much higher is a man's average life expectancy in Iceland? Round your answer to the nearest whole year.

_____

2. The average life expectancy for a woman in the United States is 79.1 years. Women in Japan have the highest average life expectancy—3.4 years higher than the United States. Estimate the average life expectancy of women in Japan. Round your answer to the nearest whole year.

_____

3. There are about 1.6093 kilometers in one mile. There are 26.2 miles in a marathon race. About how many kilometers are there in a marathon race? Round your answer to the nearest tenths.

_____

4. At top speed, a hornet can fly 13.39 miles per hour. About how many hours would it take a hornet to fly 65 miles? Round your answer to the nearest whole number.

_____

Circle the letter of the correct answer.

5. The average male human brain weighs 49.7 ounces. The average female human brain weighs 44.6 ounces. What is the difference in their weights?

   A   about 95 ounces

   B   about 7 ounces

   C   about 5 ounces

   D   about 3 ounces

6. An official hockey puck is 2.54 centimeters thick. About how thick are two hockey pucks when one is placed on top of the other?

   F   about 4 centimeters

   G   about 4.2 centimeters

   H   about 5 centimeters

   J   about 5.2 centimeters

7. Lydia earned $9.75 per hour as a lifeguard last summer. She worked 25 hours a week. About how much did she earn in 8 weeks?

   A   about $250.00

   B   about $2,000.00

   C   about $2,500.00

   D   about $200.00

8. Brent mixed 4.5 gallons of blue paint with 1.7 gallons of white paint and 2.4 gallons of red paint to make a light purple paint. About how many gallons of purple paint did he make?

   F   about 9 gallons

   G   about 8 gallons

   H   about 10 gallons

   J   about 7 gallons

Adding and Subtracting Decimals
Modeling

Essential question: *How do you add and subtract decimals?*

CC.6.NS.3

1 EXPLORE Modeling Decimal Addition

A chemist combines 0.17 mL of water and 0.49 mL of hydrogen peroxide in a beaker. How much total liquid is in the beaker?

You can use a decimal grid divided into 100 small squares to solve this problem. The entire decimal grid represents 1 unit, so each small square represents 0.01, or 1 one-hundredth.

Water	+	**Hydrogen Peroxide**	=	**Total**

How many squares are shaded to represent 0.17 mL of water?

_____

How many squares are shaded to represent 0.49 mL of hydrogen peroxide? _____

How many total squares are shaded?

_____

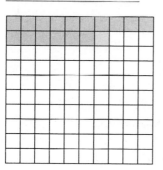 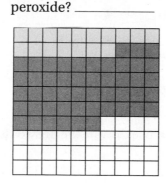

$0.17 + 0.49 = $ _____

There are _____ mL of liquid in the beaker.

TRY THIS!

Shade the grid to find each sum.

1a. $0.24 + 0.71 = $ _____

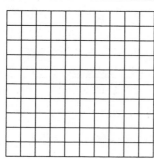

1b. $0.08 + 0.65 = $ _____

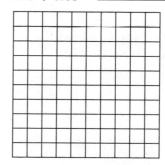

Adding and subtracting decimals are very similar to adding and subtracting whole numbers. First align the numbers by place value. Start adding or subtracting at the right and regroup when necessary. Bring down the decimal point into your answer.

2 EXAMPLE   CC.6.NS.3   Adding Decimals

Hector rode his bicycle 3.12 miles on Monday and 4.7 miles on Tuesday. How many miles did he ride in all?

Step 1 Align the decimal points.
Step 2 Add zeros as placeholders when necessary.
Step 3 Add from right to left.

	3	.	1	2
+	4	.	7	0
		.		

Hector rode _____ miles in all.

To check that your answer is reasonable, you can estimate.
Round each decimal to the nearest whole number.

$$
\begin{array}{r}
3.12 \longrightarrow 3 \\
+\,4.70 \longrightarrow +5 \\
\hline
7.82 \qquad\quad 8
\end{array}
$$

Since 8 is close to 7.82, the answer is reasonable.

TRY THIS!

Add.

2a. $0.42 + 0.27 = $ _____

2b. $0.61 + 0.329 = $ _____

2c. $3.25 + 4.6 = $ _____

2d. $17.27 + 3.88 = $ _____

REFLECT

2e. Why can you rewrite 4.7 as 4.70?

_____

_____

2f. Why is it important to align the decimal points when adding?

_____

_____

3 EXAMPLE   Subtracting Decimals

A   Mia is 160.2 centimeters tall. Rosa is 165.1 centimeters tall.
How much taller is Rosa than Mia?

Step 1 Align the decimal points.
Step 2 Add zeros as placeholders when necessary.
Step 3 Subtract from right to left, regrouping when
necessary.

	1	6	5	.	1
−	1	6	0	.	2
				.	

Rosa is _____ centimeters taller than Mia.

To check that your answer is reasonable, you can estimate.
Round each decimal to the nearest whole number.

$$165.1 \longrightarrow \boxed{}$$
$$- 160.2 \longrightarrow - \boxed{}$$

Check that your answer is close to your estimate.

B   Matthew throws a discus 58.7 meters. Zachary throws the discus
56.12 meters. How much farther did Matthew throw the discus?

Step 1 Align the decimal points.
Step 2 Add zeros as placeholders when necessary.
Step 3 Subtract from right to left, regrouping when
necessary.

	5	8	.	7	0
−	5	6	.	1	2
			.		

Matthew threw the discus _____ meters farther
than Zachary.

To check that your answer is reasonable, you can estimate.
Round each decimal to the nearest whole number.

$$58.7 \longrightarrow \boxed{}$$
$$- 56.12 \longrightarrow - \boxed{}$$

Check that your answer is close to your estimate.

TRY THIS!

Subtract.

3a. $0.91 - 0.45 =$ _____

3b. $4.7 - 0.83 =$ _____

3c. $12.17 - 9.49 =$ _____

3d. $16.04 - 5.716 =$ _____

REFLECT

3e.   How can you check a subtraction problem?

_____

_____

3f.   Use the decimals 2.47, 9.57, and 7.1 to write two different addition
facts and two different subtraction facts.

_____

Shade the grid to find each sum.

1. $0.72 + 0.19 = $ _____

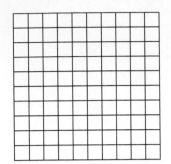

2. $0.38 + 0.4 = $ _____

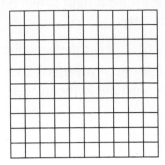

Add or subtract.

3. $54.87 + 7.48 = $ _____

4. $2.19 + 34.92 = $ _____

5. $0.215 + 3.74 = $ _____

6. $28.341 + 37.5 = $ _____

7. $5.623 + 4.19 = $ _____

8. $7.03 + 33.006 = $ _____

9. $0.24 + 1.36 + 7.005 = $ _____

10. $2.25 + 65.47 + 2.333 = $ _____

11. $9.73 - 7.16 = $ _____

12. $18.419 - 6.47 = $ _____

13. $5.006 - 3.2 = $ _____

14. $504.6 - 398.42 = $ _____

15. $25.36 - 2.004 = $ _____

16. $123.8 - 26.42 = $ _____

17. $28.6 - 0.975 = $ _____

18. $5.6 - 0.105 = $ _____

19. $25.68 + 12 = $ _____

20. $57.42 + 4 + 1.602 = $ _____

21. $150.25 - 78 = $ _____

22. $83 - 12.76 = $ _____

Use the café menu to answer each question.

23. What is the cost of a muffin and coffee?

$ _____

24. How much more does coffee cost than tea?

$ _____

25. Isaac buys 2 bagels. He has a coupon for $1.75 off. How much must Isaac pay? $ _____

26. Karen buys a pastry and a cup of tea. She pays with a $10 bill. How much change does she receive?

$ _____

Café Menu	
Muffin	$2.79
Bagel	$2.25
Pastry	$3.35
Coffee	$2.50
Tea	$1.79

Additional Practice

Find each sum or difference.

1. $8.9 + 2.4$

2. $12.7 - 9.6$

3. $18.35 - 4.16$

4. $7.21 + 11.6$

5. $0.975 + 3.8$

6. $20.66 - 9.1$

7. Tiffany's job requires a lot of driving. How many miles did she travel during the month of February? _____

Miles Tiffany Traveled

Week	1	2	3	4
Miles	210.05	195.18	150.25	165.30

8. Shelly baby-sits after school and on the weekends. How much did she earn in all for the month of April? _____

Shelly's Earnings for April

Week	1	2	3	4
Earnings	$120.50	$180.75	$205.25	$215.50

Evaluate $5.6 - a$ for each value of a.

9. $a = 3.7$

10. $a = 0.5$

11. $a = 2.8$

12. $a = 1.42$

13. $a = 0.16$

14. $a = 3.75$

15. Allen bought a box of envelopes for $2.79 and a pack of paper for $4.50. He paid with a $10 bill. How much change should he receive?

16. From a bolt of cloth measuring 25.60 yards, Tina cut a 6.8-yard piece and an 11.9-yard piece. How much material is left on the bolt?

Problem Solving

Use the table to answer the questions.

Busiest Ports in the United States

Port	Imports Per Year (millions of tons)	Exports Per Year (millions of tons)
South Louisiana, LA	30.6	57.42
Houston, TX	75.12	33.43
New York, NY & NJ	53.52	8.03
New Orleans, LA	26.38	21.73
Corpus Christi, TX	52.6	7.64

1. How many more tons of imports than exports does the Port of New Orleans handle each year?

2. How many tons of imports and exports are shipped through the port of Houston, Texas, each year in all?

Circle the letter of the correct answer.

3. Which port ships 0.39 more tons of exports each year than the port at Corpus Christi, Texas?

   A Houston

   B NY & NJ

   C New Orleans

   D South Louisiana

4. What is the difference between the imports and exports shipped in and out of Corpus Christi's port each year?

   F 45.04 million tons

   G 44.94 million tons

   H 44.96 million tons

   J 44.06 million tons

5. What is the total amount of imports shipped into the nation's 5 busiest ports each year?

   A 238.22 million tons

   B 366.47 million tons

   C 128.25 million tons

   D 109.97 million tons

6. What is the total amount of exports shipped out of the nation's 5 busiest ports each year?

   F 366.47 million tons

   G 128.25 million tons

   H 109.97 million tons

   J 238.22 million tons

Multiplying Decimals
Modeling

3-4

Essential question: *How do you multiply decimals?*

CC.6.NS.3

1 **EXPLORE** Modeling Decimal Multiplication

video tutor

Use decimal grids or area models to find each product.

A **0.3 × 0.5**

Shade 3 *columns* of the grid to represent 0.3.

Shade _____ *rows* of the grid to represent 0.5.

The shadings overlap _____ square(s).

This represents _____ hundredth(s), or 0.15.

0.3 × 0.5 = _____

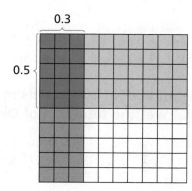

0.3

0.5

B **3.2 × 2.1**

Each row contains 3 wholes + 2 tenths.

Each column contains ____ whole(s) + ____ tenth(s).

The entire area model represents

____ whole(s) + ____ tenth(s) + ____ hundredth(s).

3.2 × 2.1 = _____

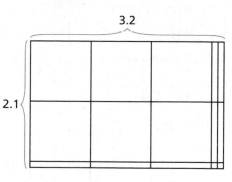

3.2

2.1

TRY THIS!

1a. Use the grid to multiply 0.3 × 0.8.

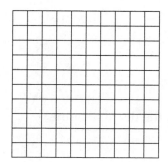

0.3 × 0.8 = _____

1b. Draw an area model to multiply 2.2 × 4.3.

2.2 × 4.3 = _____

1c. How are the products 2.1 × 3.2 and 21 × 32 alike? How are they different?

_____

_____

To multiply decimals, first multiply as you would with whole numbers. Then place the decimal point in the product. The number of decimal places in the product equals the sum of the number of decimal places in the factors.

CC.6.NS.3

2 EXAMPLE Multiplying Decimals

Dwight bought 2.4 pounds of grapes. The grapes cost $1.95 per pound. What was the total cost of Dwight's grapes?

```
   1.95     ←      2  decimal places
  × 2.4     ← +  [ ]  decimal place(s)
   780
 + 3900
  4.680     ←    [ ]  decimal place(s)
```

The grapes cost $ _____.

TRY THIS!

Multiply.

2a.
```
     12.6    ←  [ ]  decimal place(s)
   × 15.3    ← + [ ]  decimal place(s)
      378
  [     ]
 + [     ]
  _____
  [     ]    ←  [ ]  decimal place(s)
```

2b.
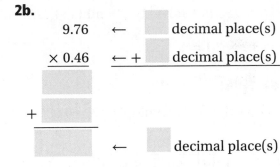
```
     9.76    ←  [ ]  decimal place(s)
   × 0.46    ← + [ ]  decimal place(s)
   [     ]
 + [     ]
  _____
  [     ]    ←  [ ]  decimal place(s)
```

REFLECT

2c. How can you use estimation to check that you have placed the decimal point correctly in your product?

_____

_____

_____

3 EXAMPLE Multiplying Decimals

A tree grows 9.25 inches per year. If the tree continues to grow at this rate, how much will the tree grow in 3.75 years?

$$9.25 \quad \leftarrow \quad \boxed{} \text{ decimal place(s)}$$
$$\times\, 3.75 \quad \leftarrow + \boxed{} \text{ decimal place(s)}$$
$$\underline{}$$
$$4625$$
$$64750$$
$$+ \underline{\boxed{}}$$
$$\boxed{} \quad \leftarrow \quad \boxed{} \text{ decimal place(s)}$$

The tree will grow _____ inches in 3.75 years.

Estimate to check whether your answer is reasonable:

Round 9.25 to the nearest whole number. _____

Round 3.75 to the nearest whole number. _____

Multiply the whole numbers. _____

Is the answer reasonable? Explain. _____

TRY THIS!

Multiply.

3a.
$$\begin{array}{r} 7.14 \\ \times\, 6.78 \\ \hline 5712 \\ \boxed{} \\ +\, \underline{\boxed{}} \\ \hline \boxed{} \end{array}$$

3b.
$$\begin{array}{r} 11.49 \\ \times\, 8.27 \\ \hline \boxed{} \\ \boxed{} \\ +\, \underline{\boxed{}} \\ \hline \boxed{} \end{array}$$

3c. Rico bicycles at an average speed of 15.5 miles per hour. What distance will Rico bicycle in 2.5 hours? _____ miles

3d. Use estimation to show that your answer to **3c** is reasonable.

_____

_____

REFLECT

3e. Compare the products 6.95×38.3 and 69.5×3.83. What do you notice? Explain.

_____

_____

PRACTICE

1. Use the grid to multiply 0.4 × 0.7.

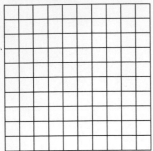

0.4 × 0.7 = _____

2. Draw an area model to multiply 1.1 × 2.4.

1.1 × 2.4 = _____

Place the decimal point in each product.

3. 3.9 × 4.6 = 1 7 9 4

4. 0.219 × 6.2 = 1 3 5 7 8

5. 14.9 × 0.092 = 1 3 7 0 8

6. 5.546 × 8.14 = 4 5 1 4 4 4

Multiply.

7. 0.18 × 0.06 = _____

8. 35.15 × 3.7 = _____

9. 0.96 × 0.12 = _____

10. 62.19 × 32.5 = _____

11. 3.4 × 4.37 = _____

12. 3.762 × 0.66 = _____

13. 11.89 × 41 = _____

14. 73.8 × 19.85 = _____

15. 12.7 × 1.83 = _____

16. 44.1 × 24.66 = _____

17. Chan Hee bought 3.4 pounds of coffee that cost $6.95 per pound. How much did he spend on coffee?

$_____

18. Adita earns $9.40 per hour working at an animal shelter. How much money will she earn for 18.5 hours of work?

$_____

Catherine tracked her gas purchases for one month.

19. How much did Catherine spend on gas in week 2?

$_____

20. How much more did she spend in week 4 than in week 1?

$_____

	Gallons	Cost per gallon ($)
Week 1	10.4	2.65
Week 2	11.5	2.54
Week 3	9.72	2.75
Week 4	10.6	2.70

Additional Practice

Find each product.

1. 0.7
   × 0.3
   _____

2. 0.05
   × 0.4
   _____

3. 8.0
   × 0.02
   _____

4. 3.5
   × 0.2
   _____

5. 12.1
   × 0.01
   _____

6. 9.0
   × 0.9
   _____

7. 0.04 • 0.58

8. 2.15 • 1.5

9. 1.73 • 0.8

10. 6.017 • 2.0

11. 3.96 • 0.4

12. 0.7 • 0.009

Evaluate 8x for each value of x.

13. $x = 0.5$

14. $x = 2.3$

15. $x = 0.74$

16. $x = 3.12$

17. $x = 0.587$

18. $x = 14.08$

19. The average mail carrier walks 4.8 kilometers in a workday. How far do most mail carriers walk in a 6-day week? There are 27 working days in July, so how far will a mail carrier walk in July?

20. A deli charges $3.45 for a pound of turkey. If Tim wants to purchase 2.4 pounds, how much will it cost?

Problem Solving

Use the table to answer the questions.

United States Minimum Wage

Year	Hourly Rate
1940	$0.30
1950	$0.75
1960	$1.00
1970	$1.60
1980	$3.10
1990	$3.80
2000	$5.15

1. At the minimum wage, how much did a person earn for a 40-hour workweek in 1950?

   _____

2. At the minimum wage, how much did a person earn for working 25 hours in 1970?

   _____

3. If you had a minimum-wage job in 1990, and worked 15 hours a week, how much would you have earned each week?

   _____

4. About how many times higher was the minimum wage in 1960 than in 1940?

   _____

Circle the letter for the correct answer.

5. Ted's grandfather had a minimum-wage job in 1940. He worked 40 hours a week for the entire year. How much did Ted's grandfather earn in 1940?

   A $12.00

   B $624.00

   C $642.00

   D $6,240.00

6. Marci's mother had a minimum-wage job in 1980. She worked 12 hours a week. How much did Marci's mother earn each week?

   F $3.72

   G $37.00

   H $37.10

   J $37.20

7. Having one dollar in 1960 is equivalent to having $5.82 today. If you worked 40 hours a week in 1960 at minimum wage, how much would your weekly earnings be worth today?

   A $40.00

   B $5.82

   C $232.80

   D $2,328.00

8. In 2000, Cindy had a part-time job at a florist, where she earned minimum wage. She worked 18 hours each week for the whole year. How much did she earn from this job in 2000?

   F $927.00

   G $4,820.40

   H $10,712.00

   J $2,142.40

© Houghton Mifflin Harcourt Publishing Company

Dividing Decimals by Whole Numbers
Modeling

Essential question: *How do you divide decimals by whole numbers?*

1 EXPLORE Modeling Decimal Division

CC.6.NS.3

Use decimal grids to find the quotient.

6.39 ÷ 3

Shade grids to model 6.39.

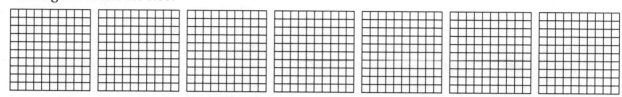

Separate the shaded grids into 3 equal groups. How many are in each group? _____

6.39 ÷ 3 = _____

Dividing decimals is very similar to dividing whole numbers. When you divide a decimal by a whole number, the placement of the decimal point in the quotient is determined by the placement of the decimal in the dividend.

2 EXAMPLE Dividing Decimals by Whole Numbers

CC.6.NS.3

A high school track is 9.76 meters wide. It is divided into 8 lanes of equal width for track and field events. How wide is each lane?

Divide using long division as with whole numbers.

Place a decimal point in the quotient directly above the decimal point in the dividend.

$$
\begin{array}{r}
1. \\
8\overline{)9.76} \\
-8 \\
\hline
17 \\
- \\
\hline
 \\
- \\
\hline
0
\end{array}
$$

Each lane is _____ meters wide.

REFLECT

2. How can you estimate to check that your quotient in 2 is reasonable?

_____

_____

1. Use decimal grids to divide $8.48 \div 4$. _____

Divide.

2. $4\overline{)29.5}$

3. $5\overline{)9.75}$

4. $7\overline{)6.44}$

5. $6\overline{)0.144}$

6. $38.5 \div 5 =$ _____

7. $23.85 \div 9 =$ _____

8. $99.48 \div 3 =$ _____

9. $13.65 \div 7 =$ _____

10. A four-person relay team completed a race in 72.4 seconds. On average, what was each runner's time? _____ second(s)

11. Daniel and three of his friends are having a party. The food for the party cost $31.20 and they agreed to share the cost equally. How much should each person pay? $ _____

12. Rachel bought 31.25 yards of fabric to make curtains for five windows in her house. If she used the same amount of fabric for each window, how many yards of fabric did she use for each window? _____ yards

Use the table for 13 and 14.

Custom Printing Costs				
Quantity	25	50	75	100
Mugs	$107.25	$195.51	$261.75	$329.00
T-shirts	$237.50	$441.00	$637.50	$829.00

13. What is the price per mug for 25 coffee mugs? $ _____

14. What is the price per T-shirt for 75 T-shirts? $ _____

15. Compare the quotients $6.39 \div 3$ and $639 \div 3$.

_____

_____

16. When using models to divide decimals, when might you want to use grids divided into tenths instead of hundredths?

_____

_____

Additional Practice

Find each quotient.

1. $0.81 \div 9$

2. $1.84 \div 4$

3. $7.2 \div 6$

4. $13.6 \div 8$

5. $4.55 \div 5$

6. $29.6 \div 8$

7. $15.57 \div 9$

8. $0.144 \div 12$

9. $97.5 \div 3$

10. $0.0025 \div 5$

11. $2.84 \div 8$

12. $18.9 \div 3$

Evaluate $2.094 \div x$ for each given value of x.

13. $x = 2$

14. $x = 4$

15. $x = 12$

16. $x = 20$

17. $x = 15$

18. $x = 30$

19. There are three grizzly bears in the city zoo. Yogi weighs 400.5 pounds, Winnie weighs 560.35 pounds, and Nyla weighs 618.29 pounds. What is the average weight of the three bears?

20. The bill for dinner came to $75.48. The four friends decided to leave a $15.00 tip. If they shared the bill equally, how much will they each pay?

Problem Solving

Write the correct answer.

1. Four friends had lunch together. The total bill for lunch came to $33.40, including tip. If they shared the bill equally, how much did they each pay?

   _____

2. There are 7.2 milligrams of iron in a dozen eggs. Because there are 12 eggs in a dozen, how many milligrams of iron are in 1 egg?

   _____

3. Kyle bought a sheet of lumber 8.7 feet long to build fence rails. He cut the strip into 3 equal pieces. How long is each piece?

   _____

4. An albatross has a wingspan greater than the length of a car—3.7 meters! Wingspan is the length from the tip of one wing to the tip of the other wing. What is the length of each albatross wing (assuming wing goes from center of body)?

   _____

Circle the letter of the correct answer.

5. The City Zoo feeds its three giant pandas 181.5 pounds of bamboo shoots every day. Each panda is fed the same amount of bamboo. How many pounds of bamboo does each panda eat every day?

   A 6.05 pounds

   B 60.5 pounds

   C 61.5 pounds

   D 605 pounds

6. Emma bought 22.5 yards of cloth to make curtains for two windows in her apartment. She used the same amount of cloth on each window. How much cloth did she use to make each set of curtains?

   F 1.125 yards

   G 10.25 yards

   H 11.25 yards

   J 11.52 yards

7. Aerobics classes cost $153.86 for 14 sessions. What is the fee for one session?

   A $10.99

   B $1.99

   C about $25.00

   D about $20.00

8. An entire apple pie has 36.8 grams of saturated fat. If the pie is cut into 8 slices, how many grams of saturated fat are in each slice?

   F 4.1 grams

   G 0.46 grams

   H 4.6 grams

   J 4.11 grams

Dividing by Decimals
Modeling

3-6

Essential question: *How do you divide by decimals?*

CC.6.NS.3

1 EXPLORE Modeling Decimal Division

Use decimal grids to find the quotient.

6.39 ÷ 2.13

Shade grids to model 6.39.

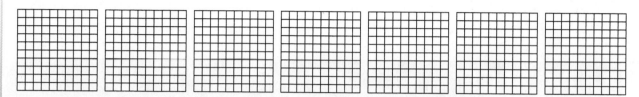

Separate the model into groups of 2.13. How many groups do you have? _____

6.39 ÷ 2.13 = _____

When dividing a decimal by a decimal, first change the divisor to a whole number by multiplying by a power of 10. Then multiply the dividend by the same power of 10.

CC.6.NS.3

2 EXAMPLE Dividing a Decimal by a Decimal

> **A** Ella uses 0.5 pound of raspberries in each raspberry cake that she makes. How many cakes can Ella make with 3.25 pounds of raspberries?

Step 1 The divisor has one decimal place, so multiply both the dividend and the divisor by 10 so that the divisor is a whole number.

$$0.5\overline{)3.25}$$

$$0.5\overline{)3.25}$$

0.5 × 10 = _____

3.25 × 10 = _____

Step 2 Divide.

$$\begin{array}{r} 6. \\ 5\overline{)32.5} \\ -30 \\ \hline 2 \\ - \\ \hline \end{array}$$

Ella can make _____ cakes.

REFLECT

2. The number of cakes that Ella can make is not equal to the quotient. Why not?

_____

_____

B Anthony spent $11.52 for some pens that were on sale for $0.72 each. How many pens did Anthony buy?

Step 1 The divisor has two decimal places, so multiply both the dividend and the divisor by 100 so that the divisor is a whole number.

$0.72\overline{)11.52}$ $0.72\overline{)11.52}$

$0.72 \times 100 =$ _____

$11.52 \times 100 =$ _____

Step 2 Divide.

$$72\overline{)1152}$$
$$-72$$
$$4$$
$$-$$

Anthony bought _____ pens.

PRACTICE

Divide.

1. $0.5\overline{)4.25}$

2. $3.1\overline{)10.261}$

3. $90 \div 0.36 =$ _____

4. $18.88 \div 1.6 =$ _____

5. Michael paid $11.48 for sliced cheese at the deli counter. The cheese cost $3.28 per pound. How much cheese did Michael buy?

_____ pound(s)

6. Elizabeth has a piece of ribbon that is 4.5 meters long. She wants to cut it into pieces that are 0.25 meter long. How many pieces of ribbon will she have?

_____ piece(s)

7. Lisa paid $43.95 for 16.1 gallons of gasoline. What was the cost per gallon, rounded to the nearest hundredth?

$ _____ per gallon

8. One inch is equivalent to 2.54 centimeters. How many inches are there in 50.8 centimeters?

_____ in.

9. Emma makes $8.25 per hour at her part-time job. She earned $123.75 last week. How many hours did she work last week?

_____ hours

10. Colson's dad bought 5.25 pounds of trail mix for a family hiking vacation. If the family eats 1.5 pounds of trail mix each day, will they have enough to last for 4 days? Explain.

_____

_____

Additional Practice

Find each quotient.

1. $9.0 \div 0.9$
2. $29.6 \div 3.7$
3. $10.81 \div 2.3$

_____ _____ _____

4. $10.5 \div 1.5$
5. $15.36 \div 4.8$
6. $9.75 \div 1.3$

_____ _____ _____

7. $20.4 \div 5.1$
8. $37.5 \div 2.5$
9. $9.24 \div 1.1$

_____ _____ _____

10. $16.56 \div 6.9$
11. $28.9 \div 8.5$
12. $14.35 \div 0.7$

_____ _____ _____

Evaluate $x \div 1.2$ for each value of x.

13. $x = 40.8$
14. $x = 1.8$
15. $x = 10.8$

_____ _____ _____

16. $x = 14.4$
17. $x = 4.32$
18. $x = 0.06$

_____ _____ _____

19. Anna is saving $6.35 a week to buy a computer game that costs $57.15. How many weeks will she have to save to buy the game?

_____

20. Ben ran a 19.5-mile race last Saturday. His average speed during the race was 7.8 miles per hour. How long did it take Ben to finish the race?

_____

Problem Solving

Write the correct answer.

1. Peter spent $6.75 on wire to build a rabbit hutch. Wire costs $0.45 per foot. How many feet of wire did Peter buy?

_____

2. Jamal drove 195.3 miles in 3.5 hours. On average, how many miles per hour did he drive?

_____

3. Lisa's family drove 830.76 miles to visit her grandparents. Lisa calculated that they used 30.1 gallons of gas. How many miles per gallon did the car average?

_____

4. A chef bought 84.5 pounds of ground beef. She uses 0.5 pound of ground beef for each hamburger. How many hamburgers can she make?

_____

Circle the letter of the correct answer.

5. Mark earned $276.36 for working 23.5 hours last week. He earned the same amount of money for each hour that he worked. What is Mark's hourly rate of pay?

   A $1.17

   B $10.76

   C $11.76

   D $117.60

6. Alicia wants to cover a section of her wall that is 2 feet wide and 12 feet long with mirrors. Each mirror tile is 2 feet wide and 1.5 feet long. How many mirror tiles does she need to cover that section?

   F 4 tiles

   G 6 tiles

   H 8 tiles

   J 12 tiles

7. John ran the city marathon in 196.5 minutes. The marathon is 26.2 miles long. On average, how many miles per hour did John run the race?

   A 7 miles per hour

   B 6.2 miles per hour

   C 8 miles per hour

   D 8.5 miles per hour

8. Shaneeka is saving $5.75 of her allowance each week to buy a new camera that costs $51.75. How many weeks will she have to save to have enough money to buy it?

   F 9 weeks

   G 9.5 weeks

   H 8.1 weeks

   J 8 weeks

Interpreting the Quotient
Going Deeper

Essential question: *How do you solve problems by interpreting the quotient?*

Many real-world situations require an exact answer to a problem. But in some cases, you may need to round your answer up or down for it to make sense in the given situation.

video tutor

CC.6.NS.3

1 EXPLORE   Interpreting Quotients

Choose the best answer to each problem. Explain your answer.

A At a bakery, 8 loaves of bread can be packaged in one box for transport. The bakery has an order for 62 loaves of bread to deliver to a grocery store today. How many boxes are needed for the shipment?

   7 boxes   7.75 boxes   8 boxes

   _____
   _____
   _____
   _____

B For a woodworking project, D'Andre needs several pieces of wood that are each 14 inches long. How many 14-inch pieces can he cut from a board that is 78.5 inches long?

   5 pieces   5.6 pieces   6 pieces

   _____
   _____
   _____
   _____

REFLECT

1a. **Reasoning** Explain how your reasoning in **A** was different than your reasoning in **B**.

   _____
   _____

TRY THIS!

1b. How many 6-ounce servings can you pour from a 33.6-ounce container? _____

PRACTICE

Solve each problem. Explain your answer.

1. A florist is placing flowers in vases to be sold in her shop. Each vase will hold 9 flowers and she has an assortment of 85 flowers to use. How many vases can she fill completely?

   _____

   _____

   _____

2. Two bags of apples weigh 8.2 pounds and cost $7.36. How many bags of apples will fit in a box with a 50 pound weight limit?

   _____

   _____

   _____

3. A company sells recycled golf balls through their online store. The golf balls are sold in packages of 6 balls. The company recently received a shipment of 200 golf balls for packaging. How many packages can be completely filled from this shipment?

   _____

   _____

4. Heather wants to burn back-up copies of some digital music on her computer. She has 140 songs to be copied. If each CD she uses will hold 18 songs, how many CDs will she need?

   _____

   _____

5. Emilio has a collection of 246 sports cards. He is buying a binder with plastic sleeves for organizing his cards. Each sleeve will hold 8 cards. How many sleeves will he need to hold his entire collection?

   _____

   _____

6. Brittany is making tote bags. She spent $18.75 on fabric that costs $5 per yard. If she uses 0.5 yard of the fabric for each bag, how many bags can she make?

   _____

   _____

Additional Practice

Circle the letter of the correct answer.

1. You spent a total of $6.75 for 15 yards of ribbon. How much did the ribbon cost per yard?

   A $0.50

   B $0.45

   C $1.35

   D $1.45

2. Buttons come in packs of 12. How many packs should you buy if you need 100 buttons?

   F 10

   G 8

   H 9

   J 12

3. Your sewing cabinet has compartments that hold 8 spools of thread each. You have 50 spools of thread. How many compartments can you fill?

   A 6

   B 7

   C 5

   D 8

4. You spent a total of $35.75 for velvet cloth. Each yard of the velvet costs $3.25. How many yards did you buy?

   F 10

   G 10.5

   H 11

   J 11.5

Write the correct answer.

5. You used a total of 67.5 yards of cotton material to make costumes for the play. Each costume used 11.25 yards of cloth. How many costumes did you make?

   _____

6. You are saving $17.00 each week to buy a new sewing machine that costs $175.50. How many weeks will you have to save to have enough money to buy the sewing machine?

   _____

7. Sequins come in packs of 75. You use 12 sequins on each costume. If you have one pack of sequins, how many costumes can you make?

   _____

8. You pay $26.28 for a subscription to Sewing Magazine. You get an issue every month for a year. How much does each issue cost?

   _____

Problem Solving

Write the correct answer.

1. Five friends split a pizza that costs $16.75. If they shared the bill equally, how much did they each pay?

_____

2. There are 45 choir members going to the recital. Each van can carry 8 people. How many vans are needed?

_____

3. Tara bought 150 beads. She needs 27 beads to make each necklace. How many necklaces can she make?

_____

4. Cat food costs $2.85 for five cans. Ben only wants to buy one can. How much will it cost?

_____

Circle the letter of the correct answer.

5. Tennis balls come in cans of 3. The coach needs 50 tennis balls for practice. How many cans should he order?

   A 16 cans

   B 17 cans

   C 18 cans

   D 20 cans

6. The rainfall for three months was 4.6 inches, 3.5 inches, and 4.2 inches. What was the average monthly rainfall during that time?

   F 41 inches

   G 12.3 inches

   H 4.3 inches

   J 4.1 inches

7. Tom has $15.86 to buy marbles that cost $1.25 each. He wants to know how many marbles he can buy. What should he do after he divides?

   A Drop the decimal part of the quotient when he divides.

   B Drop the decimal part of the dividend when he divides.

   C Round the quotient up to the next highest whole number to divide.

   D Use the entire quotient of his division as the answer.

8. Mei needs 135 hot dog rolls for the class picnic. The rolls come in packs of 10. She wants to know how many packs to buy. What should she do after she divides?

   F Drop the decimal part of the quotient when she divides.

   G Drop the decimal part of the dividend when she divides.

   H Round the quotient up to the next highest whole number.

   J Use the entire quotient of her division as the answer.

3-8

Solving Decimal Equations
Going Deeper

Essential question: *How do you solve decimal equations that contain addition or multiplication?*

Use inverse operations to solve decimal equations.

video tutor

CC.6.EE.7

1 EXAMPLE Solving Problems with Decimal Equations

A A baby lemur is weighed each week at the zoo to check its growth. One week ago it weighed 3.34 ounces. Today it weighs 3.42 ounces. How much weight did the baby lemur gain since last week?

Write and solve an equation. Let *w* be the weight gained since last week.

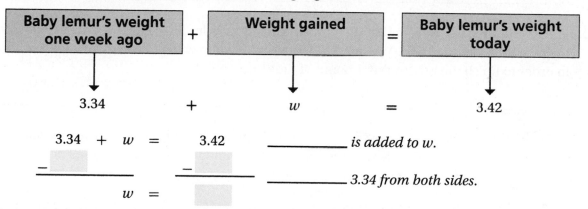

Baby lemur's weight one week ago	+	Weight gained	=	Baby lemur's weight today

3.34   +   *w*   =   3.42

3.34 + *w* = 3.42   _____ *is added to w.*

   _____ *3.34 from both sides.*

w =

The baby lemur gained _____ ounce of weight since last week.

B The area of a room is 28.125 square meters. If the length of the room is 6.25 meters, how wide is the room?

Write and solve an equation. Let *x* represent the width of the room.

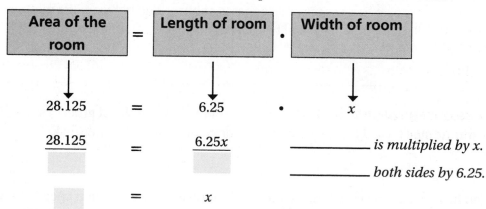

Area of the room	=	Length of room	·	Width of room

28.125   =   6.25   ·   *x*

$$\frac{28.125}{} = \frac{6.25x}{}$$

   _____ *is multiplied by x.*

   _____ *both sides by 6.25.*

= *x*

The room is _____ meters wide.

Solve each equation.

1. $16.23 + n = 33.15$

$n =$ _____

2. $25.9 + p = 51.25$

$p =$ _____

3. $135.05 = 76.525 + v$

$v =$ _____

4. $6.75m = 25.65$

$m =$ _____

5. $25.5g = 214.2$

$g =$ _____

6. $137.16 = 12.7k$

$k =$ _____

For 7–13, write and solve an equation to answer each question.

7. Abby earned $393.75 last month at her part-time job. If Abby worked a total of 37.5 hours last month, how much is she paid per hour?

_____

8. Tracy is training to run a marathon. A marathon is 26.2 miles long. He is hoping to complete the race in 3.5 hours. To the nearest tenth, how many miles will he need to average per hour in order to finish the race in this amount of time?

_____

9. Jaime is at the grocery store buying apples. He places several apples in a plastic bag and weighs them. The digital scale says they weigh 2.68 pounds. He wants to buy 4.5 pounds of apples. How many more pounds does he need?

_____

10. Mika wants to buy a new digital music player that costs $53.45. She has saved $38.50 from her babysitting jobs. How much more money does she need for the music player?

_____

11. At a zoo, a new baby marmoset has a mass of 33.6 grams at birth. The baby and its mother will be kept isolated until the baby's mass reaches 92.4 grams. How much mass must the baby marmoset gain?

_____

12. Mrs. Donaldsen bought 3.5 pounds of steak at the meat counter in her local grocery store. The total price for the steak was $19.25. What was the price per pound for the steak?

_____

13. A hot air balloon flew at 8.5 miles per hour. If the balloon traveled at a constant speed, how many hours did it take the balloon to travel 63.75 miles?

_____

Additional Practice

Solve each equation. Check your answer.

1. $a - 2.7 = 4.8$

2. $b \div 7 = 1.9$

_____

3. $w - 6.5 = 3.8$

4. $p \div 0.4 = 1.7$

_____

5. $4.5 + x = 8$

6. $b \div 3 = 2.5$

_____

7. $7.8 + s = 15.2$

8. $1.63q = 9.78$

_____

9. $0.05 + x = 2.06$

10. $1.7n = 2.38$

_____

11. $t - 6.08 = 12.59$

12. $9q = 16.2$

_____

13. $w - 8.9 = 10.3$

14. $1.4n = 3.22$

_____

15. $t - 12.7 = 0.8$

16. $3.8 + a = 6.5$

_____

17. The distance around a square photograph is 12.8 centimeters. What is the length of each side of the photograph?

18. You buy two rolls of film for $3.75 each. You pay with a $10 bill. How much change should you get back?

_____

Problem Solving

Write the correct answer.

1. Bee hummingbirds weigh only 0.0056 ounces. They have to eat half their body weight every day to survive. How much food does a bee hummingbird have to eat each day?

2. The desert locust, a type of grasshopper, can jump 10 times the length of its body. The locust is 1.956 inches long. How far can it jump in one leap?

3. In 1900, there were about 1.49 million people living in California. In 2000, the population was 33.872 million. How much did the population grow between 1900 and 2000?

4. Juanita has $567.89 in her checking account. After she deposited her paycheck and paid her rent of $450.00, she had $513.82 left in the account. How much was her paycheck?

Circle the letter of the correct answer.

5. The average body temperature for people is 98.6°F. The average body temperature for most dogs is 3.4°F higher than for people. The average body temperature for cats is 0.5°F lower than for dogs. What is the normal body temperature for dogs and cats?

   A dogs: 101.5°F; cats 102°F

   B dogs: 102°F; cats 101.5°F

   C dogs: 102.5°F; cats 103°F

   D dogs: 102.5°F; cats 102.5°F

6. Seattle, Washington, is famous for its rainy climate. Winter is the rainiest season there. From November through December the city gets an average of 5.85 inches of rain each month. Seattle usually gets 6 inches of rain in December. What is the city's average rainfall in November?

   F 6 inches

   G 5.925 inches

   H 5.8 inches

   J 5.7 inches

7. The equation to convert from Celsius to Kelvin degrees is $K = 273.16 + C$. If it is 303.66°K outside, what is the temperature in Celsius degrees?

   A 576.82°C

   B 30.5°C

   C 305°C

   D 257.68°C

8. The distance around a square mirror is 6.8 feet. Which of the following equations finds the length of each side of the mirror?

   F $6.8 - x = 4$

   G $x \div 4 = 6.8$

   H $4x = 6.8$

   J $6.8 + 4 = x$

CHAPTER 3

Problem Solving Connections

Welcome Back! Elizabeth is an event planner who has been hired to plan a class reunion. The class has 275 people and 256 will be attending. Elizabeth must plan the seating, decorations, and food. She then needs to determine how much to charge each guest so that all costs are covered.

1 Seating

The cost sheet shows the types of tables available, the cost per table, and the cost per tablecloth.

A How many round tables would be necessary to seat all of the guests?

Type of Table	Seats	Cost per Table ($)	Cost per Tablecloth ($)
Round	8	5.00	3.75
Rectangular	12	7.50	4.35

B How many rectangular tables would be necessary to seat all of the guests?

C Which table, round or rectangular, would be cheaper for the reunion? How much cheaper?

D A name card will be placed at each seat. Elizabeth finds that 36 name cards come in a package. How many packages will she need? Explain.

2 Decorations and Favors

A The school colors are blue and white. Elizabeth bought 84 blue balloons for $10.92. What is the cost per balloon?

B Elizabeth wants to make balloon bouquets that each have 7 blue balloons and 8 white balloons. If the price per balloon is the same for both colors of balloons, will $20 buy enough balloons for 12 bouquets? Explain.

C Elizabeth has 87.75 feet of banner paper. How many banners can she make that are 11.25 feet long? Explain.

D Elizabeth plans to hand out door prizes as the guests arrive. Every 6th guest will receive a mug, and every 14th guest will receive a T-shirt. How many mugs and T-shirts should Elizabeth order?

E Elizabeth has two 8.5-pound bags of mints. She plans to put 0.5 pound on each rectangular table. Does she have enough mints?

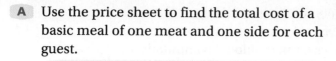

3 Food and Drink

A Use the price sheet to find the total cost of a basic meal of one meat and one side for each guest.

Meal Options	Price per Plate ($)
1 meat, 1 side	9.25
2 meats, 1 side	10.25
Additional sides	0.75
Salad	1.45

B How would you determine how much more it would cost to serve each guest a salad rather than an additional side?

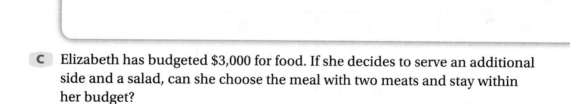

C Elizabeth has budgeted $3,000 for food. If she decides to serve an additional side and a salad, can she choose the meal with two meats and stay within her budget?

D Elizabeth purchases a container of punch mix that, when mixed with water, makes 640 ounces of punch. Elizabeth has 8-ounce drinking glasses. She assumes that each person will drink 2 glasses of punch. Show how to determine how many people can be served with one container of punch.

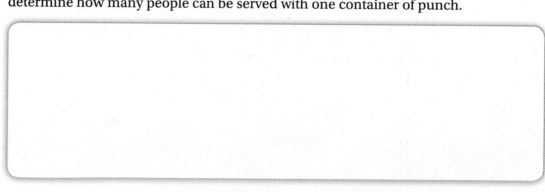

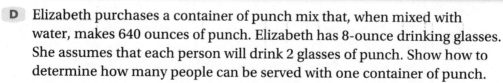

© Houghton Mifflin Harcourt Publishing Company

Answer the Question

A Elizabeth's budget for the class reunion is shown. Help
her complete the budget using some of your answers from previous
questions. You may also have to perform additional computations.

Class Reunion Budget			
Item	Number of Items/Packages	Cost per Item	Total Cost
Rectangular tables		$11.85	
Name cards		$5.10	
Balloons		$0.13	
Sign	1	$25.25	
T-shirts		$7.50	
Mugs		$5.00	
Mints		$5.50	
Meals	256	$11.45	
Punch		$4.25	
Pie	16	$6.75	
Cake	7	$12.00	
Elizabeth's Fee			$1,800.00
Total Cost			

B Based on your total cost, determine the amount each guest should
pay to attend the reunion. Would $20 per person be enough to cover
all of the expenses? Explain. How much would you charge? Justify
your answer.

Performance Task

CHAPTER 3

COMMON
CORE

CC.6.NS.3
CC.6.EE.6
CC.6.EE.7

⭐ **1.** Darla's dad gives her 2 dimes and 3 pennies. She now has 76 cents. How much money did Darla have originally? Write and solve an equation to find the answer.

⭐ **2.** Three judges score a dive at a competition. One judge gives a score of 9.15. The lowest score was 0.25 less than this score. The highest score was 0.35 more than the lowest score. Find the lowest and highest scores.

3. Amy spends $10.62 at the bookstore. She buys 3 identical notebooks, and a pen for $1.99. She pays $0.26 tax.

   a. How much does Amy spend on all 3 notebooks before tax? Explain.

   b. Explain how you can write an equation to determine the price of one notebook. Then solve your equation.

4. Rebecca and three of her friends have lunch. The bill comes out to $33.86 without tip.

   a. Rebecca claims that there is no way to split the bill so that everyone pays the same amount. Is she correct? Explain why or why not.

   b. The group wants to leave a tip of at least $4 but no more than $6. What amount of tip can they leave so that the total, bill plus tip, can be split evenly among them? Explain how you found your answer.

Name _____ Class _____ Date _____

SELECTED RESPONSE

1. The table shows the weights of different types of golf balls. Which golf ball is the heaviest?

Golf Ball	Weight (oz)
FlyFar	1.593
D-Drive	1.661
LaunchLoft	1.624
Arrow	1.6
Red Star	1.619

   A. D-Drive   C. Red Star

   B. LaunchLoft   D. FlyFar

2. A snail travels 0.03 mile per hour. How far will the snail travel in 36.8 hours?

   F. 0.1104 miles   H. 11.04 miles

   G. 1.104 miles   J. 110.4 miles

3. A rectangular garden has the dimensions shown in the figure.

7.48 meters

15.6 meters

   What is the perimeter of the garden?

   A. 16.24 meters   C. 46.16 meters

   B. 23.08 meters   D. 116.688 meters

4. Solve the equation $x - 4.5 = 17$

   F. $x = 3.8$ H. $x = 21.5$

   G. $x = 12.5$ J. $x = 76.5$

5. Rusty has $25.45 in the bank and $16.18 in his wallet. He wants to purchase a sweater that costs $49.99. How much more money does he need?

   A. $41.63   C. $24.54

   B. $33.81   D. $8.36

6. Adam drove from his house directly to one of the destinations shown in the table. Adam's trip odometer read 248.9 miles when he left home and 316.3 miles when he reached his destination. What was his destination?

Destination	Distance from Adam's House
Museum	64.6 miles
Baseball stadium	67.4 miles
Theater	70.4 miles
Historical landmark	66.4 miles
Mall	71.4 miles

   F. Mall

   G. Theater

   H. Historical landmark

   J. Baseball stadium

7. Which of the following quotients has the greatest value?

   A. $0.075 \div 6$ C. $0.75 \div 0.06$

   B. $7.5 \div 0.006$ D. $0.75 \div 0.6$

8. Leon had some change in his pocket. Then a friend loaned him $0.25. Now Leon has $1.45 in his pocket. Which equation can be used to find the original amount of money m that Leon had in his pocket?

   F. $m + 0.25 = 1.45$

   G. $1.45 = m - 0.25$

   H. $m + 1.45 = 0.25$

   J. $m = 1.45(0.25)$

9. An automated call machine can handle 8.86 minutes of calls before it sends a report. How many reports would it send for 53.16 minutes of calls?

A. 0.06 report   **C.** 6 reports

B. 0.6 report   **D.** 60 reports

10. In 2007, Jacksonville Jaguars running back Maurice Jones-Drew averaged 4.6 yards per carry on 167 carries. He also averaged 10.2 yards per catch on 40 catches. Which is the best estimate of the total yards gained by Jones-Drew in 2007?

F. 255 yards   **H.** 750 yards

G. 400 yards   **J.** 1,150 yards

CONSTRUCTED RESPONSE

11. You deposited $45.25 in your checking account, but instead of adding $45.25 to your balance, the bank accidentally subtracted $45.25. How much money should the bank add to your account to correct the mistake? Explain.

12. Is the quotient $4.5 \div 0.9$ greater or less than 4.5? Why?

13. Maria earned $7.40 per hour at her part-time job. She worked at least 15.75 hours each week. Did she make more or less than $400 in 4 weeks? Justify your answer.

14. Apples cost $1.29 per pound. How much would a bag of apples weighing 4.7 pounds cost? (Round your answer to the nearest cent.)

15. A bridge is 21.6 meters long. A nearby tunnel is 2.3 times as long as the bridge. How long is the tunnel?

16. Explain how to draw a model to find the quotient of $2.4 \div 3$. What is this quotient?

17. Tom has $15.86 to buy marbles that cost $1.25 each. He wants to know how many marbles he can buy. What should he do after he divides? How many marbles can be buy?

18. Kelly needs to make 8 ladders for the school play. Each ladder has 9 rungs and each rung is 1.6 ft in length.

a. How many feet of wood are needed to make the rungs for one ladder?

b. If the rungs of the ladder are cut from 12ft-long pieces of wood, how many pieces of wood does Kelly need to buy to make all 8 ladders? Explain.

Number Theory and Fractions

Chapter Focus

You will use area models to find factors of numbers and then find the common factors for two numbers. You will find and use the greatest common factor of two numbers in a problem situation. Equivalent expressions are useful in simplifying expressions and solving equations. You will identify and write equivalent expressions. You have compared and ordered decimals. Now you will compare and order decimals and fractions including mixed numbers. Fractions that name the same amount are called equivalent fractions. You will model fractions, write fractions in simplest form, and solve problems with fractions in simplest form. Finally, you will learn to convert between mixed numbers and improper fractions.

Chapter at a Glance

COMMON CORE

Lesson	Standards for Mathematical Content
4-1 Factors and Prime Factorization	C.C6.NS.4
4-2 Greatest Common Factor	CC.6.NS.4
4-3 Equivalent Expressions	CC.6.EE.2b, CC.6.EE.4
4-4 Decimals and Fractions	CC.6.NS.6c
4-5 Equivalent Fractions	CC.6.NS.4
4-6 Mixed Numbers and Improper Fractions	PREP FOR CC.6.NS.1
4-7 Comparing and Ordering Fractions	CC.6.NS.7
Problem Solving Connections	
Performance Task	
Assessment Readiness	

CHAPTER 4

Unpacking the Standards

Understanding the standards and the vocabulary terms in the standards will help you know exactly what you are expected to learn in this chapter.

CHAPTER 4

COMMON CORE CC.6.NS.4

Find the greatest common factor of two whole numbers less than or equal to 100 and the least common multiple of two whole numbers less than or equal to 12. Use the distributive property to express a sum of two whole numbers 1–100 with a common factor as a multiple of a sum of two whole numbers with no common factor.

Key Vocabulary

greatest common factor (GCF) *(máximo común divisor (MCD))* The largest common factor of two or more given numbers.

What It Means to You

You will determine the greatest common factor of two numbers and solve real-world problems involving the greatest common factor.

EXAMPLE

There are 12 boys and 18 girls in Ms. Ruiz's science class. The students must form lab groups. Each group must have the same number of boys and the same number of girls. What is the greatest number of groups Ms. Ruiz can make if every student must be in a group?

factors of 12: 1, 2, 3, 4, ⑥, 12

factors of 18: 1, 2, 3, ⑥, 9, 18

The GCF of 12 and 18 is 6. The greatest number of groups Ms. Ruiz can make is 6.

COMMON CORE CC.6.EE.3

Apply the properties of operations to generate equivalent expressions.

Key Vocabulary

equivalent expression *(expresión equivalente)* Equivalent expressions have the same value for all values of the variables.

What It Means to You

Given an algebraic expression, you will write equivalent expressions.

EXAMPLE

$3(1 + 27m)$

$= 3 \cdot 1 + 3 \cdot 27m$ *Apply the Distributive Property.*

$= 3 + 81m$ *Multiply.*

$= 81m + 3$ *Apply the Commutative Property.*

$= 3^4m + 3$ *Write the coefficient of $81m$ as 3^4.*

CC.6.NS.6c

Find and position integers and other rational numbers on a horizontal or vertical number line diagram; find and position pairs of integers and other rational numbers on a coordinate plane.

Key Vocabulary

integer *(entero)* A member of the set of whole numbers and their opposites.

rational number *(número racional)* A number that can be written in the form $\frac{a}{b}$, where a and b are integers and $b \neq 0$.

What It Means to You

You will use a number line to order a set of rational numbers.

EXAMPLE

Use a number line to order the fractions and decimals from least to greatest.

$$0.5, \frac{1}{5}, 0.37$$

First, rewrite the fraction as a decimal. $\frac{1}{5} = 0.2$

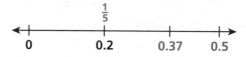

The numbers in order from least to greatest are $\frac{1}{5}$, 0.37, and 0.5.

CC.6.NS.7b

Write, interpret, and explain statements of order for rational numbers in real-world contexts.

What It Means to You

You will use your knowledge of rational numbers to describe and explain real-world situations.

EXAMPLE

Rachel and Hannah have $1\frac{2}{3}$ cups cabbage. They need $1\frac{1}{2}$ cups to make potstickers. Do they have enough for the recipe?

Compare the whole number parts.

$1 = 1$ The whole number parts are equal.

Find equivalent fractions with 6 as the denominator.

$$\frac{2}{3} = \frac{\blacksquare}{6} \qquad\qquad \frac{1}{2} = \frac{\blacksquare}{6}$$

$$\frac{2 \cdot 2}{3 \cdot 2} = \frac{4}{6} \qquad\qquad \frac{1 \cdot 3}{2 \cdot 3} = \frac{3}{6}$$

$$\frac{2}{3} = \frac{4}{6} \qquad\qquad \frac{1}{2} = \frac{3}{6}$$

Compare the like fractions. $\frac{4}{6} > \frac{3}{6}$ so, $\frac{2}{3} > \frac{1}{2}$.

Since $1\frac{2}{3}$ cups is more than $1\frac{1}{2}$ cups, they have enough cabbage.

CHAPTER 4

Key Vocabulary

common factor *(factor común)* A number that is a factor of two or more numbers.

equivalent expression *(expresión equivalente)* Equivalent expressions have the same value for all values of the variables.

equivalent fractions *(fracciones equivalentes)* Fractions that name the same amount or part.

factor *(factor)* A number that is multiplied by another number to get a product.

greatest common factor *(GCF) (máximo común divisor (MCD))* The largest common factor of two or more given numbers.

improper fraction *(fracción impropia)* A fraction in which the numerator is greater than or equal to the denominator.

proper fraction *(fracción propia)* A fraction in which the numerator is less than the denominator.

simplest form *(of a fraction)* *(mínima expresión (de una fracción))* A fraction is in simplest form when the numerator and denominator have no common factors other than 1.

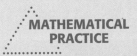

MATHEMATICAL PRACTICE The Common Core Standards for Mathematical Practice describe varieties of expertise that mathematics educators at all levels should seek to develop in their students. Opportunities to develop these practices are integrated throughout this program.

1. Make sense of problems and persevere in solving them.
2. Reason abstractly and quantitatively.
3. Construct viable arguments and critique the reasoning of others.
4. Model with mathematics.
5. Use appropriate tools strategically.
6. Attend to precision.
7. Look for and make use of structure.
8. Look for and express regularity in repeated reasoning.

CHAPTER 4

4-1

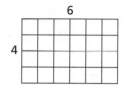

video tutor

Factors and Prime Factorization
Modeling: Factors

Essential question: *How can you model factors?*

The **factors** of a number are any whole numbers that divide evenly into the number. A number is divisible by each of its factors.

Prime factors are those factors of a number that are prime numbers. Recall that a *prime number* is a number whose only two factors are 1 and itself. Any number that is not prime is a *composite number*.

CC.6.NS.4

1 **EXPLORE** Modeling Factors

Use grid paper to show different area models for the number 24.

The number 24 can be modeled by drawing a rectangle that is 4 units wide and 6 units long. The dimensions of the rectangle, 4 and 6, are factors of 24. So, $4 \times 6 = 24$.

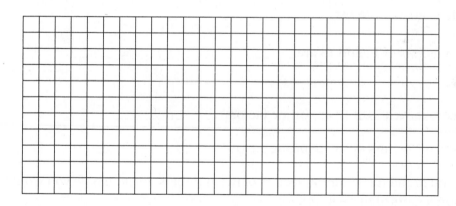

What other factor pairs of 24 can be modeled?
Use the grid below to draw the area models. _____

List all the factors of 24: _____, _____, _____, 4, 6, _____, _____, and _____

REFLECT

1a. Examine the grid models at the right. Explain why the models show that 11 is a prime number and 15 is a composite number.

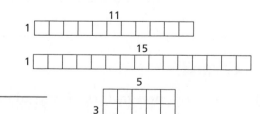

_____

_____

1b. Use grid paper to model two prime numbers and two composite numbers. List all the factors of each number.

A number that is factor of two or more whole numbers is a **common factor** of those numbers. For example, 3 is a common factor of 12 and 18.

CC.6.NS.4

2 EXPLORE   Finding Common Factors

Use grid paper to show all of the different area models for 12 and all of the different area models for 18.

Complete the models for each number.

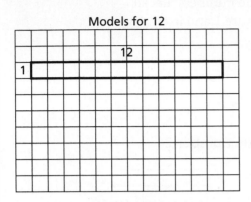

Models for 12

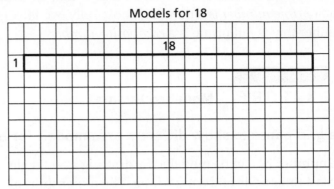

Models for 18

List all the factors of 12: _____

List all the factors of 18: _____

Which numbers are in both lists? _____

The common factors of 12 and 18 are _____, _____, _____, and _____.

REFLECT

2a. Which of the factors of 12 are prime factors? _____

2b. Which of the factors of 18 are prime factors? _____

2c. In ❷ you found the common factors of two numbers. Explain how you would find the common factors of three numbers.

_____

_____

_____

TRY THIS!

Find the common factors, if any, of each pair of numbers.

2d. 21 and 35   **2e.** 16 and 28   **2f.** 36 and 48

_____   _____   _____

Additional Practice

List all of the factors of each number.

1. 15

2. 24

3. 33

_____

_____

4. 72

5. 48

6. 95

_____

_____

7. 66

8. 87

9. 36

_____

_____

Find the common factors, if any, of each pair of numbers.

10. 33 and 44

11. 49 and 56

12. 30 and 42

_____

13. 36 and 39

14. 20 and 48

15. 35 and 125

_____

16. 45 and 54

17. 85 and 100

18. 32 and 48

_____

19. James has an assigned seat for his flight to Denver. The seats on the plane are numbered 1–49. James's seat number is an odd number greater than 10 that is factor of 100. What is his seat number for the flight?

_____

Problem Solving

Write the correct answer.

1. The area of a rectangle is the product of its length and width. If a rectangular board has an area of 30 square feet, what are the possible measurements of its length and width?

_____

_____

2. Jenna is cutting ribbon to make bows. She has two lengths of ribbon, one 24 inches long and one 36 inches long. She wants to cut the ribbon into equal lengths and not have any ribbon left over. Into what lengths can she cut the ribbon?

_____

_____

3. Franklin bought a 32-ounce bottle of orange juice and a 48-ounce bottle of apple juice. He wants to divide all of the juice into equal-sized servings and not have any juice left over. Into what serving sizes can Franklin divide the juice?

_____

_____

4. Mr. Samuels has 24 students in his math class. He wants to divide the students into equal groups, and he wants the number of students in each group to be prime. What are his choices for group sizes? How many groups can he make?

_____

_____

Circle the letter of the correct answer.

5. Julie has 48 pencils in her collection. She wants to divide the pencils into equal groups. Which could **not** represent Julie's pencils?

    A 4 groups of 12 pencils

    B 7 groups of 6 pencils

    C 16 groups of 3 pencils

    D 2 groups of 24 pencils

6. What prime numbers are factors of both 60 and 105?

    F 2 and 3

    G 2 and 5

    H 3 and 5

    J 5 and 7

7. Olaf wants to cut two strips of wood into equal lengths for a craft project. The strips of wood are 18 inches long and 36 inches long. Into what lengths can Olaf cut the strips of wood so that he has no wood left over?

    A 1-inch, 2-inch, 3-inch, 4-inch

    B 6-inch, 8-inch, 9-inch, 12-inch

    C 1-inch, 2-inch, 3-inch, 6-inch, 9-inch

    D 18-inch and 24-inch

8. Tim's younger brother, Bryant, just had a birthday. Bryant's age only has one factor, and is not a prime number. How old is Bryant?

    F 10 years old

    G 7 years old

    H 3 years old

    J 1 year old

Greatest Common Factor
Going Deeper

Essential question: *How do you find and use the greatest common factor of two whole numbers?*

CC.6.NS.4

1 EXPLORE   Greatest Common Factor

A florist plans to make bouquets of roses and tulips. She has 18 roses and 30 tulips. Each bouquet must have the same number of roses and the same number of tulips. She wants to use all of the flowers. What are the possible bouquets she can make?

A   Complete the tables below.

Roses

Number of bouquets	1	2	3	6	9	18
Number of roses in each bouquet	18	9				

Tulips

Number of bouquets	1	2	3	5	6	10	15	30
Number of tulips in each bouquet	30							

B   Can the florist make five bouquets? Why or why not?

_____

🔑 If a number is a factor of two or more counting numbers, it is called a *common factor* of those numbers.

C   What are the common factors of 18 and 30? What do they represent in this situation?

_____

🔑 The **greatest common factor (GCF)** of two or more counting numbers is the greatest factor shared by the numbers.

D   What is the GCF of 18 and 30? _____

If the florist wants the number of bouquets to be as large as possible, how many bouquets can she make? _____

How many roses will be in each bouquet? _____

How many tulips will be in each bouquet? _____

One way to find the GCF of two numbers is to list all of their factors.

2 EXAMPLE Greatest Common Factor

A baker has 24 blueberry muffins and 36 apple muffins to divide into boxes for sale. Each box must have the same number of blueberry muffins and the same number of apple muffins. What is the greatest number of boxes that the baker can make using all of the muffins? How many blueberry muffins and how many apple muffins will be in each box?

A List the factors of 24 and 36. Then circle the common factors.

Factors of 24: _____, _____, _____, _____, _____, _____, _____, _____

Factors of 36: _____, _____, _____, _____, _____, _____, _____, _____, _____

B What do the common factors represent in this situation?

_____

C What is the GCF of 24 and 36? _____

D The greatest number of boxes that the baker can make is _____. There will

be _____ blueberry muffin(s) and _____ apple muffin(s) in each box.

TRY THIS!

List the factors to find the GCF of each pair of numbers.

2a. 14 and 35 _____   **2b.** 20 and 28 _____

2c. The sixth-grade class is competing in the school field day. There are 32 girls and 40 boys who want to participate in the relay race. Each team must have the same number of girls and the same number of boys. What is the greatest number of teams that can be formed? How many boys and how many girls will be on each team?

_____

REFLECT

2d. What is the GCF of two numbers when one number is a multiple of the other? Give an example.

_____

2e. What is the GCF of two prime numbers? Give an example.

_____

© Houghton Mifflin Harcourt Publishing Company

You can use the Distributive Property to rewrite a sum of two or more numbers as a product of their GCF and another number.

3 EXPLORE   Distributive Property

You can use grid paper to draw area models of 45 and 60. Here are all of the possible area models of 45.

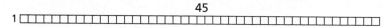

45

1

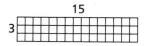

15

3

9

5

A What do the side lengths of the area models above (1, 3, 5, 9, 15, and 45) represent? _____

B On your own grid paper, show all of the possible area models of 60.

C What side lengths do the area models of 45 and 60 have in common?

_____

What do these side lengths represent? _____

D What is the greatest common side length? What does it represent?

_____

E Write 45 as a product of the GCF and another number. _____

Write 60 as a product of the GCF and another number. _____

F Use your answers above to rewrite 45 + 60.

$45 + 60 = 15 \times \boxed{} + 15 \times \boxed{}$

Use the Distributive Property and your answer above to write 45 + 60 as a product of the GCF and another number.

$15 \times \boxed{} + 15 \times \boxed{} = 15 \times \left(\boxed{} + \boxed{} \right) = 15 \times \boxed{}$

TRY THIS!

Write each sum as a product of the GCF of the two numbers.

3a. 27 + 18 _____   **3b.** 120 + 36 _____

REFLECT

3c. Does the same process work with subtraction? For example, can you write 120 − 36 as a product of the GCF and another number? Explain.

_____

List the factors of each number.

1. 16 _____

2. 39 _____

3. 50 _____

Find the GCF of each pair of numbers.

4. 40 and 48 _____

5. 10 and 45 _____

6. 6 and 21 _____

7. 60 and 72 _____

8. 21 and 40 _____

9. 28 and 32 _____

10. 28 and 70 _____

11. 45 and 81 _____

12. 30 and 45 _____

13. 55 and 77 _____

14. Mrs. Davis is sewing vests. She has 16 green buttons and 24 yellow buttons. Each vest will have the same number of yellow buttons and the same number of green buttons. What is the greatest number of vests Mrs. Davis can make using all of the buttons?

_____ vests

15. A baker has 27 wheat bagels and 36 plain bagels that will be divided into boxes. Each box must have the same number of wheat bagels and the same number of plain bagels. What is the greatest number of boxes the baker can make using all of the bagels?

_____ boxes

16. Lola is putting appetizers on plates. She has 63 meatballs and 84 cheese cubes. She wants both kinds of food on each plate, and each plate must have the same number of meatballs and the same number of cheese cubes. What is the greatest number of plates she can make using all of the appetizers?

_____ plates

17. The Delta High School marching band has 54 members. The Swanton High School marching band has 90 members. The bands are going to march in a parade together. The director wants to arrange the bands into the same number of rows. What is the greatest number of rows in which the two bands can be arranged?

_____ rows

Write each sum as a product of the GCF of the two numbers.

18. $75 + 90$

_____

19. 36 and 45

_____

20. $56 + 64$

_____

21. $48 + 14$

_____

Additional Practice

Find the GCF of each set of numbers.

1. 12 and 15 _____

2. 18 and 24 _____

3. 15 and 25 _____

4. 16 and 24 _____

5. 36 and 45 _____

6. 24 and 54 _____

7. 48 and 64 _____

8. 27 and 72 _____

9. 55 and 77 _____

10. 16, 28, and 48 _____

11. 15, 35, and 95 _____

12. 20, 30, and 80 _____

13. 18, 36, and 54 _____

14. 27, 36, and 45 _____

15. 21, 49, and 63 _____

16. 25, 35, and 45 _____

17. 28, 42, and 63 _____

18. 25, 75, and 115 _____

19. Mr. Thompson's sixth-grade class is competing in the school field day. There are 16 boys and 12 girls in his class. He divided the class into the greatest number of teams possible with the same number of boys on each team and the same number of girls on each team. How many teams were made if each person was on a team? How many girls were on each team? How many boys?

_____

20. Barbara is making candy bags for her birthday party. She has 24 lollipops, 12 candy bars, and 42 pieces of gum. She wants each bag to have the same number of each kind of candy. What is the greatest number of bags she can make if all the candy is used? How many pieces of each kind of candy will be in each bag?

_____

_____

Problem Solving

Write the correct answer.

1. Carolyn has 24 bottles of shampoo, 36 tubes of hand lotion, and 60 bars of lavender soap to make gift baskets. She wants to have the same number of each item in every basket. What is the greatest number of baskets she can make without having any of the items left over?

_____

_____

2. There are 40 girls and 32 boys who want to participate in the relay race. If each team must have the same number of girls and boys, what is the greatest number of teams that can race? How many boys and girls will be on each team?

_____

_____

3. Ming has 15 quarters, 30 dimes, and 48 nickels. He wants to group his money so that each group has the same number of each coin. What is the greatest number of groups he can make? How many of each coin will be in each group? How much money will each group be worth?

_____

_____

_____

4. A gardener has 27 tulip bulbs, 45 tomato plants, 108 rose bushes, and 126 herb seedlings to plant in the city garden. He wants each row of the garden to have the same number of each kind of plant. What is the greatest number of rows that the gardener can make if he uses all the plants?

_____

_____

_____

Circle the letter of the correct answer.

5. Kim packed 6 boxes with identical supplies. It was the greatest number she could pack and use all the supplies. Which of these is her supply list?

  A 24 pencils, 36 pens, 10 rulers

  B 12 rulers, 30 pencils, 45 pens

  C 42 pencils, 18 rulers, 72 pens

  D 60 pens, 54 pencils, 32 rulers

6. The sum of three numbers is 60. Their greatest common factor is 4. Which of the following lists shows these three numbers?

  F 4, 16, 36

  G 8, 20, 32

  H 14, 16, 30

  J 10, 18, 32

Equivalent Expressions
Connection: Parts of an Expression

Essential question: *How can you identify and write equivalent expressions?*

CC.6.EE.2b

1 **E X P L O R E** Definitions

A Write the definitions of these words in your own words.

variable _____

_____

constant _____

_____

algebraic expression _____

_____

B In the expressions $9a$, $5y$, $6n$, and $12x$, the blue numbers are *coefficients*.
Write a definition of *coefficient* in your own words.

coefficient _____

_____

C The expression $5y + z - 8$ has three terms. The expression $15 + x$ has two terms.
The expression $5c$ has one term. Write a definition of *term* in your own words.

term _____

_____

D Compare your definitions in **B** and **C** to those of other students and discuss
any differences in them. If necessary, make changes to your definitions.

E Use words from the box to complete each sentence.

factor	product	quotient	sum	difference

$15 + x$ represents a _____ of two terms.

$9a$ represents the _____ of 9 and a.

$p \div 3$ represents a _____ .

$12 - x$ is a _____ of two terms.

1. **Conjecture** What is the coefficient of a term that consists of a single variable? For example, what is the coefficient of x? _____

CC.6.EE.2b

2 EXPLORE   Describing Expressions

There may be several different ways to describe a given expression.

A   Write each description on individual index cards or sticky notes.

algebraic expression	sum of two terms	product of two factors	sum of a quotient and a constant	product of a coefficient and a variable

B   Write each of the following expressions at the top of its own sheet of paper. Then place the index card(s) or sticky note(s) that describe an expression onto its paper. Write the descriptions you placed on each paper next to the expression.

$\frac{9a}{5} + 32$ _____

_____

$3(m + 1)$ _____

_____

$7c$ _____

_____

$5 + 9$ _____

_____

C   Compare your answers in **B** with those of other students and make changes to them, if necessary.

TRY THIS!

Write an algebraic expression that matches each description.

2a.   A product of two variables _____

2b.   A sum of a product and a constant _____

Equivalent expressions are expressions that simplify to the same value for any number(s) substituted for the variable(s). For example, the expression $y + y + y$ is equivalent to $3y$ because the two expressions will have the same value for any number that is substituted for y.

3 EXPLORE   Identifying Equivalent Expressions

Match the expressions in List A with their equivalent expressions in List B.

List A	List B
$5x + 65$	$5x + 1$
$5(x + 1)$	$5x + 5$
$1 + 5x$	$5(13 + x)$

A One way to test whether two expressions might be equivalent is to evaluate them for the same value of the variable. Evaluate each of the expressions in the lists for $x = 3$.

List A	List B
$5(3) + 65 = $ ☐	$5(3) + 1 = $ ☐
$5(3 + 1) = $ ☐	$5(3) + 5 = $ ☐
$1 + 5(3) = $ ☐	$5(13 + 3) = $ ☐

B Which pair(s) of expressions have the same value for $x = 3$?

_____

C How could you further test whether the expressions in each pair are equivalent?

_____

_____

D Do you think the expressions in each pair are equivalent? Why or why not?

_____

_____

REFLECT

3a. Lisa evaluated the expressions $2x$ and x^2 for $x = 2$ and found that both expressions were equal to 4. Lisa concluded that $2x$ and x^2 are equivalent expressions. How could you show Lisa that she is incorrect?

_____

_____

3b. What does **3a** demonstrate about expressions?

_____

Properties of operations can be used to identify equivalent expressions.

Properties of Operations	Examples
Commutative Property of Addition: When adding, changing the order of the numbers does not change the sum.	$3 + 4 = 4 + 3$
Commutative Property of Multiplication: When multiplying, changing the order of the numbers does not change the product.	$2 \times 4 = 4 \times 2$
Associative Property of Addition: When adding more than two numbers, the grouping of the numbers does not change the sum.	$(3 + 4) + 5 = 3 + (4 + 5)$
Associative Property of Multiplication: When multiplying more than two numbers, the grouping of the numbers does not change the product.	$(2 \times 4) \times 3 = 2 \times (4 \times 3)$
Distributive Property: Multiplying a number by a sum or difference is the same as multiplying by each number in the sum or difference and then adding or subtracting.	$6(2 + 4) = 6(2) + 6(4)$ $8(5 - 3) = 8(5) - 8(3)$

CC.6.EE.3

4 EXAMPLE Writing Equivalent Expressions

Use one of the properties in the table above to write an expression that is equivalent to $x + 3$.

The operation in the expression is _____.

Which property of this operation can be applied to $x + 3$?

_____

Use this property to write an equivalent expression:

$x + 3 =$ _____

TRY THIS!

For each expression, use a property to write an equivalent expression. Tell which property you used.

4a. $(ab)c =$ _____

4b. $3y + 4y =$ _____

Recall that terms are the parts of an expression that are added or subtracted. A term may contain variables, constants, or both. **Like terms** are terms with the same variable(s) raised to the same power(s). All constants are like terms.

$12 + 3y^3 + 4x + 2y^3$ $3y^3$ and $2y^3$ are like terms.

$5 + 8x + 13$ 5 and 13 are like terms.

5 EXAMPLE Identifying Like Terms

Identify the like terms in the list.

$$5a \quad 3y^3 \quad 7t \quad x^2 \quad 4x \quad y \quad 2y^3 \quad 2t \quad 2a \quad 2a^2$$

First, identify the terms that have the same variable.

Terms with a: _____   Terms with t: _____

Terms with x: _____   Terms with y: _____

Within each list above, circle the terms that have the same exponent.

The like terms are _____ and _____; _____ and _____; _____ and _____.

REFLECT

5. The terms y and $2y^3$ contain the same variable but are not like terms.
Why not? _____

When an expression contains like terms, you can use properties to combine the like terms into a single term. This results in an expression that is equivalent to the original expression.

6 EXAMPLE Combining Like Terms

Combine like terms.

A $6x^2 - 4x^2$

$6x^2$ and $4x^2$ are like terms.

$$6x^2 - 4x^2 = x^2(6 - 4) \qquad \textit{Distributive Property}$$

$$= x^2 \left(\boxed{} \right) \qquad \textit{Subtract inside the parentheses.}$$

$$= \boxed{} \; x^2 \qquad \textit{Commutative Property of Multiplication}$$

$$6x^2 - 4x^2 = \underline{\hspace{2cm}}$$

B $3a + 2(b + 5a)$

$$3a + 2(b + 5a) = 3a + 2b + 2(5a) \qquad \textit{Distributive Property}$$

$$= 3a + 2b + (2 \cdot 5)a \qquad \textit{Associative Property of Multiplication}$$

$$= 3a + 2b + \boxed{} \; a \qquad \textit{Multiply 2 and 5.}$$

$$= 3a + 10a + 2b \qquad \underline{\hspace{3cm}} \textit{Property of Addition}$$

$$= (3 + 10)a + 2b \qquad \textit{Distributive Property}$$

$$= \boxed{} \; a + 2b \qquad \textit{Add inside the parentheses.}$$

$$3a + 2(b + 5a) = \underline{\hspace{3cm}}$$

Combine like terms.

6a. $8y - 3y = $ _____

6b. $6x^2 + 4(x^2 - 1) = $ _____

6c. $4a^5 - 2a^5 + 4b + b = $ _____

6d. $8m + 14 - 12 + 4n = $ _____

PRACTICE

Write an algebraic expression that matches each description.

1. An expression with 3 terms _____

2. A product of two factors, where one factor is a difference of two terms

_____

3. Draw lines to match the expressions in List A with their equivalent expressions in List B.

List A	List B
$4 + 4b$	$4b - 4$
$4(b - 1)$	$4(b + 1)$
$4b + 1$	$1 + 4b$

For each expression, use a property to write an equivalent expression. Tell which property you used.

4. $ab = $ _____

5. $x + 13 = $ _____

6. $5(3x - 2) = $ _____

7. $2 + (a + b) = $ _____

Circle the like terms in each list.

8. $3a$ $16a$ 5 y $2a^2$

9. $5x^3$ $3y$ $7x^3$ $4x$ 21

10. $6b^2$ $2a^2$ $4a^3$ b^2 b

11. $12t^2$ $4x^3$ a $4t^2$ 1 $2t^2$

12. $32y$ 5 $3y^2$ 17 y^3 6

13. $10k^2$ m 9 $2m$ $10k$

Combine like terms.

14. $7x^4 - 5x^4 = $ _____

15. $2x + 3x + 4 = $ _____

16. $6b + 7b - 10 = $ _____

17. $32y + 5y = $ _____

18. $y + 4 + 3(y + 2) = $ _____

19. $7a^2 - a^2 + 16 = $ _____

20. $7a^3 - 2a^3 = $ _____

21. $5x + 3(y + 4x) = $ _____

22. $6b^2 - 4b^2 + 6a + 2a = $ _____

23. $3x + 7 - 2 + 5y = $ _____

Additional Practice

Factor the sum of terms as a product of the GCF and a sum.

1. $18 + 20$

2. $35 + 15$

3. $12 + 66$

4. $24 + 40$

5. $52 + 28$

6. $3 + 33$

7. $10y + 15$

8. $18s + 21$

9. $49m + 7$

10. $56 + 24x$

11. $80 + 25z$

12. $32b + 48$

Write four equivalent expressions for each given expression.

13. $50 - 10$

14. $42 + 18$

15. $24x - 8x$

16. $5n + 15n$

17. $4(2 + 7p)$

18. $3(6m + 3)$

19. Kara's backpack contains 4 boxes of pencils. Each box contains p pencils. Kara's backpack also contains 6 pens. Write three equivalent expressions for the total number of pencils and pens in Kara's backpack.

20. Juan buys c children's tickets at $8 each. He also buys one adult ticket for $12. Write three equivalent expressions for the total cost of the tickets.

Problem Solving

Write the correct answer.

1. A vase contains *r* roses and 6 tulips. Write two equivalent expressions for the total number of flowers in the vase.

_____

2. Keisha bikes 5 miles on Monday and *m* miles on Tuesday. Write two equivalent expressions for the total number of miles she bikes on Monday and Tuesday.

_____

3. Tristan buys *b* boxes of granola that cost $4 each. He also buys one box of crackers that costs $2. Write three equivalent expressions for the total amount Tristan spends.

_____

_____

4. A refrigerator contains *c* cartons, each of which holds 12 eggs. There are also 8 eggs on the counter. Write three equivalent expressions for the total number of eggs.

_____

_____

Circle the letter of the correct answer.

5. The expression $40 + 28m$ gives the total cost, in dollars, of joining a gym and using the gym for *m* months. Which of these expressions can also be used to find the total cost?

   A $28 + 40m$

   B $4(10 + 7m)$

   C $40(1 + 28m)$

   D $2(20 + m)$

6. The height, in feet, of an elevator above the ground after *s* seconds is represented by $20s + 64$. Which of these expressions can also be used to find the height of the elevator?

   F $2(10s + 64)$

   G $5(4s + 12)$

   H $64s + 20$

   J $4(5s + 16)$

7. The expression $12n + 18$ represents the total cost, in dollars, of catering a party for *n* people. Which of the following shows the expression written as the product of the GCF and a sum?

   A $6(2n + 3)$

   B $3(4n + 6)$

   C $2(6n + 9)$

   D $12(n + 18)$

8. The ideal cooking time, in minutes, for a turkey that weighs *p* pounds is given by the expression $15 + 20p$. Which of the following shows the expression written as the product of the GCF and a sum?

   F $15p + 20$

   G $15(1 + 20p)$

   H $5(3 + 20p)$

   J $5(3 + 4p)$

4-4

Decimals and Fractions
Going Deeper: Comparing and Ordering

Essential question: *How can you compare and order decimals and fractions?*

One way to compare a decimal and a fraction is to compare each value to $\frac{1}{2}$.

video tutor

CC.6.NS.6c

1 EXPLORE   Comparing a Decimal and a Fraction

Thomas measured rainfall for his science class for two days. On Monday he measured $\frac{3}{8}$ inch of rain. On Tuesday he measured 0.63 inch of rain. On which day did it rain the most?

Step 1 Compare $\frac{3}{8}$ to $\frac{1}{2}$.

Graph $\frac{3}{8}$ on the number line.

```
 ← + + + + + + + + →
   0     1/4    1/2    3/4    1
```

Explain how you knew where to graph $\frac{3}{8}$ on the number line.

_____

Is $\frac{3}{8}$ greater than $\frac{1}{2}$ or less than $\frac{1}{2}$? _____

Step 2 Compare 0.63 to $\frac{1}{2}$.

Graph 0.63 on the number line.

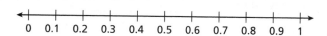

```
 ← + + + + + + + + + + + →
   0  0.1 0.2 0.3 0.4 0.5 0.6 0.7 0.8 0.9 1
```

Which decimal on the number line is equivalent to $\frac{1}{2}$? _____

Is 0.63 greater than $\frac{1}{2}$ or less than $\frac{1}{2}$? _____

Since $\frac{3}{8} < \frac{1}{2}$ and $0.63 > \frac{1}{2}$, then 0.63 ▢ $\frac{3}{8}$.

So, it rained the most on _____.

TRY THIS!

Compare. Write < or >.

1a. $\frac{2}{5}$ ▢ 0.55   **1b.** $\frac{3}{4}$ ▢ 0.34   **1c.** $\frac{7}{8}$ ▢ 0.48   **1d.** 0.45 ▢ $\frac{4}{7}$

1e. Explain how the number lines show the comparison in **1**.

_____

_____

_____

1f. Explain how to compare $\frac{5}{9}$ to $\frac{1}{2}$.

_____

_____

1g. Suppose a fraction and a decimal were both greater than $\frac{1}{2}$. How might you compare them?

_____

_____

_____

CC.6.NS.6c

2 EXPLORE   Ordering Decimals and Fractions

Tamara found eight old wrenches. The sizes marked on some of them were fractions and some were decimals. She wrote all of the sizes on a sheet of paper to show to her father. She wants to arrange the values in order from least to greatest.

0.4	$\frac{5}{8}$	0.7
0.65	$\frac{3}{8}$	0.35
0.2	$\frac{1}{4}$	

Step 1 Use division to convert the fractions to decimals.

$\frac{3}{8} = 3 \div 8 =$ ⬜ $\frac{1}{4} = 1 \div 4 =$ ⬜ $\frac{5}{8} = 5 \div 8 =$ ⬜

Step 2 Graph each value on the number line.

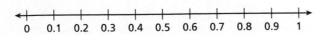

```
←┼───┼───┼───┼───┼───┼───┼───┼───┼───┼───┼→
 0  0.1 0.2 0.3 0.4 0.5 0.6 0.7 0.8 0.9  1
```

Write the fractions and decimals in order from *least to greatest*.

_____

Additional Practice

Compare. Write < or >.

1. 0.23 ___ $\dfrac{2}{5}$

2. $\dfrac{1}{9}$ ___ 0.1

3. $\dfrac{2}{3}$ ___ 0.59

4. 0.35 ___ $\dfrac{3}{4}$

5. $\dfrac{5}{8}$ ___ 0.42

6. 0.75 ___ $\dfrac{7}{8}$

7. $\dfrac{3}{5}$ ___ 0.4

8. 0.8 ___ $\dfrac{5}{6}$

9. $\dfrac{3}{8}$ ___ 0.5

10. $\dfrac{7}{10}$ ___ 0.75

11. 0.82 ___ $\dfrac{4}{5}$

12. $\dfrac{7}{20}$ ___ 0.32

Order the fractions and decimals from least to greatest.

13. $\dfrac{1}{4}$, 0.7, $\dfrac{3}{5}$

14. 0.25, $\dfrac{1}{8}$, 0.3

15. $\dfrac{9}{10}$, 0.49, $\dfrac{1}{2}$

_____   _____   _____

Order the fractions and decimals from greatest to least.

16. 0.13, $\dfrac{1}{10}$, 0.9

17. $\dfrac{2}{5}$, 0.7, $\dfrac{2}{3}$

18. 0.65, $\dfrac{4}{5}$, $\dfrac{3}{4}$

_____   _____   _____

19. Derrick has a dollar bill and three dimes, Jane has a dollar bill and one quarter, and Kelly has a dollar bill and ten nickels. Who has the most money? the least?

_____

20. It rained three and one half inches in April. In May it rained $3\dfrac{3}{4}$ inches, and in June it rained 3.6 inches. Write the months in order from the greatest to the least amount of rain.

_____

Problem Solving

Electricity is measured in amperes, or the rate electrical currents flow. A high ampere measurement means that a lot of electricity is being used. The table below shows the average amount of electricity some household appliances use per hour. Use the table to answer the questions.

1. Which uses more electricity in an hour, a 25-inch TV or a computer and printer?

   _____

2. Which uses less electricity in an hour, a blender or a popcorn popper?

   _____

3. List the appliances in order of electricity used per hour from greatest to least.

   _____

   _____

   _____

Electricity Use in the Home

Appliance	Amps per Hour
Blender	2.5
Coffeemaker	$6\frac{2}{3}$
Computer and printer	$1\frac{5}{6}$
Microwave	12.5
Popcorn popper	$2\frac{1}{12}$
25-inch TV	1.25

Circle the letter of the correct answer.

4. Daniel, Natalie, and Sean each ordered a small pizza for lunch. Daniel ate $\frac{5}{8}$ of his pizza, Natalie had 0.5 of her pizza, and Sean ate $\frac{2}{5}$ of his pizza. List the names in order of amount of pizza eaten from least to greatest.

   A Sean, Daniel, Natalie

   B Sean, Natalie, Daniel

   C Daniel, Natalie, Sean

   D Natalie, Sean, Daniel

5. Jonie, Kim, Lauren, and Tanisha are training for a triathlon. Each day Jonie runs $3\frac{4}{5}$ miles, Kim runs 3.6 miles, Lauren runs 3.25 miles, and Tanisha runs $3\frac{1}{2}$ miles. Who runs the most miles each day?

   F Jonie

   G Kim

   H Lauren

   J Tanisha

4-5

Equivalent Fractions
Modeling

Essential question: *How do you write equivalent fractions?*

Fractions that name the same amount are called **equivalent fractions**.

One $\frac{1}{2}$ fraction bar models the same amount as two $\frac{1}{4}$ fraction bars. $\frac{1}{2}$ is equivalent to $\frac{2}{4}$.

$\frac{1}{2}$	
$\frac{1}{4}$	$\frac{1}{4}$

video tutor

CC.6.NS.4

1 **EXPLORE** Modeling Equivalent Fractions

Kyle needs to measure $\frac{3}{4}$ pound of salt for an experiment. When he checks the drawer of his lab table, the only weights he has for the balance scale are $\frac{1}{8}$ pound and $\frac{1}{16}$ pound weights. How many $\frac{1}{8}$ pound weights does he need to place on the scale to equal $\frac{3}{4}$ pound?

You can use fraction bars to model equivalent fractions to find how many eighths are equivalent to $\frac{3}{4}$.

Start with three $\frac{1}{4}$ fraction bars. Draw $\frac{1}{8}$ fraction bars along the bottom of the row of $\frac{1}{4}$ fraction bars until the two rows are equal in length.

$\frac{1}{4}$	$\frac{1}{4}$	$\frac{1}{4}$

$\frac{1}{8}$	$\frac{1}{8}$

How many $\frac{1}{8}$ fraction bars are equal to $\frac{3}{4}$? _____

The model shows that $\frac{3}{4} = \frac{}{8}$.

Kyle needs to use _____ $\frac{1}{8}$ pound weights.

REFLECT

1a. **What if?** Suppose Kyle used the $\frac{1}{16}$ pound weights to equal $\frac{3}{4}$ pound. How many $\frac{1}{16}$ pound weights would he need? Explain.

_____

_____

1b. Explain how you could use a model to find how many sixths are equivalent to $\frac{2}{3}$.

_____

_____

_____

© Houghton Mifflin Harcourt Publishing Company

A fraction is in **simplest form** when the only common factor of the numerator and denominator is 1.

2 E X A M P L E   Writing Fractions in Simplest Form

Write $\frac{18}{48}$ in simplest form.

A   Use common factors.

List the factors of 18. _____

List the factors of 48. _____

What are the common factors of 18 and 48? _____

Divide both the numerator and denominator of $\frac{18}{48}$ by a common factor other than 1.

$$\frac{18}{48} = \frac{18 \div 2}{48 \div \boxed{}} = \frac{\boxed{}}{\boxed{}}$$

Continue dividing by a common factor until the only common factor is _____.

$$\frac{9}{24} = \frac{9 \div \boxed{}}{24 \div \boxed{}} = \frac{\boxed{}}{\boxed{}}$$

B   Use the greatest common factor.

What is the GCF of 18 and 48? _____

Divide both the numerator and denominator of $\frac{18}{48}$ by the GCF.

$$\frac{18}{48} = \frac{18 \div \boxed{}}{48 \div \boxed{}} = \frac{\boxed{}}{\boxed{}}$$

C   Use a ladder diagram.

Begin by dividing the numerator and denominator of $\frac{18}{48}$ by any common factor. Continue dividing by a common factor until the numerator and denominator have no remaining common factors other than 1.

$$\begin{array}{r} 2\overline{)18/48} \\ 3\overline{)9/24} \\ \boxed{}/\boxed{} \end{array}$$ *First divide numerator and denominator by 2.*
Then divide the results by 3.

So, _____ is the simplest form of $\frac{18}{48}$.

REFLECT

2a. Which method would you use to write $\frac{24}{40}$ in simplest form? Why?

_____

_____

Write each fraction in simplest form.

2b. $\frac{12}{30}$ _____ **2c.** $\frac{35}{45}$ _____ **2d.** $\frac{27}{63}$ _____ **2e.** $\frac{42}{72}$ _____

CC.6.NS.4

3 **EXAMPLE** Solving Problems with Fractions in Simplest Form

Households in the United States spend money on a variety of items. The graph shows the various spending categories for the average household. Each category is shown as a fraction of total monthly expenses.

Which category can be written as $\frac{17}{50}$ in simplest form?

Identify each category with a fraction that is not in simplest form.

_____

_____

_____

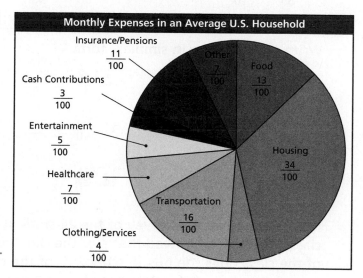

Write those fractions in simplest form.

$\frac{34}{100} =$ ____ $\frac{4}{100} =$ ____ $\frac{16}{100} =$ ____ $\frac{5}{100} =$ ____

_____ has a fraction that can be written as $\frac{17}{50}$ in simplest form.

REFLECT

3a. In the graph the fraction for Food is $\frac{13}{100}$. Is this fraction in simplest form? If not, write it in simplest form. Explain your answer.

_____

_____

3b. Explain what happens when you simplify a fraction like $\frac{4}{4}$ or $\frac{10}{10}$.

_____

_____

_____

Determine if each pair of fractions is equivalent. Write yes or no.

1. $\frac{4}{8}$ and $\frac{5}{10}$

2. $\frac{3}{5}$ and $\frac{7}{9}$

3. $\frac{6}{9}$ and $\frac{14}{20}$

4. $\frac{21}{35}$ and $\frac{6}{10}$

5. $\frac{72}{96}$ and $\frac{35}{45}$

6. $\frac{27}{27}$ and $\frac{41}{41}$

Write each fraction in simplest form.

7. $\frac{6}{9}$ _____

8. $\frac{5}{30}$ _____

9. $\frac{10}{22}$ _____

10. $\frac{16}{40}$ _____

11. $\frac{63}{90}$ _____

12. $\frac{36}{54}$ _____

13. $\frac{64}{88}$ _____

14. $\frac{68}{70}$ _____

15. $\frac{42}{98}$ _____

Mrs. Goddard took a survey of the 24 students in her 3rd period science class. The survey showed that $\frac{5}{8}$ of the class has at least 1 sibling, $\frac{15}{24}$ of the class rides the bus to school, $\frac{7}{24}$ of the class has a job during the summer, and $\frac{3}{12}$ of the class has at least 2 pets.

16. Which of the fractions are equivalent? _____

17. What fraction of the class rides the bus to school? Is this fraction in simplest form? Explain your answer.

_____

_____

18. Write the fraction from **17** in simplest form.

_____

19. Which other fraction is not in simplest form? Write that fraction in simplest form.

_____

20. Suppose you have a friend who was absent the day your teacher taught this lesson. How would you explain the process of writing a fraction in simplest form to your friend?

_____

_____

_____

Additional Practice

Find two equivalent fractions for each fraction.

1. $\frac{3}{6}$

2. $\frac{4}{7}$

3. $\frac{11}{13}$

_____

4. $\frac{2}{15}$

5. $\frac{5}{14}$

6. $\frac{8}{9}$

_____

7. $\frac{2}{21}$

8. $\frac{24}{48}$

9. $\frac{25}{100}$

_____

Find the missing numbers that make the fractions equivalent.

10. $\frac{4}{7} = \frac{?}{28}$

11. $\frac{2}{9} = \frac{?}{54}$

12. $\frac{36}{4} = \frac{?}{1}$

_____

13. $\frac{56}{8} = \frac{?}{2}$

14. $1\frac{3}{5} = \frac{?}{25}$

15. $1\frac{4}{7} = \frac{?}{42}$

_____

Write each fraction in simplest form.

16. $\frac{15}{25}$

17. $\frac{8}{36}$

18. $\frac{12}{18}$

19. $\frac{10}{24}$

_____

20. Billy had 24 trading cards. He gave 7 of his cards to Miko and 9 of his cards to Teri. What fraction of his original 24 cards does Billy have left? Write two equivalent fractions for that amount.

_____

21. Beth and Kristine ride their bikes to school in the morning. Beth has to ride $1\frac{7}{32}$ miles. Kristine has to ride $\frac{39}{32}$ miles. Who rides the farthest to reach school? Explain.

_____

Problem Solving

About 60 million Americans exercise 100 times or more each year. Their top activities and the fraction of those 60 million people who did them are shown on the circle graph. Use the graph to answer the questions.

1. Which two activities did the same number of people use to keep in shape?

_____

_____

2. Which activity had the most participants? Write an equivalent fraction for that activity's participants.

_____

_____

3. Which activity had the fewest participants? Write two equivalent fractions for that activity's participants.

_____

_____

Exercise in the U.S.

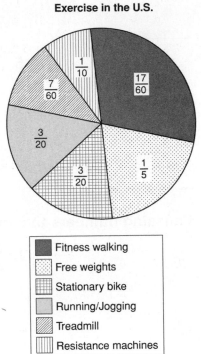

Fitness walking
Free weights
Stationary bike
Running/Jogging
Treadmill
Resistance machines

Circle the letter of the correct answer.

4. Which activity did $\frac{3}{15}$ of the people use to exercise?

 A free weights

 B treadmill

 C fitness walking

 D stationary bike

5. Which activity did $\frac{35}{300}$ of the people use to stay healthy?

 F running/jogging

 G resistance machines

 H free weights

 J treadmill

6. An average-sized person can burn about $6\frac{1}{2}$ calories a minute while riding a bike. Which of the following is equivalent to that amount?

 A $1\frac{2}{2}$ C $6\frac{2}{4}$

 B $5\frac{6}{2}$ D $6\frac{2}{6}$

7. An average-sized person can burn about 11.25 calories a minute while jogging. Which of the following is not equivalent to that amount?

 F $11\frac{1}{4}$ H $11\frac{2}{8}$

 G $11\frac{1}{2}$ J $11\frac{3}{12}$

Mixed Numbers and Improper Fractions
Modeling

Essential question: *How do you convert between mixed numbers and fractions?*

A fraction whose numerator is greater than its denominator is called an **improper fraction**. The fraction $\frac{8}{5}$ is an improper fraction.

A **proper fraction** is one in which the numerator is less than the denominator.

video tutor

PREP FOR CC.6.NS.1

1 EXPLORE · Using a Model to Write Improper Fractions as Mixed Numbers

Write $\frac{7}{3}$ as a mixed number.

Step 1 Complete the model by drawing $\frac{1}{3}$ fraction pieces to model $\frac{7}{3}$.

Step 2 Arrange the fraction pieces into groups that represent 1 whole and draw the model. Count the number of wholes and the number of leftover $\frac{1}{3}$ pieces.

There are _____ whole(s) and _____ leftover $\frac{1}{3}$ piece(s), so $\frac{7}{3} =$ _____.

TRY THIS!

Draw fraction pieces to model each improper fraction. Then use the model to write the improper fraction as a mixed number.

1a. $\frac{9}{4}$ _____

1b. $\frac{7}{2}$ _____

1c. $\frac{11}{8}$ _____

1d. Describe two ways that you could write $\frac{22}{8}$ as a mixed number.

_____

_____

_____

1e. Suppose you model $\frac{22}{8}$ with $\frac{1}{8}$ fraction bars and then model $\frac{11}{4}$ with $\frac{1}{4}$ fraction bars. How will the two models compare? Explain.

_____

_____

_____

PREP FOR **CC.6.NS.1**

2 EXPLORE Using a Model to Write Mixed Numbers as Improper Fractions

Write $1\frac{3}{5}$ as an improper fraction.

Step 1 Complete the model by drawing $\frac{1}{5}$ fraction pieces to model $1\frac{3}{5}$.

$\frac{1}{5}$	$\frac{1}{5}$	$\frac{1}{5}$	$\frac{1}{5}$	$\frac{1}{5}$

Step 2 Count the total number of $\frac{1}{5}$ fraction pieces in your model.

There is a total of _____ $\frac{1}{5}$ pieces, so $1\frac{3}{5} =$ _____.

TRY THIS!

Draw fraction pieces to model each mixed number. Then use the model to write the mixed number as an improper fraction.

2a. $3\frac{3}{4}$ _____

2b. $2\frac{5}{6}$ _____

Additional Practice

Write each mixed number as an improper fraction.

1. $3\frac{1}{2}$

2. $2\frac{1}{3}$

3. $5\frac{1}{4}$

_____

_____

_____

4. $1\frac{3}{7}$

5. $3\frac{3}{4}$

6. $4\frac{1}{3}$

_____

_____

_____

7. $2\frac{3}{5}$

8. $3\frac{5}{6}$

9. $7\frac{1}{3}$

_____

_____

_____

Write each improper fraction as a mixed number or whole number. Tell whether your answer is a mixed number or whole number.

10. $\frac{17}{3}$

11. $\frac{40}{8}$

12. $\frac{48}{7}$

_____

_____

_____

13. $\frac{33}{10}$

14. $\frac{50}{8}$

15. $\frac{83}{9}$

_____

_____

_____

16. $\frac{104}{8}$

17. $\frac{121}{6}$

18. $\frac{78}{11}$

_____

_____

_____

19. The hotel ordered an extra-long rug for a hallway that is $\frac{123}{2}$ feet long. What is the rug's length in feet and inches? Remember, 1 foot = 12 inches.

_____

20. During this year's football-throwing contest, John threw the ball $49\frac{2}{3}$ feet. Sharon threw the ball 51 feet. Who threw the ball $\frac{153}{3}$ feet?

_____

Problem Solving

Write the correct answer.

1. If stretched end-to-end, the total length of the blood vessels inside your body could wrap around Earth's equator $\frac{5}{2}$ times! Write this fact as a mixed number.

   _____

2. In 2000, the average 12-year-old child in the United States earned an allowance of 9 dollars and $\frac{7}{25}$ cents a week. Write this amount as an improper fraction and a decimal.

   _____

3. The normal body temperature for a rattlesnake is between $53\frac{3}{5}$ °F and $64\frac{2}{5}$ °F. Write this range as improper fractions.

   _____

4. A professional baseball can weigh no less than $\frac{45}{9}$ ounces and no more than $\frac{21}{4}$ ounces. Write this range as mixed numbers.

   _____

Circle the letter of the correct answer.

5. Betty needs a piece of lumber that is $\frac{14}{3}$ feet long. Which size should she look for at the hardware store?

   A $3\frac{1}{3}$ feet

   C $4\frac{2}{3}$ feet

   B $3\frac{1}{4}$ feet

   D $4\frac{1}{4}$ feet

6. What operations are used to change a mixed number to an improper fraction?

   F multiplication and addition

   G division and subtraction

   H division and addition

   J multiplication and subtraction

7. Adult bees only eat nectar, the substance in flowers used to make honey. A bee could fly 4 million miles on the energy it would get from eating $\frac{9}{2}$ liters of nectar. What is this amount of nectar written as a mixed number.

   A $9\frac{1}{2}$ liters

   C $4\frac{1}{9}$ liters

   B $4\frac{1}{2}$ liters

   D $2\frac{1}{2}$ liters

8. An astronaut who weighs 250 pounds on Earth would weigh $41\frac{1}{2}$ pounds on the moon. What is the astronaut's moon weight written as an improper fraction?

   F $\frac{41}{2}$ pounds

   H $\frac{82}{2}$ pounds

   G $\frac{42}{2}$ pounds

   J $\frac{83}{2}$ pounds

Comparing and Ordering Fractions
Going Deeper

Essential question: *How can you compare and order fractions?*

video tutor

CC.6.NS.7

1 E X P L O R E   **Using Models to Compare Fractions**

A **Compare $\frac{2}{3}$ and $\frac{1}{3}$.**

Shade the model to show $\frac{2}{3}$.

Shade the model to show $\frac{1}{3}$.

How are $\frac{2}{3}$ and $\frac{1}{3}$ the same? _____

How does the model show the comparison?

_____

To compare fractions with the same denominator, compare the

_____.

2 ☐ 1, so $\frac{2}{3}$ ☐ $\frac{1}{3}$.

B **Compare $\frac{3}{4}$ and $\frac{3}{5}$.**

Shade the model to show $\frac{3}{4}$.

Shade the model to show $\frac{3}{5}$.

How are $\frac{3}{4}$ and $\frac{3}{5}$ the same? _____

How does the model show the comparison?

_____

To compare fractions with the same numerator, compare the

_____.

5 ☐ 4, so $\frac{3}{4}$ ☐ $\frac{3}{5}$.

1a. There are two identical pizzas. One is cut into four equal-sized pieces and the other is cut into five equal-sized pieces. Which would be a larger serving, 3 pieces from the first pizza or 3 pieces from the second pizza? Explain.

_____

_____

_____

1b. How could you compare $\frac{4}{5}$ and $\frac{2}{3}$?

_____

_____

CC.6.NS.7

2 EXAMPLE Ordering Fractions and Mixed Numbers

On the ninth hole during a charity golf tournament, the organizers held a closest-to-the-hole contest. The table shows the distance from the hole for each of the three closest shots.

Golfer	Jenae	Kaylon	Pinkie
Distance (ft)	$6\frac{2}{3}$	$8\frac{5}{6}$	$6\frac{1}{4}$

Put the distances in order from *closest* to *farthest* from the hole.

Step 1 Compare the whole number parts.

$$6 \quad \boxed{} \quad 6 \qquad 6 \quad \boxed{} \quad 8$$

Step 2 Compare the fraction parts.
Find equivalent fractions with the same denominator.

$$6\frac{2 \times 4}{3 \times \boxed{}} = 6\frac{\boxed{}}{\boxed{}} \qquad 6\frac{1 \times \boxed{}}{4 \times \boxed{}} = 6\frac{\boxed{}}{\boxed{}}$$

Step 3 Compare the numerators.

$$6\frac{\boxed{}}{\boxed{}} < 6\frac{\boxed{}}{\boxed{}} < 8\frac{5}{6}$$

From closest to farthest, the distances are _____.

TRY THIS!

Compare. Write <, >, or =.

2a. $\frac{4}{7}$ $\boxed{}$ $\frac{6}{7}$

2b. $\frac{4}{5}$ $\boxed{}$ $\frac{4}{9}$

2c. $3\frac{4}{9}$ $\boxed{}$ $3\frac{5}{8}$

2d. In ② , you compared two fractions or mixed numbers at a time. How might you compare three or more fractions at the same time? Give an example involving three fractions.

_____

_____

_____

_____

3 E X A M P L E Ordering Decimals and Fractions

During last year's baseball season, Kolbe's batting average was 0.450 and Phil's was 0.390. After the first 6 games this season, Kolbe's batting average is $\frac{8}{20}$ and Phil's is $\frac{3}{10}$. Write the fractions and decimals in order from least to greatest.

Write the decimals in words and then as fractions.

0.450 = _____ hundredths = _____

0.390 = _____ hundredths = _____

Now graph the four fractions on the number line below.

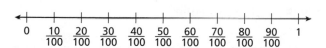

From least to greatest, the order is _____

REFLECT

3a. Explain another way the fractions and decimals could be compared in ③ .

_____

TRY THIS!

List the numbers in order from greatest to least.

3b. $\frac{2}{3}$, 0.65, 0.28, $\frac{1}{4}$ _____   **3c.** 0.54, $\frac{7}{8}$, $\frac{5}{9}$, 0.92 _____

Compare. Write <, >, or =.

1. $\frac{2}{5}$ ☐ $\frac{4}{5}$

2. $7\frac{13}{20}$ ☐ $7\frac{7}{10}$

3. $\frac{27}{30}$ ☐ $\frac{9}{10}$

4. $\frac{7}{9}$ ☐ $\frac{3}{4}$

5. $3\frac{3}{4}$ ☐ $3\frac{3}{5}$

6. $11\frac{1}{3}$ ☐ $11\frac{5}{12}$

List the numbers in order from least to greatest.

7. $\frac{4}{5}$, 0.76, 0.82, $\frac{3}{4}$ _____

8. 0.18, $\frac{1}{6}$, $\frac{2}{9}$, 0.15 _____

9. 0.38, $\frac{11}{20}$, $\frac{3}{8}$, 0.54 _____

10. $\frac{61}{100}$, 0.33, 0.6, $\frac{17}{50}$ _____

List the numbers in order from greatest to least.

11. $\frac{23}{100}$, 0.25, 0.29, $\frac{13}{50}$ _____

12. 0.72, $\frac{3}{4}$, $\frac{7}{10}$, 0.69 _____

13. $\frac{19}{20}$, 0.94, 0.98, $\frac{9}{10}$ _____

14. 0.78, $\frac{4}{9}$, $\frac{23}{30}$, 0.46 _____

15. This morning Alex's dog ate $\frac{5}{6}$ pound of dog food. Gina's dog ate $\frac{5}{8}$ pound of dog food. Whose dog ate more food? Explain.

_____

16. Mr. Jennings handed back test papers today. Carlos missed $11\frac{3}{4}$ points on the test. Aisha missed $11\frac{1}{4}$ points. Who missed fewer points? Explain.

_____

_____

17. Andy ran a total of $4\frac{1}{8}$ miles on the school track. Brea ran a total of 4.15 miles. Who ran farther? Explain.

_____

18. Eli and his friends meet at the park every Saturday morning. Eli lives $2\frac{5}{6}$ miles from the park. Aaron lives $3\frac{1}{8}$ miles from the park and Tom lives $2\frac{2}{3}$ miles from the park. List the friends in order of the distance they live from the park from greatest to least.

_____

Additional Practice

Compare. Write <, >, or =.

1. $\dfrac{4}{7}$ — $\dfrac{3}{5}$
2. $\dfrac{1}{8}$ — $\dfrac{2}{3}$
3. $\dfrac{1}{4}$ — $\dfrac{2}{5}$

4. $\dfrac{7}{8}$ — $\dfrac{5}{6}$
5. $\dfrac{18}{24}$ — $\dfrac{3}{4}$
6. $\dfrac{4}{5}$ — $\dfrac{8}{12}$

Order the fractions from least to greatest.

7. $\dfrac{1}{2}, \dfrac{2}{5}, \dfrac{1}{3}$
8. $\dfrac{2}{5}, \dfrac{3}{4}, \dfrac{2}{3}$
9. $\dfrac{3}{7}, \dfrac{5}{6}, \dfrac{4}{5}$

_____ _____ _____

10. $\dfrac{5}{9}, \dfrac{3}{7}, \dfrac{2}{3}$
11. $\dfrac{3}{8}, \dfrac{2}{7}, \dfrac{3}{5}$
12. $\dfrac{2}{7}, \dfrac{1}{8}, \dfrac{2}{5}$

_____ _____ _____

Order the fractions from greatest to least.

13. $\dfrac{1}{6}, \dfrac{2}{7}, \dfrac{1}{5}$
14. $\dfrac{3}{7}, \dfrac{4}{9}, \dfrac{2}{3}$
15. $\dfrac{2}{5}, \dfrac{3}{10}, \dfrac{2}{3}$

_____ _____ _____

16. $\dfrac{4}{5}, \dfrac{7}{10}, \dfrac{1}{12}$
17. $\dfrac{3}{8}, \dfrac{3}{4}, \dfrac{4}{9}$
18. $\dfrac{4}{7}, \dfrac{3}{5}, \dfrac{5}{6}$

_____ _____ _____

19. David ran $4\dfrac{1}{4}$ miles, Shane ran $4\dfrac{1}{2}$ miles, and Matt ran $4\dfrac{5}{8}$ miles. Who ran the farthest?

_____

20. Darius and Anita both took the same test. Darius answered $\dfrac{5}{6}$ of the questions correctly, and Anita answered $\dfrac{6}{7}$ correctly. Who got the higher score on the test?

_____

Problem Solving

The table shows what fraction of Earth's total land area each of the continents makes up. Use the table to answer the questions.

1. Which continent makes up the most of Earth's land?

   _____

2. Which continent makes up the least part of Earth's land?

   _____

3. Explain how you would compare the part of Earth's total land area that Australia and Europe make up.

   _____

   _____

Earth's Land

Continent	Fraction of Earth's Land
Africa	$\frac{1}{5}$
Antarctica	$\frac{1}{10}$
Asia	$\frac{3}{10}$
Australia	$\frac{1}{20}$
Europe	$\frac{7}{100}$
North America	$\frac{4}{25}$
South America	$\frac{6}{50}$

Circle the letter of the correct answer.

4. Which of these continents covers the greatest part of Earth's total land area?

   A North America

   B South America

   C Europe

   D Australia

5. Which of these continents covers the least part of Earth's total land area?

   F Africa

   G Antarctica

   H Asia

   J Australia

6. Which of the following lists shows the continents written in order from the greatest part of Earth's total land they cover to the least part?

   A Asia, Africa, North America

   B Africa, Asia, North America

   C Asia, South America, North America

   D North America, Asia, South America

7. Which of the following lists shows the continents written in order from the least part of Earth's total land they cover to the greatest part?

   F Antarctica, Europe, South America

   G South America, Antarctica, Europe

   H Australia, Europe, Antarctica

   J Antarctica, Europe, Australia

CHAPTER 4

Problem Solving Connections

Snack Attack! A group of friends start a business selling healthy snack boxes. They decide that each box will contain samples of fruit chews and trail mix. Because they will be shipping some of the boxes, they want to choose snacks with the least possible weight. Which snacks should they include in the boxes and how many of each should there be?

COMMON CORE

CC.6.NS.4
CC.6.NS.7
CC.6.EE.3
CC.6.EE.4

1 Comparing Fruit Chews

Rafael collects information on different brands of fruit chews. The table shows the weights of 6 different brands.

Fruit Chews	
Brand	**Weight (lb)**
Bonny's	$\frac{3}{8}$
Fresh Max	0.18
Sunshine	$\frac{3}{15}$
Golden	$\frac{16}{100}$
Taste King	$\frac{7}{35}$
Avalanche	0.28

A Write the weights of Fresh Max and Avalanche as fractions in simplest form.

Fresh Max: _____   Avalanche: _____

B Do any of the packages have the same weight? Explain.

C Rafael thinks the group should not consider any brand of fruit chews if the package weighs more than $\frac{1}{4}$ lb. Which brand or brands does Rafael think the group should not consider? Why?

D List the brands of fruit chews in order from lightest to heaviest. Include each weight written as a decimal.

	Lightest ——————————————→ Heaviest					
Brand						
Weight (lb)						

2 Comparing Trail Mixes

Alyssa collects information on different brands of trail mix. The table shows the weights of 6 different brands.

Trail Mix	
Brand	**Weight (oz)**
Energize	$2\frac{1}{3}$
Mountain	$\frac{9}{4}$
Jonah's	$3\frac{1}{5}$
A-Plus	$3\frac{2}{3}$
Cruncho	$\frac{12}{5}$
Red Star	$\frac{7}{2}$

A Write the weights of Energize, Jonah's, and A-Plus as improper fractions.

Energize: _____ Jonah's: _____

A-Plus: _____

B Write the weights of Mountain, Cruncho, and Red Star as mixed numbers.

Mountain: _____ Cruncho: _____ Red Star: _____

C List the brands of trail mix below in order from lightest to heaviest. Include each weight written as a mixed number.

	Lightest ⟶ Heaviest					
Brand						
Weight (oz)						

D Alyssa thinks the group should not consider any brand of trail mix if the package weighs more than $3\frac{1}{4}$ oz. Which brand or brands does Alyssa think the group should not consider? Why?

3 What Goes in the Box?

The group members prepare a budget for their first batch of snack boxes. They find that they have enough money to buy 32 packages of fruit chews and 48 packages of trail mix. The group wants each box to contain the same number of packages of fruit chews and the same number of packages of trail mix. They also want to be sure no snacks are left over after preparing the boxes.

A Is it possible to make exactly 12 boxes of snacks? Why or why not?

B Is it possible to make exactly 8 boxes of snacks? If so, how many of each type of snack would be in each box?

C What are all the possible numbers of snack boxes that the group can make? Explain how you know.

D The group members decide they want to make the greatest possible number of snack boxes. How many boxes will they make? How many packages of fruit chews and trail mix will each box contain?

4 Choosing the Box

The group members want to have special cardboard boxes made. Mikiko gathers data from three companies that make boxes. The table shows the cost of ordering b boxes from each company.

Cardboard Boxes	
Company	Cost of b Boxes ($)
Graphix	$3(b + 2)$
Print City	$2b + 4 + b + 2$
Super Pack	$3b + 4$

A Use a property to write an equivalent expression for the cost of ordering b boxes from Graphix. Tell which property you used.

B Do any of the companies have the same cost for ordering b boxes? Explain.

C The group wants to have the boxes printed as inexpensively as possible. Which company should Mikiko recommend to the group? Why?

5 Answer the Question

A The group members decide that each box should contain different types of fruit chews and different types of trail mix. Remember that the group wants to make the greatest possible number of boxes and they want each box to be as light as possible.

Look back over your work. Which brands of fruit chews and trail mix should each box contain?

B Tyrell needs to fill out an order form for the group. Complete the form below to show how the group can make the snack boxes as light as possible and as inexpensive as possible. (You may not need to use all the rows in the form.)

Fruit Chews		
Brand of Fruit Chew	Number of Packages in Each Snack Box	Total Number of Packages to Order
Trail Mix		
Brand of Trail Mix	Number of Packages in Each Snack Box	Total Number of Packages to Order
Boxes		
Company	Number of Boxes to Order	Total Cost of Boxes

Performance Task

COMMON CORE

CC.6.NS.4
CC.6.NS.7
CC.6.EE.3
CC.6.EE.4

★ **1.** An animal shelter has 24 large cages and 42 small cages that need to be cleaned. The director of the shelter wants to divide the work so that each person cleans the same number of large cages and the same number of small cages. What is the largest number of people he can use to do the work, and how many large and small cages will each person clean? Explain your reasoning.

★ **2.** Francis is baking cookies. The recipe for chocolate chip cookies calls for $2\frac{2}{3}$ cups of flour, the recipe for peanut butter cookies calls for 2.75 cups, and the recipe for ginger snaps calls for $\frac{5}{2}$ cups. If Francis wants to use as little flour as possible, which cookie should he make? Explain your reasoning.

★ **3.** Marty and Cindy are packing books in boxes for storage. Marty has packed 126 books
★ and Cindy has packed 144. Each box contains the same number of books.

a. What is the greatest common factor of 126 and 144? Explain how you found it.

b. Write an expression equivalent to 126 + 144 using the Distributive Property and the greatest common factor.

c. The greatest common factor is also the number of books that fit in a box. Interpret the expression you wrote in terms of the boxes and books Marty and Cindy have packed.

4. As a project for gym class, Marcus is designing a field for a new sport. The field is in the shape shown. The areas of the two smaller rectangles are 228 and 132 square meters. All sides have lengths which are whole numbers.

← width

a. What is the greatest possible width of the field? Explain how you found your answer.

b. What are the lengths of the two rectangles that make up the field? Show your work.

c. Marcus decides to change the length of the smaller rectangle but keep the width the same. He says the new area of the smaller rectangle is 136 square meters, and the length is a whole number. Is this possible? Explain why or why not.

Name _____ Class _____ Date _____

SELECTED RESPONSE

1. Find the GCF of 72 and 96.

   A. 13   **C.** 144

   B. 24   **D.** 3

2. Factor the sum of terms as a product of the GCF and a sum: $60 + 72$.

   F. $12(5 + 6)$ **H.** $2(30 + 36)$

   G. $12(20 + 24)$ **J.** $4(15 + 18)$

3. A sixth-grade class has 12 boys and 8 girls. The teacher wants to divide them into groups that have the same number of boys and the same number of girls. What is the greatest possible number of groups the teacher can make?

   A. 4 groups   **C.** 6 groups

   B. 8 groups   **D.** 2 groups

4. Identify the terms in the expression $3x^2 + 9x - 8$.

   F. $3x^2$, $9x$ and 8   **H.** x^2 and x

   G. 3, 9, and 8   **J.** $3x^2$ and $9x$

5. In the expression $3x^2 + 6x - 9$, 3 and 6 are examples of which of the following?

   A. terms   **C.** coefficients

   B. constants   **D.** factors

6. Which expression is NOT equivalent to the expression $45 - 18$

   F. $3(15 - 6)$ **H.** $(5 - 2)9$

   G. 27   **J.** $9(5 - 18)$

7. Which expression is equivalent to $3x - 4 + 2(2 + 4x)$?

   A. $11x$ **C.** $9x$

   B. $11x - 8$ **D.** $9x - 8$

8. Which number is between $\frac{3}{4}$ and 0.8?

   F. 0.78

   G. $\frac{2}{3}$

   H. 0.85

   J. $\frac{1}{2}$

9. Which number is the greatest?

   A. $\frac{4}{9}$ **C.** $\frac{7}{8}$

   B. $\frac{3}{4}$ **D.** $\frac{8}{9}$

10. Order the fractions $\frac{1}{2}, \frac{4}{7}, \frac{3}{8}$ from least to greatest.

   F. $\frac{3}{8}, \frac{4}{7}, \frac{1}{2}$

   G. $\frac{3}{8}, \frac{1}{2}, \frac{4}{7}$

   H. $\frac{1}{2}, \frac{3}{8}, \frac{4}{7}$

   J. $\frac{4}{7}, \frac{1}{2}, \frac{3}{8}$

11. Find the value of 3^5.

   A. 15   **C.** 125

   B. 81   **D.** 243

12. Mary Ann needs $\frac{3}{7}$ cup of sugar to bake a cake. She has $\frac{3}{5}$ cup. Does she have enough to bake the cake?

   F. yes   **G.** no

13. Karen has 30 photos from a trip to Dallas and 48 photos from a trip to Austin. She wants to put all of the photos in an album so that the photos from each trip are in separate sections. She also wants the same number of photos on each page. What is the greatest number of photos she can put on each page?

   A. 4   **C.** 8

   B. 6   **D.** 12

CONSTRUCTED RESPONSE

14. Write the sum as a product of the GCF and a sum: $39 + 91$.

_____

15. At the pet fair, there are 42 dogs and 35 cats. The pets must be split into small groups so that there are the same number of dogs in each group and the same number of cats in each group. What is the greatest number of groups that can be made so that each animal is in a group? Explain how you determined your answer.

_____

_____

_____

_____

_____

_____

_____

_____

_____

_____

_____

16. There are 5 books in a series of books Mia and Toby are reading. Mia has read $1\frac{3}{4}$ of the books and Toby has read $1\frac{1}{7}$ of the books. Who has read more of the series? Explain your answer.

_____

_____

_____

_____

_____

_____

_____

_____

17. Is the following statement true or false? Explain.

$$4\frac{3}{5} = 4\frac{21}{35}$$

_____

_____

_____

Fraction Operations

Chapter Focus

You will find the least common multiple of two numbers in a problem situation. You will use your knowledge of least common multiples to find the least common denominator of two fractions in order to add or subtract. Solving equations involving addition, subtraction, multiplication, and division of mixed numbers will also be taught in this chapter.

Chapter at a Glance

COMMON CORE

Lesson		Standards for Mathematical Content
5-1	Least Common Multiple	CC.6.NS.4
5-2	Adding and Subtracting with Unlike Denominators	CC.6.NS.4
5-3	Regrouping to Subtract Mixed Numbers	CC.6.EE.7
5-4	Solving Fraction Equations: Addition and Subtraction	CC.6.EE.7
5-5	Multiplying Mixed Numbers	PREP FOR CC.6.NS.1
5-6	Dividing Fractions and Mixed Numbers	CC.6.NS.1
5-7	Solving Fraction Equations: Multiplication and Division	CC.6.EE.7
	Problem Solving Connections	
	Performance Task	
	Assessment Readiness	

Unpacking the Standards

Understanding the standards and the vocabulary terms in the standards will help you know exactly what you are expected to learn in this chapter.

COMMON CORE **CC.6.EE.7**

Solve real-world and mathematical problems by writing and solving equations of the form $x + p = q$ and $px = q$ for cases in which p, q and x are all nonnegative rational numbers.

Key Vocabulary

rational number (*número racional*)
A number that can be written in the form $\frac{a}{b}$, where a and b are integers and $b \neq 0$.

What It Means to You

You will use your knowledge of operations to solve equations.

EXAMPLE

On average, a person in Costa Rica consumes $132\frac{1}{4}$ lb of sugar per year. If the average person in Costa Rica consumes $24\frac{1}{4}$ lb less than the average person in the U.S., what is the average sugar consumption per year by a person in the U.S.?

Let u represent the average amount of sugar consumed in the U.S.

$$u - 24\frac{1}{4} = 132\frac{1}{4}$$
$$\underline{+24\frac{1}{4} \quad +24\frac{1}{4}}$$
$$u = 156\frac{2}{4}$$
$$u = 156\frac{1}{2}$$

On average, a person in the U.S. consumes $156\frac{1}{2}$ lb of sugar per year.

CC.6.NS.4

Find the greatest common factor of two whole numbers less than or equal to 100 and the least common multiple of two whole numbers less than or equal to 12. Use the distributive property to express a sum of two whole numbers 1—100 with a common factor as a multiple of a sum of two whole numbers with no common factor.

Key Vocabulary

least common multiple (LCM) *(mínimo común denominador (m.c.d.))* The smallest number, other than zero, that is a multiple of two or more given numbers.

What It Means to You

You will determine the least common multiple of two numbers and solve real-world problems involving the least common multiple.

EXAMPLE

Lydia's family will provide juice boxes and granola bars for 24 players. Juice comes in packs of 6, and granola bars in packs of 8. What is the least number of packs needed so that each player has a drink and granola bar and there are none left over?

6: 6, 12, 18, 24, 30, …

8: 8, 16, 24, 32, …

There are 24 juice boxes and 24 granola bars. Lydia's family should buy 4 packs of juice and 3 packs of granola bars.

 CC.6.NS.1

Interpret and compute quotients of fractions, and solve word problems involving division of fractions by fractions, e.g., by using visual fraction models and equations to represent the problem.

Key Vocabulary

quotient *(cociente)* The result when one number is divided by another.
fraction *(fracción)* A number in the form $\frac{a}{b}$, where $b \neq 0$.
equation *(ecuación)* A mathematical sentence that shows that two expressions are equivalent.

What It Means to You

You will learn how to divide two fractions. You will also understand the relationship between multiplication and division.

EXAMPLE

Zachary is making vegetable soup. The recipe makes $6\frac{3}{4}$ cups of soup. How many $1\frac{1}{2}$ cup servings will the recipe make?

$$6\frac{3}{4} \div 1\frac{1}{2}$$

$$= \frac{27}{4} \div \frac{3}{2}$$

$$= \frac{27}{4} \cdot \frac{2}{3}$$

$$= \frac{9}{2}$$

$$= 4\frac{1}{2}$$

The recipe will make $4\frac{1}{2}$ servings.

CHAPTER 5

Key Vocabulary

least common denominator *(LCD)(mínimo común denominador (m.c.d.))* The least common multiple of two or more denominators.

least common multiple *(LCM) (mínimo común múltiplo (m.c.m.))* The smallest number, other than zero, that is a multiple of two or more given numbers.

reciprocal *(recíproco)* One of two numbers whose product is 1.

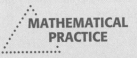

MATHEMATICAL PRACTICE

The Common Core Standards for Mathematical Practice describe varieties of expertise that mathematics educators at all levels should seek to develop in their students. Opportunities to develop these practices are integrated throughout this program.

1. Make sense of problems and persevere in solving them.
2. Reason abstractly and quantitatively.
3. Construct viable arguments and critique the reasoning of others.
4. Model with mathematics.
5. Use appropriate tools strategically.
6. Attend to precision.
7. Look for and make use of structure.
8. Look for and express regularity in repeated reasoning.

Least Common Multiple
Going Deeper

Essential question: *How do you find the least common multiple of two numbers?*

video tutor

CC.6.NS.4

1 EXPLORE Least Common Multiple

For the next 100 days, Shannon will be training for a biathlon. She will swim every 6 days and bicycle every 8 days. On what days will she both swim and bicycle?

Step 1 Shade each day Shannon will swim.

Step 2 Circle each day Shannon will bicycle.

Shannon will both swim and bicycle on days _____.

The numbers of the days that Shannon will swim and bicycle are common multiples of 6 and 8.

⚷ The **least common multiple (LCM)** is the least common multiple of two or more counting numbers.

1	2	3	4	5	6	7	8	9	10
11	12	13	14	15	16	17	18	19	20
21	22	23	24	25	26	27	28	29	30
31	32	33	34	35	36	37	38	39	40
41	42	43	44	45	46	47	48	49	50
51	52	53	54	55	56	57	58	59	60
61	62	63	64	65	66	67	68	69	70
71	72	73	74	75	76	77	78	79	80
81	82	83	84	85	86	87	88	89	90
91	92	93	94	95	96	97	98	99	100

What is the LCM of 6 and 8? What does it represent in this situation?

_____

CC.6.NS.4

2 EXAMPLE Least Common Multiple

A store is holding a grand opening promotion. Every 3rd customer receives a free key chain and every 4th customer receives a free magnet. Which customer will be the first to receive both a key chain and a magnet?

List the multiples of each number. Circle the common multiples.

Multiples of 3: _____, _____, _____, _____, _____, _____, _____, _____, _____

Multiples of 4: _____, _____, _____, _____, _____, _____, _____, _____, _____

What is the LCM of 3 and 4? _____

The first customer to get both a key chain and a magnet is _____.

List multiples to find the LCM of each pair of numbers.

2a. 4 and 9 _____

2b. 18 and 24 _____

2c. What is the LCM of two numbers when one number is a multiple of the other? Give an example.

_____

_____

2d. What is the LCM of two numbers that have no common factors greater than 1? Give an example.

_____

_____

PRACTICE

Find the LCM of each pair of numbers.

1. 6 and 9 _____

2. 9 and 21 _____

3. 8 and 56 _____

4. 16 and 24 _____

5. 12 and 30 _____

6. 6 and 10 _____

7. At a restaurant, after every 12th visit you receive a free beverage. After every 15th visit you receive a free dessert. At which visit will you first receive a free beverage and a free dessert?   Visit _____

8. Starting today (day 1) Lee will walk his dog Fido every 3rd day and his dog Fifi every 5th day. On which day will Lee first walk both dogs together?   Day _____

Use the train schedule for 9 and 10.

9. The red line and the blue line trains just arrived at the station. When will they next arrive at the station at the same time? In _____ minutes

10. All three trains just arrived at the station. When will they next all arrive at the station at the same time? In _____ minutes

Train Schedule	
Train	**Arrives Every...**
Red line	8 minutes
Blue line	10 minutes
Yellow line	12 minutes

Additional Practice

Find the least common multiple (LCM).

1. 2 and 5 _____

2. 4 and 3 _____

3. 6 and 4 _____

4. 6 and 8 _____

5. 5 and 9 _____

6. 4 and 5 _____

7. 10 and 15 _____

8. 8 and 12 _____

9. 6 and 10 _____

10. 3, 6, and 9 _____

11. 2, 5, and 10 _____

12. 4, 7, and 14 _____

13. 3, 5, and 9 _____

14. 2, 5, and 8 _____

15. 3, 9, and 12 _____

16. Mr. Stevenson is ordering shirts and hats for his Boy Scout troop. There are 45 scouts in the troop. Hats come in packs of 3, and shirts come in packs of 5. What is the least number of packs of each he should order so that each scout will have 1 hat and 1 shirt, and none will be left over?

_____

17. Tony wants to make 36 party bags. Glitter pens come in packs of 6. Stickers come in sheets of 4, and balls come in packs of 3. What is the least number of each package he should buy to have 1 of each item in every party bag, and no supplies left over?

_____

18. Glenda is making 30 school supply baskets. Notepads come in packs of 5. Erasers come in packs of 15, and markers come in packs of 3. What is the least number of each package she should buy to have 1 of each item in every basket, and no supplies left over?

_____

Problem Solving

Use the table to answer the questions.

1. You want to have an equal number of plastic cups and paper plates. What is the least number of packs of each you can buy?

_____

_____

2. You want to invite 48 people to a party. What is the least number of packs of invitations and napkins you should buy to have one for each person and none left over?

_____

_____

Party Supplies

Item	Number per Pack
Invitations	12
Balloons	30
Paper plates	10
Paper napkins	24
Plastic cups	15
Noise makers	5

Circle the letter of the correct answer.

3. You want to have an equal number of noisemakers and balloons at your party. What is the least number of packs of each you can buy?

  A 1 pack of balloons and 1 pack of noise makers

  B 1 pack of balloons and 2 packs of noise makers

  C 1 pack of balloons and 6 packs of noise makers

  D 6 packs of balloons and 1 pack of noise makers

5. The LCM for three items listed in the table is 60 packs. Which of the following are those three items?

  A balloons, plates, noise makers

  B noise makers, invitations, balloons

  C napkins, cups, plates

  D balloons, napkins, plates

4. You bought an equal number of packs of plates and cups so that each of your 20 guests would have 3 cups and 2 plates. How many packs of each item did you buy?

  F 1 pack of cups and 1 pack of plates

  G 3 packs of cups and 4 packs of plates

  H 4 packs of cups and 3 packs of plates

  J 4 packs of cups and 4 packs of plates

6. To have one of each item for 120 party guests, you buy 10 packs of one item and 24 packs of the other. What are those two items?

  F plates and invitations

  G balloons and cups

  H napkins and plates

  J invitations and noise makers

Adding and Subtracting with Unlike Denominators

Reasoning

Essential question: *How do you use a common denominator to add and subtract fractions?*

To add or subtract unlike fractions, rewrite the fractions using a common denominator, or the least common denominator. The **least common denominator (LCD)** is the least common multiple (LCM) of two or more denominators.

CC.6.NS.4

1 EXAMPLE   Adding Three Unlike Fractions

Wakenda is baking three different kinds of cookies. One recipe uses $\frac{1}{3}$ cup of butter, another uses $\frac{1}{2}$ cup, and the third uses $\frac{3}{4}$ cup. In all, how many cups of butter does she need for her cookies?

You can multiply the denominators to find a common denominator.

Common denominator: ☐ × ☐ × ☐ = ☐

$$\frac{1}{3} \rightarrow \frac{1 \times \Box}{3 \times \Box} \rightarrow \frac{\quad}{\quad}$$ *Multiply numerator and denominator by* ☐ .

$$\frac{1}{2} \rightarrow \frac{1 \times \Box}{2 \times \Box} \rightarrow \frac{\quad}{\quad}$$ *Multiply numerator and denominator by* ☐ .

$$+ \frac{3}{4} \rightarrow \frac{3 \times \Box}{4 \times \Box} \rightarrow + \frac{\quad}{\quad}$$ *Multiply numerator and denominator by* ☐ .

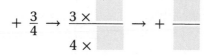
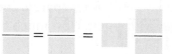

$$\frac{\quad}{\quad} = \frac{\quad}{\quad} = \Box \frac{\quad}{\quad}$$ *Add the numerators.*
Simplify.
Then write as a mixed number.

Wakenda needs _____ cups of butter for her cookies.

REFLECT

1. What is the least common denominator (LCD) for the fractions in **1** ? Explain how the steps of the solution would be different if the LCD was used.

_____

_____

_____

2 EXAMPLE Adding and Subtracting Unlike Fractions

Eduardo is using canvas for two projects. One project requires $\frac{1}{6}$ yard of canvas and the other requires $\frac{1}{4}$ yard of canvas. Eduardo has $\frac{2}{3}$ yard of canvas. After completing both projects, how much canvas will he have left over?

Add parentheses to the expression to model this situation.

$$\frac{2}{3} - \frac{1}{6} + \frac{1}{4}$$

Simplify the expression using the order of operations.

$\frac{2}{3} - \left(\frac{1}{6} + \frac{1}{4}\right) = \frac{2}{3} \quad - \left(\frac{}{} + \frac{}{}\right)$ *The LCD is _____.*

$= \frac{2}{3} \quad - \frac{}{}$ *Perform operations within parentheses.*

$= \frac{}{} - \frac{}{}$ *The LCD is _____.*

$= \frac{}{} = \frac{}{}$ *Subtract. Write the difference in simplest form.*

Eduardo will have _____ yard of canvas left.

PRACTICE

1. The Santoso family went hiking at a state park near their home. They hiked three trails, one $\frac{5}{8}$-mile long, one $\frac{1}{6}$-mile long, and one $\frac{3}{4}$-mile long. How far did they hike? _____

2. Kaleb needs $\frac{3}{4}$ pint of blue paint. He has two partial containers, one with $\frac{3}{8}$ pint and the other with $\frac{1}{4}$ pint. How much more blue paint does he need? _____

3. **Error Analysis** On the first day of his cross-country skiing vacation, Marvin skied $\frac{1}{5}$ mile in the morning and $\frac{1}{2}$ mile in the afternoon. At the end of the day Marvin said he had skied $\frac{3}{10}$ mile altogether. Use mental math to explain why his total was not reasonable.

_____

_____

Additional Practice

Add or subtract. Write each answer in simplest form.

1. $\frac{6}{7} + \frac{1}{3}$

2. $\frac{3}{7} - \frac{2}{5}$

3. $\frac{1}{4} + \frac{3}{8}$

_____

4. $\frac{7}{8} - \frac{2}{3}$

5. $\frac{1}{6} + \frac{3}{5}$

6. $\frac{5}{6} - \frac{2}{3}$

_____

7. $\frac{5}{9} - \frac{1}{3}$

8. $\frac{7}{8} + \frac{3}{4}$

9. $\frac{5}{12} - \frac{1}{6}$

_____

10. $\frac{4}{5} - \frac{7}{11}$

11. $\frac{4}{9} + \frac{5}{6}$

12. $\frac{5}{8} + \frac{2}{3}$

_____

Evaluate each expression for $b = \frac{1}{3}$. Write your answer in simplest form.

13. $b + \frac{5}{8}$

14. $\frac{7}{9} - b$

15. $\frac{2}{7} + b$

_____

16. $b + b$

17. $\frac{11}{12} - b$

18. $\frac{3}{4} - b$

_____

19. There are three grades in Mona's middle school—sixth, seventh, and eighth. One-third of the students are in sixth grade and $\frac{1}{4}$ are in seventh grade. What fraction of the schools' students are in eighth grade?

_____

20. Kyle is making a dessert that calls for $\frac{4}{5}$ cup of crushed cookies. If he has already crushed $\frac{7}{10}$ cup, how much more does he need?

_____

Problem Solving

Use the circle graph to answer the questions. Write each answer in simplest form.

1. On which two continents do most people live? How much of the total population do they make up together?

_____

_____

2. How much of the world's population live in either North America or South America?

_____

_____

3. How much more of the world's total population lives in Asia than in Africa?

_____

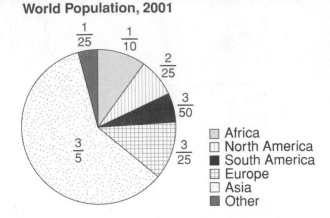

World Population, 2001

$\frac{1}{25}$ $\frac{1}{10}$ $\frac{2}{25}$ $\frac{3}{50}$ $\frac{3}{5}$ $\frac{3}{25}$

☐ Africa
⊞ North America
■ South America
⊞ Europe
⊡ Asia
■ Other

Circle the letter of the correct answer.

4. How much of Earth's total population do people in Asia and Africa make up all together?

   A $\frac{3}{10}$ of the population

   B $\frac{2}{5}$ of the population

   C $\frac{7}{10}$ of the population

   D $\frac{7}{5}$ of the population

5. What is the difference between North America's part of the total population and Africa's part?

   F Africa has $\frac{1}{50}$ more.

   G Africa has $\frac{1}{50}$ less.

   H Africa has $\frac{9}{50}$ more.

   J Africa has $\frac{9}{50}$ less.

6. How much more of the population lives in Europe than in North America?

   A $\frac{1}{25}$ of the population

   B $\frac{1}{5}$ of the population

   C $\frac{1}{15}$ of the population

   D $\frac{1}{10}$ of the population

7. How much of the world's population lives in North America and Europe?

   F $\frac{1}{25}$ of the population

   G $\frac{1}{15}$ of the population

   H $\frac{1}{5}$ of the population

   J $\frac{1}{20}$ of the population

5-3

Regrouping to Subtract Mixed Numbers
Connection: Subtraction Property of Equality

Essential question: *How do you use the Subtraction Property of Equality to solve a problem involving mixed numbers?*

Recall that the Subtraction Property of Equality says the same number can be subtracted from both sides of an equation and the two sides will remain equal.

CC.6.EE.7

1 **E X A M P L E** Using the Subtraction Property of Equality with Fractions

Megan spent $2\frac{5}{6}$ hours yesterday finishing her science project. She spent a total of $5\frac{1}{2}$ hours on the project in all. How much time had she spent on the project before yesterday?

Let *x* represent the time Megan spent on the project before yesterday.

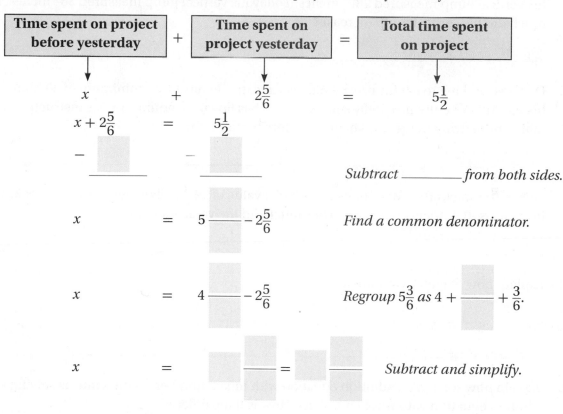

Time spent on project before yesterday		Time spent on project yesterday		Total time spent on project
	+		=	
x	+	$2\frac{5}{6}$	=	$5\frac{1}{2}$

$$x + 2\frac{5}{6} = 5\frac{1}{2}$$

$$- \boxed{} \qquad - \boxed{}$$

$\underline{} \qquad \underline{}$ *Subtract _____ from both sides.*

$$x = 5\frac{\boxed{}}{\boxed{}} - 2\frac{5}{6}$$ *Find a common denominator.*

$$x = 4\frac{\boxed{}}{\boxed{}} - 2\frac{5}{6}$$ *Regroup $5\frac{3}{6}$ as $4 + \frac{\boxed{}}{\boxed{}} + \frac{3}{6}$.*

$$x = \frac{\boxed{}}{\boxed{}} = \frac{\boxed{}}{\boxed{}}$$ *Subtract and simplify.*

Megan had spent _____ hours on the project before yesterday.

REFLECT

1. Explain why you needed to regroup $5\frac{3}{6}$ in **1**.

_____

_____

Solve each equation. Write the answer in simplest form.

1. $x + 1\frac{3}{4} = 2\frac{1}{2}$ **2.** $m + 3\frac{8}{9} = 5\frac{2}{3}$ **3.** $k + 5\frac{3}{4} = 8\frac{2}{5}$

$x =$ _____ $m =$ _____ $k =$ _____

For 4–7, write and solve an addition equation to answer each question. Write the answer in simplest form.

4. Mandy has been watching an icicle grow from the end of a gutter on her house. Yesterday she measured the length of the icicle at $16\frac{3}{4}$ inches. Today when she measured the icicle it was $19\frac{5}{8}$ inches long. How many inches did the icicle grow?

_____

5. Collin has been training to increase his vertical jumping ability. Before he started training, his vertical jump measured $28\frac{7}{10}$ inches. Today his vertical jump measured $38\frac{1}{4}$ inches. How much did his vertical jump increase?

_____

6. Devin is working to get his private pilot certificate. He must fly a minimum of 20 hours with his instructor before he can fly solo. So far he has flown $8\frac{3}{4}$ hours with his instructor. How many more flying hours does he need before he can solo?

_____

7. One of the stocks that Mrs. Jones owns had a value of $19\frac{3}{8}$ dollars per share last week. Today its value is $21\frac{1}{4}$ dollars per share. How much did the value increase?

_____

8. Explain how to check your answer in **7**.

_____

_____

9. Explain how solving an addition equation with mixed numbers is the same as solving an addition equation with whole numbers. How is it the different?

_____

_____

_____

_____

Additional Practice

Subtract. Write each answer in simplest form.

1. $4 - 2\frac{3}{8}$

2. $5\frac{1}{6} - 2\frac{2}{3}$

3. $14 - 8\frac{2}{9}$

_____

4. $19\frac{1}{7} - 5\frac{1}{3}$

5. $7\frac{1}{4} - 3\frac{5}{8}$

6. $10\frac{1}{5} - 5\frac{7}{10}$

_____

7. $1\frac{1}{6} - \frac{7}{9}$

8. $9\frac{1}{4} - 1\frac{7}{16}$

9. $6\frac{1}{5} - 3\frac{1}{4}$

_____

Solve each equation. Write the answer in simplest form.

10. $x + 1\frac{5}{6} = 2\frac{2}{3}$

11. $2\frac{1}{6} + n = 3\frac{5}{12}$

12. $y + 3\frac{1}{4} = 5\frac{1}{3}$

$x =$ _____

$n =$ _____

$y =$ _____

13. $10\frac{9}{10} + k = 12\frac{2}{5}$

14. $m + 4\frac{5}{6} = 5\frac{1}{2}$

15. $s + 2\frac{1}{3} = 5\frac{1}{12}$

$k =$ _____

$m =$ _____

$s =$ _____

16. Tim had 6 feet of wrapping paper for Kylie's birthday present. He used $3\frac{3}{8}$ feet of the paper to wrap her gift. How much paper did Tim have left? _____

17. At his last doctor's visit, Pablo was $60\frac{1}{2}$ inches tall. At today's visit, he measured $61\frac{1}{6}$ inches. How much did Pablo grow between visits? _____

18. Yesterday, Danielle rode her bike for $5\frac{1}{2}$ miles. Today, she rode her bike for $6\frac{1}{4}$ miles. How much farther did Danielle ride her bike today? _____

Problem Solving

Write the correct answer in simplest form.

1. The average person in the United States eats $6\frac{13}{16}$ pounds of potato chips each year. The average person in Ireland eats $5\frac{15}{16}$ pounds. How many more pounds of potato chips do Americans eat per year?

_____

2. The average person in the United States eats $270\frac{1}{16}$ pounds of meat each year. The average person in Australia eats $238\frac{1}{2}$ pounds. How much more meat do Americans eat a year than people in Australia?

_____

3. The average Americans eats $24\frac{1}{2}$ pounds of ice cream every year. The average person in Israel eats $15\frac{4}{5}$ pounds. How much more ice cream do Americans eat each year?

_____

4. People in Switzerland eat the most chocolate—26 pounds a year per person. Most Americans eat $12\frac{9}{16}$ pounds each year. How much more chocolate do the Swiss eat?

_____

5. The average person in the United States chews $1\frac{9}{16}$ pounds of gum each year. The average person in Japan chews $\frac{7}{8}$ pound. How much more gum do Americans chew?

_____

6. Norwegians eat the most frozen foods—$78\frac{1}{2}$ pounds per person each year. Most Americans eat $35\frac{15}{16}$ pounds. How much more frozen food do people in Norway eat?

_____

Circle the letter of the correct answer.

7. Most people around the world eat $41\frac{7}{8}$ pounds of sugar each year. Most Americans eat $66\frac{3}{4}$ pounds. How much more sugar do Americans eat than the world's average?

   A $25\frac{7}{8}$ pounds more

   B $25\frac{1}{8}$ pounds more

   C $24\frac{7}{8}$ pounds more

   D $24\frac{1}{8}$ pounds more

8. The average person eats 208 pounds of vegetables and $125\frac{5}{8}$ pounds of fruit each year. How many more pounds of vegetables do most people eat than fruit?

   F $83\frac{5}{8}$ pounds more

   G $82\frac{3}{8}$ pounds more

   H $123\frac{5}{8}$ pounds more

   J $83\frac{3}{8}$ pounds more

Solving Fraction Equations: Addition and Subtraction
Reasoning

Essential question: *How do you solve addition and subtraction equations with fractions?*

video tutor

CC.6.EE.7

1 EXAMPLE Solving Equations with Fractions

The U.S. Postal Service has priority mail packages that ship for a flat rate. The flat-rate boxes and their dimensions are given in the table.

Package Type	Dimensions (inches)		
	Length	Width	Height
Small Flat-Rate Box	$8\frac{5}{8}$	$5\frac{3}{8}$	$1\frac{5}{8}$
Medium Flat-Rate Box #1	$13\frac{5}{8}$	$11\frac{7}{8}$	$3\frac{3}{8}$
Medium Flat-Rate Box #2	11	$8\frac{1}{2}$	$5\frac{1}{2}$
Large Flat-Rate Box	12	12	$5\frac{1}{2}$

Which box has a width that is $3\frac{1}{8}$ inches longer than the width of the small flat-rate box?

Write an equation. Let x represent the width of the unknown box.

Width of unknown box	−	Width of small flat-rate box	=	Difference between widths

$$x \quad - \quad 5\frac{3}{8} \quad = \quad 3\frac{1}{8}$$

$x - 5\frac{3}{8} = 3\frac{1}{8}$ *Add* _____

$\quad + \boxed{} \qquad + \boxed{}$ *to both sides.*

$x \qquad = \underline{\qquad} = \underline{\qquad}$ inches   *Add and simplify.*

The _____ is the unknown box.

1a. A large flat-rate box is stacked on top of another box for a total height of $8\frac{7}{8}$ inches. Write and solve an equation to identify the second box.

_____

REFLECT

1b. Explain how to check your answer in **1a.**

_____

_____

PRACTICE

The table gives the length of the largest example of each shark type in an aquarium. Use the information in the table to write and solve an equation for 1–3. Write the answer in simplest form.

1. Which shark is $1\frac{5}{8}$ foot longer than the blacktip reef shark?

_____

Type	Length (feet)
Blacktip Reef Shark	$4\frac{3}{4}$
Bonnethead Shark	$3\frac{5}{8}$
Bull Shark	$9\frac{1}{2}$
Nurse Shark	$11\frac{1}{3}$
Sandbar Shark	$6\frac{3}{8}$
Zebra Shark	$7\frac{1}{4}$

2. The length of the nurse shark is $4\frac{1}{12}$ feet longer than the length of which other shark?

_____

3. The combined length of the zebra shark and another shark is $10\frac{7}{8}$ feet. What is the other shark?

_____

4. **What's the Error?** Kaye solved the equation $x - 3\frac{1}{3} = 7\frac{2}{5}$. Her work is shown at the right. What error did she make?

_____

_____

$$x - 3\frac{1}{3} = 7\frac{2}{5}$$
$$x - 3\frac{1}{3} - 3\frac{1}{3} = 7\frac{2}{5} - 3\frac{1}{3}$$
$$x = 7\frac{6}{15} - 3\frac{5}{15}$$
$$x = 4\frac{1}{15}$$

Additional Practice

Solve each equation. Write the solution in simplest form. Check your answers.

1. $5\frac{1}{4} = x + \frac{7}{16}$

2. $6\frac{1}{4} = z + 1\frac{5}{8}$

_____

3. $2\frac{2}{7} = n - 4\frac{2}{3} - 1\frac{1}{3}$

4. $a - 2\frac{2}{11} = 2\frac{5}{22} - 1\frac{2}{11}$

_____

5. $k + 3\frac{3}{4} = 5\frac{2}{3} - 1\frac{1}{3}$

6. $r + 6 = 9\frac{2}{5} - 2\frac{1}{2}$

_____

7. $11\frac{2}{5} = q - 4\frac{2}{7} + 2\frac{1}{7}$

8. $4\frac{2}{5} - 2\frac{1}{2} = p + \frac{3}{10}$

_____

9. $\frac{3}{8} + \frac{1}{6} = c - 4\frac{5}{6}$

10. $2\frac{1}{4} + c = 2\frac{1}{3} + 1\frac{1}{6}$

_____

11. A seamstress raised the hem on Helen's skirt by $1\frac{1}{3}$ inches. The skirt's original length was 16 inches. What is the new length?

_____

12. The bike trail is $5\frac{1}{4}$ miles long. Jessie has already cycled $2\frac{5}{8}$ miles of the trail. How much farther does she need to go to finish the trail?

_____

Problem Solving

Write the correct answer in simplest form.

1. It usually takes Brian $1\frac{1}{2}$ hours to get to work from the time he gets out of bed. His drive to the office takes $\frac{3}{4}$ hour. How much time does he spend getting ready for work?

_____

2. Before he went to the hairdresser, Shel's hair was $7\frac{1}{4}$ inches long. When he left the salon, it was $5\frac{1}{2}$ inches long. How much of his hair did Shel get cut off?

_____

3. One lap around the gym is $\frac{1}{3}$ mile. Kim has already run 5 times around. If she wants to run 2 miles total, how much farther does she have to go?

_____

4. Darius timed his speech at $5\frac{1}{6}$ minutes. His time limit for the speech is $4\frac{1}{2}$ minutes. How much does he need to cut from his speech?

_____

Circle the letter of the correct answer.

5. Mei and Alex bought the same amount of food at the deli. Mei bought $1\frac{1}{4}$ pounds of turkey and $1\frac{1}{3}$ pounds of cheese. Alex bought $1\frac{1}{2}$ pounds of turkey. How much cheese did Alex buy?

   A $1\frac{1}{12}$ pounds　　C $1\frac{1}{4}$ pounds

   B $1\frac{1}{6}$ pounds　　D $4\frac{1}{12}$ pounds

6. When Lynn got her dog, May, she weighed $10\frac{1}{2}$ pounds. During the next 6 months, she gained $8\frac{4}{5}$ pounds. At her one-year check-up she had gained another $4\frac{1}{3}$ pounds. How much did May weigh when she was 1 year old?

   F $22\frac{19}{30}$ pounds　G $23\frac{19}{30}$ pounds

   H $23\frac{29}{30}$ pounds　　J $23\frac{49}{50}$ pounds

7. Kay picked up 2 planks of wood at the hardware store. One is $6\frac{1}{4}$ feet long and the other is $5\frac{5}{8}$ feet long. How much should she cut from the first plank to make them the same length?

   A $\frac{5}{8}$ foot　　　C $1\frac{3}{8}$ feet

   B $\frac{1}{2}$ foot　　　D $1\frac{5}{8}$ feet

8. Charlie used $3\frac{3}{4}$ cups of flour to make a cake. She had $\frac{1}{2}$ cup of flour left over. Which equation can you use to find how much flour she had before baking the cake?

   F $x + \frac{1}{2} = 3\frac{3}{4}$　　H $3\frac{3}{4} - \frac{1}{2} = x$

   G $x - 3\frac{3}{4} = \frac{1}{2}$　　J $3\frac{3}{4} - x = \frac{1}{2}$

© Houghton Mifflin Harcourt Publishing Company

Multiplying Mixed Numbers
Modeling

Essential question: *How do you multiply mixed numbers?*

You can use area models to find the product of a fraction and a mixed number.

PREP FOR **CC.6.NS.1**

1 EXPLORE **Multiplying Mixed Numbers Using Models**

video tutor

Three-fourths of a $3\frac{2}{3}$ acre piece of land has been set aside as a bird sanctuary. How many acres will be used as the bird sanctuary?

Think of $\frac{3}{4}$ of $3\frac{2}{3}$ as $\frac{3}{4} \times 3\frac{2}{3}$.

Use an area model to find the product $\frac{3}{4} \times 3\frac{2}{3}$.

Step 1 Shade $3\frac{2}{3}$ rectangles.

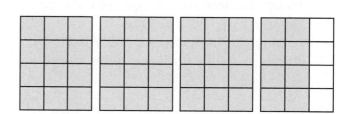

Step 2 Since you are multiplying by $\frac{3}{4}$, divide each rectangle into fourths.

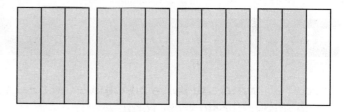

Step 3 Now shade 3 of the 4 parts of each rectangle.

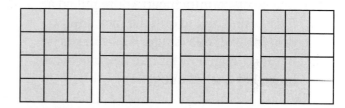

What fraction does each of the small rectangles represent? _____

How many small rectangles have been shaded twice? _____

So, $\frac{3}{4} \times 3\frac{2}{3} =$ _____ $=$ _____, or _____.

_____ acres will be used as a bird sanctuary.

2 EXAMPLE — Multiplying Whole Numbers and Mixed Numbers

The judge at an instrumental music contest will hear 9 more students play their solos before the next break. If each student's solo lasts $4\frac{1}{2}$ minutes, how many more minutes of music will the judge hear before break?

Write an expression for the total amount of time: _____

$9 \times 4\frac{1}{2} =$ _____ $\times 4\frac{1}{2}$ *Write the whole number as a fraction.*

$=$ _____ $\times$ _____   *Rewrite $4\frac{1}{2}$ as an improper fraction.*

$=$ _____   *Multiply numerators. Multiply denominators.*

$=$ _____   *Write the product as a mixed number.*

The judge will hear _____ more minutes of music before the break.

PRACTICE

For 1–4, write and solve an expression to answer each question. Write the answer in simplest form.

1. At a cross-country meet, Andre pulled a muscle and had to quit the race after running $\frac{4}{5}$ of the first lap. If each lap is $2\frac{1}{4}$ miles long, how far had he gone before he had to stop running?

2. Mykala runs around a lake at a city park to stay in shape. The length of the route she runs is $5\frac{3}{10}$ miles. She runs this route 4 times each week. How many miles does she run each week?

3. The larger center circle on a basketball court is 12 feet in diameter. The distance around a circle can be found by multiplying its diameter by $3\frac{1}{7}$. What is the distance around the larger center circle?

4. The area of a rectangle is found by multiplying its length and its width. If the length of the floor of a rectangular garage is $7\frac{2}{3}$ yards and its width is $4\frac{1}{2}$ yards, what is the area of the garage floor?

5. **Conjecture** How would you multiply three mixed numbers?

_____

_____

_____

_____

Additional Practice

Multiply. Write each answer in simplest form.

1. $1\frac{2}{3} \cdot \frac{4}{5}$

2. $1\frac{7}{8} \cdot \frac{4}{5}$

3. $2\frac{3}{4} \cdot \frac{1}{5}$

_____

4. $2\frac{1}{6} \cdot \frac{2}{3}$

5. $2\frac{2}{5} \cdot \frac{3}{8}$

6. $1\frac{3}{4} \cdot \frac{5}{6}$

_____

7. $1\frac{1}{6} \cdot \frac{3}{5}$

8. $\frac{2}{9} \cdot 2\frac{1}{7}$

9. $2\frac{3}{11} \cdot \frac{7}{10}$

_____

Find each product. Write the answer in simplest form.

10. $\frac{6}{7} \cdot 1\frac{1}{4}$

11. $\frac{5}{8} \cdot 1\frac{3}{5}$

12. $2\frac{4}{9} \cdot \frac{1}{6}$

_____

13. $1\frac{3}{10} \cdot 1\frac{1}{3}$

14. $2\frac{1}{2} \cdot 2\frac{1}{2}$

15. $1\frac{2}{3} \cdot 3\frac{1}{2}$

_____

16. Dominick lives $1\frac{3}{4}$ miles from his school. If his mother drives him half the way, how far will Dominick have to walk to get to school?

_____

17. Katoni bought $2\frac{1}{2}$ dozen donuts to bring to the office. Since there are 12 donuts in a dozen, how many donuts did Katoni buy?

_____

Problem Solving

Use the recipe to answer the questions.

CHOCOLATE CHIP COOKIES Servings: 1 batch
$1\frac{2}{3}$ cups flour
$\frac{3}{4}$ teaspoon baking soda
$\frac{1}{2}$ cup white sugar
$2\frac{1}{3}$ cups semisweet chocolate chips
$\frac{1}{2}$ cup brown sugar
$\frac{3}{4}$ cup butter
1 egg
$1\frac{1}{4}$ teaspoons vanilla

1. If you want to make $2\frac{1}{2}$ batches, how much flour would you need?

   _____

2. If you want to make only $1\frac{1}{2}$ batches, how many cups of chocolate chips would you need?

   _____

3. You want to bake $3\frac{1}{4}$ batches. How much vanilla do you need in all?

   _____

Choose the letter for the best answer.

4. If you make $1\frac{1}{4}$ batches, how much baking soda would you need?

   A $\frac{3}{16}$ teaspoon   C $\frac{3}{5}$ teaspoon

   B $\frac{5}{16}$ teaspoon   D $\frac{15}{16}$ teaspoon

5. How many cups of white sugar do you need to make $3\frac{1}{2}$ batches of cookies?

   F $3\frac{1}{2}$ cups   H $1\frac{1}{2}$ cups

   G $1\frac{3}{4}$ cups   J $1\frac{1}{4}$ cups

6. Dan used $2\frac{1}{4}$ cups of butter to make chocolate chip cookies using the above recipe. How many batches of cookies did he make?

   A 3 batches   C 5 batches

   B 4 batches   D 6 batches

7. One bag of chocolate chips holds 2 cups. If you buy five bags, how many cups of chips will you have left over after baking $2\frac{1}{2}$ batches of cookies?

   F $4\frac{1}{6}$ cups   H $2\frac{1}{3}$ cups

   G $5\frac{5}{6}$ cups   J $\frac{1}{3}$ cups

5-6

Dividing Fractions and Mixed Numbers
Modeling

Essential question: *How do you divide fractions and mixed numbers?*

video tutor

CC.6.NS.1

1 EXPLORE — **Modeling Fraction Division**

You have $\frac{3}{4}$ cup of salsa for making burritos. Each burrito requires $\frac{1}{8}$ cup of salsa. How many burritos can you make?

To find the number of burritos that can be made, you need to determine how many $\frac{1}{8}$ s are in $\frac{3}{4}$.

How many $\frac{1}{8}$ s are there in $\frac{3}{4}$? _____

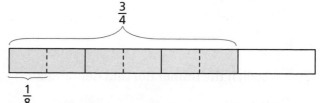

You have enough salsa to make _____ burritos.

REFLECT

1a. Division can be checked by using multiplication. What would you multiply to check your answer above?

_____

TRY THIS!

1b. How many burritos could you make with $\frac{1}{2}$ cup of salsa? _____

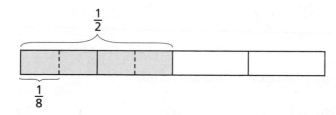

1c. Five people share $\frac{1}{2}$ pound of chocolate equally. How much chocolate does each person receive? _____ pound

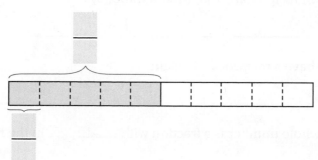

Another way to divide fractions is to use *reciprocals*.
Two numbers whose product is 1 are **reciprocals**. To find the
reciprocal of a fraction, switch the numerator and denominator.

$$\frac{\text{numerator}}{\text{denominator}} \cdot \frac{\text{denominator}}{\text{numerator}} = 1$$

CC.6.NS.1
2 EXAMPLE Reciprocals

Find the reciprocal of each fraction or mixed number.

A $\frac{5}{8}$

Switch the numerator and denominator: ——

The reciprocal of $\frac{5}{8}$ is ——.

Check:

$$\frac{}{} \times \frac{5}{8} = \frac{}{} = 1$$

B $\frac{1}{6}$

Switch the numerator and denominator: ——

Simplify:

The reciprocal of $\frac{1}{6}$ is ☐.

C $1\frac{2}{7}$

Change to an improper fraction: $1\frac{2}{7} = $ ——

Switch the numerator and denominator: ——

The reciprocal of $1\frac{2}{7}$ is ——.

TRY THIS!

Find the reciprocal of each fraction or mixed number.

2a. $\frac{7}{8}$ _____

2b. $\frac{9}{15}$ _____

2c. $\frac{1}{11}$ _____

2d. $2\frac{4}{5}$ _____

REFLECT

2e. Is any number its own reciprocal? If so, what number(s)?

_____

2f. Does every number have a reciprocal? Explain.

_____

2g. The reciprocal of a whole number is a fraction with _____ in the numerator.

© Houghton Mifflin Harcourt Publishing Company

Notice that dividing by a whole number is equivalent to multiplying by its reciprocal. This is also true when dividing by fractions. To divide by a fraction, multiply by its reciprocal.

$$24 \div 3 = 8$$
$$24 \times \frac{1}{3} = 8$$

CC.6.NS.1

3 EXAMPLE Using Reciprocals to Divide Fractions

Divide.

A $\frac{5}{8} \div \frac{5}{6}$

Step 1 Rewrite the problem as multiplication using the reciprocal of the second fraction.

$$\frac{5}{8} \div \frac{5}{6} = \frac{5}{8} \times \underline{\hphantom{xx}}$$

Step 2 Multiply and simplify.

$$\frac{5}{8} \times \underline{\hphantom{xx}} = \frac{30}{40}$$

$$\frac{30}{40} = \underline{\hphantom{xx}}$$

$$\frac{5}{8} \div \frac{5}{6} = \underline{\hspace{2cm}}$$

B $1\frac{3}{7} \div \frac{2}{5}$

Step 1 Convert the mixed number to a fraction.

$$1\frac{3}{7} = \underline{\hphantom{xx}}$$

Step 2 Rewrite the problem as multiplication using the improper fraction and the reciprocal of the second fraction.

$$1\frac{3}{7} \div \frac{2}{5} = \underline{\hphantom{xx}} \div \frac{2}{5} = \underline{\hphantom{xx}} \times \underline{\hphantom{xx}}$$

Step 3 Multiply and simplify.

$$\underline{\hphantom{xx}} \times \underline{\hphantom{xx}} = \underline{\hphantom{xx}}$$

$$= \underline{\hphantom{xx}}, \text{ or } 3\underline{\hphantom{xx}}$$

$$1\frac{3}{7} \div \frac{2}{5} = \underline{\hspace{2cm}}$$

TRY THIS!

Divide.

3a. $\frac{9}{10} \div \frac{2}{5} = \underline{\hspace{2cm}}$

3b. $2\frac{9}{10} \div \frac{3}{5} = \underline{\hspace{2cm}}$

4 EXAMPLE Solving Problems Involving Area

The area of a rectangular flower bed is $6\frac{1}{2}$ square feet. The width of the flower bed is $\frac{3}{4}$ foot. What is the length? (*Hint:* area = length × width)

To find the length of the flower bed, divide the area by the width.

$$6\frac{1}{2} \div \frac{3}{4} = \underline{} \div \frac{3}{4}$$

$$= \underline{} \times \underline{} = \underline{} = \underline{} = \underline{}$$

| $A = 6\frac{1}{2}$ ft^2 | $w = \frac{3}{4}$ ft |

$\ell = ?$

The length of the flower bed is _____ feet.

PRACTICE

Find the reciprocal of each fraction or mixed number.

1. $\frac{2}{5}$ _____

2. $\frac{1}{9}$ _____

3. $\frac{5}{3}$ _____

4. $\frac{4}{11}$ _____

5. $4\frac{1}{5}$ _____

6. $3\frac{1}{8}$ _____

Divide.

7. $\frac{4}{3} \div \frac{5}{3} =$ _____

8. $\frac{3}{10} \div \frac{4}{5} =$ _____

9. $\frac{1}{2} \div \frac{2}{5} =$ _____

10. $\frac{8}{9} \div \frac{1}{2} =$ _____

11. $4\frac{1}{4} \div \frac{3}{4} =$ _____

12. $4 \div 1\frac{1}{8} =$ _____

13. A recipe for one loaf of banana bread requires $\frac{2}{3}$ cup of oil. You have 2 cups of oil. How many loaves of banana bread can you make? _____ loaves

14. Ayita made $5\frac{1}{2}$ cups of trail mix. She wants to divide the trail mix into $\frac{3}{4}$ cup servings. How many servings will she have? _____ serving(s)

15. Dao has $2\frac{3}{8}$ pounds of hamburger meat. He is making $\frac{1}{4}$-pound burgers. How many hamburgers can he make? _____ hamburger(s)

16. A rectangular piece of land has an area of $\frac{3}{4}$ square mile and is $\frac{1}{2}$ mile wide. What is the length? _____ mile(s)

17. Write a real-world problem whose solution requires dividing the fractions $\frac{1}{3}$ and $\frac{3}{4}$. Then solve your problem.

_____

_____

Additional Practice

Find the reciprocal.

1. $\frac{5}{7}$

2. $\frac{9}{8}$

3. $\frac{3}{5}$

_____

4. $\frac{1}{10}$

5. $\frac{4}{9}$

6. $\frac{13}{14}$

_____

7. $1\frac{1}{3}$

8. $2\frac{4}{5}$

9. $3\frac{1}{6}$

_____

Divide. Write each answer in simplest form.

10. $\frac{5}{6} \div 5$

11. $2\frac{3}{4} \div 1\frac{4}{7}$

12. $\frac{7}{8} \div \frac{2}{3}$

_____

13. $3\frac{1}{4} \div 2\frac{3}{4}$

14. $\frac{9}{10} \div 3$

15. $\frac{3}{4} \div 9$

_____

16. $2\frac{6}{9} \div \frac{6}{7}$

17. $\frac{5}{6} \div 2\frac{3}{10}$

18. $2\frac{1}{8} \div 3\frac{1}{4}$

_____

19. The rope in the school gymnasium is $10\frac{1}{2}$ feet long. To make it easier to climb, the gym teacher tied a knot in the rope every $\frac{3}{4}$ foot. How many knots are in the rope? _____

20. Mr. Fulton bought $12\frac{1}{2}$ pounds of ground beef for the cookout. He plans on using $\frac{1}{4}$ pound of beef for each hamburger. How many hamburgers can he make? _____

21. Mrs. Marks has $9\frac{1}{4}$ ounces of fertilizer for her plants. She plans on using $\frac{3}{4}$ ounce of fertilizer for each plant. How many plants can she fertilize? _____

Problem Solving

Write the correct answer in simplest form.

1. Horses are measured in units called *hands*. One inch equals $\frac{1}{4}$ hand. The average Clydesdale horse is $17\frac{1}{5}$ hands high. What is the horse's height in inches? in feet?

_____

2. Cloth manufacturers use a unit of measurement called a *finger*. One finger is equal to $4\frac{1}{2}$ inches. If 25 inches are cut off a bolt of cloth, how many fingers of cloth were cut?

_____

3. People in England measure weights in units called *stones*. One pound equals $\frac{1}{14}$ of a stone. If a cat weighs $\frac{3}{4}$ stone, how many pounds does it weigh?

_____

4. The hiking trail is $\frac{9}{10}$ mile long. There are 6 markers evenly posted along the trail to direct hikers. How far apart are the markers placed?

_____

Choose the letter for the best answer.

5. A cake recipe calls for $1\frac{1}{2}$ cups of butter. One tablespoon equals $\frac{1}{16}$ cup. How many tablespoons of butter do you need to make the cake?

   A 24 tablespoons

   B 8 tablespoons

   C $\frac{3}{32}$ tablespoon

   D 9 tablespoons

6. Printed letters are measured in units called *points*. One point equals $\frac{1}{72}$ inch. If you want the title of a paper you are typing on a computer to be $\frac{1}{2}$ inch tall, what type point size should you use?

   F 144 point

   G 36 point

   H $\frac{1}{36}$ point

   J $\frac{1}{144}$ point

7. Phyllis bought 14 yards of material to make chair cushions. She cut the material into pieces $1\frac{3}{4}$ yards long to make each cushion. How many cushions did Phyllis make?

   A 4 cushions

   B 6 cushions

   C 8 cushions

   D $24\frac{1}{2}$ cushions

8. Dry goods are sold in units called *pecks* and *bushels*. One peck equals $\frac{1}{4}$ bushel. If Peter picks $5\frac{1}{2}$ bushels of peppers, how many pecks of peppers did Peter pick?

   F $1\frac{3}{8}$ pecks

   G 11 pecks

   H 20 pecks

   J 22 pecks

Solving Fraction Equations: Multiplication and Division

Going Deeper: Multiplication Equations

Essential question: *How do you solve multiplication and division equations with fractions?*

Recall that the Division Property of Equality says that when you divide both sides of an equation by the same nonzero number, the two sides will remain equal.

video tutor

CC.6.EE.7

1 EXAMPLE Solving Multiplication Equations with Fractions

Randy told his parents that $\frac{2}{3}$ of the players on his baseball team are going to attend a college game next Saturday. If 16 players are going to the game, how many players are on his team?

Let x represent the number of players on Randy's baseball team.

Fraction of players going to game		Number of players on the team		Number of players going to the game
$\frac{2}{3}$	$\cdot$	x	$=$	16

By what fraction is x multiplied? _____ What is its reciprocal? _____

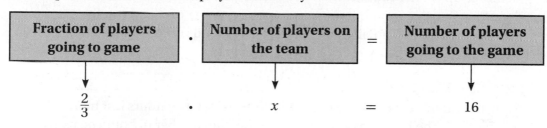

$$\frac{2}{3}x = 16$$

$$\frac{2}{3}x \div \frac{2}{3} = 16 \div \frac{2}{3} \qquad \textit{Divide both sides by } \frac{2}{3}.$$

$$\underline{\quad} \cdot \frac{2}{3}x = \underline{\quad} \cdot \frac{16}{1} \qquad \textit{Multiply both sides by the reciprocal of } \frac{2}{3}.$$

$$x = \underline{\quad} \text{ or } \boxed{} \qquad \textit{Multiply and simplify.}$$

There are _____ players on Randy's baseball team.

REFLECT

1. Is $\frac{2}{3}x$ the same as $\frac{2x}{3}$? Explain.

_____

_____

Solve each equation. Write the answer in simplest form.

1. $\frac{3}{5}a = 21$

$a =$ _____

2. $30 = \frac{4}{7}b$

$b =$ _____

3. $\frac{5d}{8} = 15$

$d =$ _____

4. $\frac{7}{10}n = 8$

$n =$ _____

5. $4w = \frac{5}{9}$

$w =$ _____

6. $\frac{2t}{15} = 5$

$t =$ _____

7. $9 = \frac{4}{9}x$

$x =$ _____

8. $12 = \frac{7}{8}k$

$k =$ _____

9. $\frac{4}{5}z = \frac{10}{11}$

$z =$ _____

For 10–15, write and solve an equation to answer each question. Write the answer in simplest form.

10. Janet has an exercise routine that she follows every day. So far today, she has done $\frac{5}{12}$ of the sit-ups in her routine. If she has done 75 sit-ups so far, how many sit-ups does she include in her daily exercise routine?

_____

11. So far today, Amir has chatted with 18 of his friends on his favorite social network web site. If this number represents $\frac{2}{5}$ of his total number of friends on the site, how many friends does he have on this social network?

_____

12. Mara is using her mom's cake recipe. To make a smaller cake, she is making just $\frac{3}{4}$ of the recipe. If she uses 2 teaspoons of vanilla, how much vanilla does the full recipe use?

_____

13. Kobe worked 35 hours last month. This is $\frac{5}{6}$ of the number of hours he usually works in a month. How many hours does Kobe usually work in a month?

_____

14. Stephen has twice as many baseball cards as Drew. If you divide the number of cards that Stephen has by 3, the result is 12. How many baseball cards does each boy have?

_____

_____

15. Mark rode his bike on a trail Saturday. He stopped for a rest $\frac{3}{5}$ of the way along the trail. The mile marker where he stopped says he is $7\frac{1}{2}$ miles from where he started. How long is the bike trail?

_____

16. Will the solution of $\frac{3}{4}b = 8$ be less than 8 or greater than 8?

_____

_____

Additional Practice

Solve each equation. Write the answer in simplest form. Check you answers.

1. $\frac{1}{4}x = 6$

2. $2t = \frac{4}{7}$

3. $\frac{3}{5}a = 3$

_____

_____

4. $\frac{r}{6} = 8$

5. $\frac{2b}{9} = 4$

6. $3y = \frac{4}{5}$

_____

_____

7. $\frac{2}{3}d = 5$

8. $2f = \frac{1}{6}$

9. $4q = \frac{2}{9}$

_____

_____

10. $\frac{1}{2}s = 2$

11. $\frac{h}{7} = 5$

12. $\frac{1}{4}c = 9$

_____

_____

13. $5g = \frac{5}{6}$

14. $3k = \frac{1}{9}$

15. $\frac{3x}{5} = 6$

_____

_____

16. It takes 3 buckets of water to fill $\frac{1}{3}$ of a fish tank. How
many buckets are needed to fill the whole tank? _____

17. Jenna got 12, or $\frac{3}{5}$, of her answers on the test right.
How many questions were on the test? _____

18. It takes Charles 2 minutes to run $\frac{1}{4}$ of a mile. How long
will it take Charles to run a mile? _____

Problem Solving

Solve.

1. The number of T-shirts is multiplied by $\frac{1}{2}$ and the product is 18. Write and solve an equation for the number of T-shirts, where t represents the number of T-shirts.

_____

2. The number of students is divided by 18 and the quotient is $\frac{1}{6}$. Write and solve an equation for the number of students, where s represents the number of students.

_____

3. The number of players is multiplied by $2\frac{1}{2}$ and the product is 25. Write and solve an equation for the number of players, where p represents the number of players.

_____

4. The number of chairs is divided by $\frac{1}{4}$ and the quotient is 12. Write and solve an equation for the number of chairs, where c represents the number of chairs.

_____

Circle the letter of the correct answer.

5. Paco bought 10 feet of rope. He cut it into several $\frac{5}{6}$-foot pieces. Which equation can you use to find how many pieces of rope Paco cut?

   A $\frac{5}{6} \div 10 = x$ C $10 \div x = \frac{5}{6}$

   B $\frac{5}{6} \div x = 10$ D $10x = \frac{5}{6}$

6. Each square on the graph paper has an area of $\frac{4}{9}$ square inch. What is the length and width of each square?

   F $\frac{1}{9}$ inch   H $\frac{2}{9}$ inch

   G $\frac{2}{3}$ inch   J $\frac{1}{3}$ inch

7. Which operation should you use to solve the equation $6x = \frac{3}{8}$?

   A addition
   B subtraction
   C multiplication
   D division

8. A fraction divided by $\frac{2}{3}$ is equal to $1\frac{1}{4}$. What is that fraction?

   F $\frac{1}{3}$ H $\frac{1}{4}$

   G $\frac{5}{6}$ J $\frac{1}{2}$

CHAPTER 5

Problem Solving Connections

On the Shelf Mia is planning to build a storage unit for her video games. She wants to make a storage unit that has a short top shelf for remote controls and other accessories, and two taller shelves to hold the games. What dimensions should she use for the storage unit and approximately how many games will it hold?

COMMON CORE

CC.6.NS.1
CC.6.NS.4
CC.6.EE.7

1 Find the Height of the Top Shelf

The storage unit is made from 6 boards (A through F) and a rectangular piece of cardboard for the back panel. Each board is $\frac{5}{8}$ inch thick.

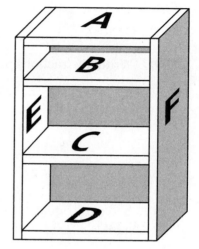

A The storage unit is $24\frac{1}{2}$ inches tall and the bottom shelves are both $8\frac{3}{4}$ inches high, as shown in the bottom figure. Mia wants to know the height of the top shelf, x. She first calculates the lengths y and z. Write a sum of fractions that gives the length y. Then find y.

B The length z is the overall height of the storage unit minus the thickness of board A. Write a difference of fractions that gives the length z. Then find z.

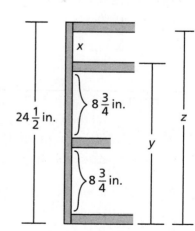

C How can you write a difference of fractions to find x, the height of the top shelf?

D Find the height of the top shelf.

2 Find the Depth of the Storage Unit

The figure shows board D, which forms the base of the storage unit. The width of this board is also the depth of the storage unit.

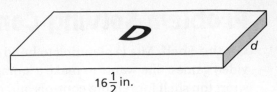

16½ in.

A Mia knows that the length of board D is $16\frac{1}{2}$ inches. and the area of the board is $140\frac{1}{4}$ square inches. Write an equation that can be used to find the width of the board, *d*.

B Write the fractions in the equation as improper fractions.

C Solve the equation for *d*. What is the depth of the storage unit?

D The 6 boards A through F all have the same width and same thickness. This means they can all be cut from one long board. Write an expression that gives the length of this board.

E What is the length of the long board that can be used to make boards A through F?

F Explain how to find the length of this board in feet.

---

3 Find the Dimensions of the Back Panel

The back panel of the storage unit is a rectangular piece of cardboard. It completely covers the back of the storage unit and fits perfectly, right to the edge.

A What is the height h of the back panel. How do you know?

B Explain how to find the width w of the back panel.

C Find the width w of the back panel.

D Mia wants to cover the pack panel with paper that looks like wood. She has a sheet of this paper with an area of 430 square inches. Will this sheet be big enough to cover the back panel? Why or why not?

4 Answer the Question

Look back over your work to answer the following questions about the dimensions of the storage unit and the number of games it will hold.

A Complete the figure by filling in the missing dimensions.

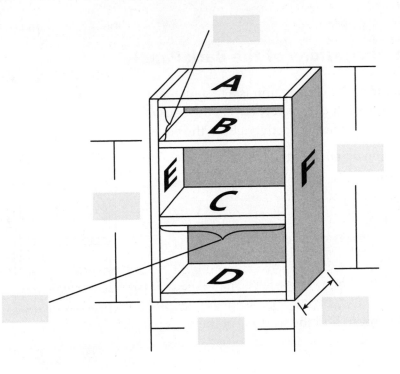

B Mia wants to know approximately how many games will fit on the shelves. Each game is packaged in a box that is about $\frac{3}{4}$ in. thick. Explain how to estimate the number of games that will fit on the two bottom shelves of the storage unit.

$\frac{3}{4}$ in.

C How many more games could Mia fit in the storage unit if she stacks some of the boxes horizontally on the top shelf? (Assume there is only enough room for one such stack.)

Performance Task

COMMON
CORE

CC.6.NS.1
CC.6.NS.4
CC.6.EE.6
CC.6.EE.7

⭐ **1.** The equation $\frac{h}{3} = 2\frac{1}{3}$ can be used to find how many $\frac{1}{3}$-pound hamburgers can be made from $2\frac{1}{3}$ pounds of ground beef. Solve the equation and interpret the solution. Show your work.

⭐ **2.** Erin, Dwayne, and Maria all log onto the same social network on the same day. After that, Erin logs on every 4 days, Dwayne logs on every 6 days, and Maria logs on every 8 days. How long will it be before all three log on the same day? Explain how found your answer.

⭐⭐ **3.** Vakesh practiced soccer $5\frac{3}{4}$ hours this week. He practiced $4\frac{1}{3}$ hours on weekdays and the rest over the weekend.

a. Write an equation you could use to find the hours w that Vakesh practiced over the weekend.

b. What is the least common multiple of the denominators of $5\frac{3}{4}$ and $4\frac{1}{3}$?
Show your work.

c. Solve the equation. Show your work.

⭐⭐⭐ **4.** Todd is painting a banner on a wall in the cafeteria. The banner is in the shape of a rectangle and has a blue background. Todd has enough blue paint to cover $1\frac{1}{2}$ square yards of wall. The banner will be $\frac{2}{3}$ yard wide. Todd wants to use all of the blue paint.

a. Write and solve an equation to find the height of the banner.

b. The school colors are blue and yellow, so Todd wants to add yellow rectangles on the left and right sides of the blue rectangle. The yellow rectangles will be 10 inches wide and the same height as the blue rectangle. What will be the total area of the two yellow bars?

Name _____ Class _____ Date _____

SELECTED RESPONSE

1. Find the least common multiple (LCM) of 8 and 10.

   A. 24   **C.** 40

   B. 42   **D.** 30

2. Each student needs a pencil and an eraser to take a test. If pencils come 8 in a box and erasers come 10 in a bag, what is the least number of boxes and bags needed for 40 students to each have a pencil and an eraser?

   F. 5 boxes of pencils, 4 bags of erasers

   G. 4 boxes of pencils, 5 bags of erasers

   H. 2 boxes of pencils, 2 bags of erasers

   J. 8 boxes of pencils, 10 bags of erasers

3. Renee works at the Candy Boutique making gift candy arrangements. Each arrangement must have the same number of truffles and the same number of hard candies. If she has 16 truffles and 24 hard candies and uses all of the pieces of candy, what is the greatest number of arrangements she can make?

   A. 2   **C.** 6

   B. 3   **D.** 8

4. Lauren visits the park every 3 days and goes to the library every 10 days. If Lauren does both of these today, how many days will pass before Lauren gets to do them both on the same day again?

   F. 13 days   **H.** 30 days

   G. 60 days   **J.** 7 days

5. Two stacks of books together are $7\frac{1}{2}$ inches tall. If one stack is $4\frac{3}{4}$ inches tall, how tall is the other?

   A. $3\frac{1}{7}$ inches   **C.** $2\frac{8}{5}$ inches

   B. $2\frac{3}{4}$ inches   **D.** 3 inches

6. Solve the equation $\frac{7}{9}w = 7$. Express your answer in simplest form.

   F. $w = 3\frac{49}{9}$ **H.** $w = 9$

   G. $w = \frac{1}{9}$ **J.** $w = \frac{9}{49}$

7. Solve the equation $13r = \frac{3}{7}$. Express your answer in simplest form.

   A. $r = \frac{91}{3}$ **C.** $r = \frac{39}{7}$

   B. $r = \frac{7}{39}$ **D.** $r = \frac{3}{91}$

8. In a fish tank, $\frac{8}{11}$ of the fish have a red stripe on them. If 16 of the fish have red stripes, how many total fish are in the tank?

   F. 21 fish   **H.** 20 fish

   G. 22 fish   **J.** 26 fish

9. Solve $p + 2\frac{4}{5} = 4\frac{1}{2}$

   A. $p = 1\frac{3}{10}$ **C.** $p = 2\frac{3}{10}$

   B. $p = 1\frac{7}{10}$ **D.** $p = 2\frac{7}{10}$

10. Solve the equation. Choose the answer in simplest form.

$$4x = \frac{8}{7}$$

   F. $\frac{1}{28}$ **H.** $\frac{2}{7}$

   G. $\frac{1}{7}$ **J.** $\frac{7}{2}$

CONSTRUCTED RESPONSE

11. Find the LCM of 4, 10 using prime factorization.

_____

_____

_____

_____

12. Hamburger buns come in packages of 8. Hamburger patties come in packages of 10. Neil would like to buy the smallest number of hamburger buns and hamburger patties so that he will have exactly one hamburger patty per bun. How many packages of hamburger buns and hamburger patties must he buy?

_____

_____

_____

_____

13. Slices of cheese come in packs of 8. Eggs come in packs of 12. What is the fewest number of omelettes you can make using one egg and one piece of cheese without having any eggs or cheese left over? Show your work.

_____

_____

_____

14. A box weighs $3\frac{7}{8}$ pounds. This box is $\frac{3}{4}$ pound lighter than a second box. How much does the second box weigh? Show your work.

_____

_____

_____

_____

_____

_____

_____

15. Curtains measuring 4 feet wide are bought for a window. But when they are hung, they cover only $\frac{3}{4}$ of the window. How wide is the window? Show your work.

_____

_____

_____

_____

_____

_____

_____

Proportional Relationships

Chapter Focus

You will write ratios, find equivalent ratios, and compare unit rates. Tables are great tools for finding equivalent ratios. You will use tables to find equivalent ratios and to compare ratios. You will explore ordered pairs in tables and graphs to better understand ratios. Proportional reasoning using equivalent ratios will help you solve real-world and mathematical problems. Understanding the relationship among fractions, decimals, and percents will allow you to change from one form to another and to compare fractions, decimals, and percents. Finally, you will find the percent of a number and solve problems involving percents.

Chapter at a Glance

COMMON CORE

CHAPTER 7

Unpacking the Standards

Understanding the standards and the vocabulary terms in the standards will help you know exactly what you are expected to learn in this chapter.

 CC.6.RP.3b

Solve unit rate problems including those involving unit pricing and constant speed.

Key Vocabulary

unit rate *(tasa unitaria)* A rate in which the second quantity in the comparison is one unit.

What It Means to You

You will solve problems involving unit rates and unit prices.

EXAMPLE

A 2-liter bottle of soda costs $2.02. A 3-liter bottle of the same soda costs $2.79. Which is the better deal?

2-liter bottle	**3-liter bottle**
$\dfrac{\$2.02}{2\text{ liters}}$	$\dfrac{\$2.79}{3\text{ liters}}$
$\dfrac{\$2.02 \div 2}{2\text{ liters} \div 2}$	$\dfrac{\$2.79 \div 3}{3\text{ liters} \div 3}$
$\dfrac{\$1.01}{1\text{ liter}}$	$\dfrac{\$0.93}{1\text{ liter}}$

The 3-liter bottle is the better deal.

 CC.6.RP.3

Use ratio and rate reasoning to solve real-world and mathematical problems, e.g., by reasoning about tables of equivalent ratios, tape diagrams, double number line diagrams, or equations.

Key Vocabulary

ratio *(razón)* A comparison of two quantities by division.
rate *(tasa)* A ratio that compares two quantities measured in different units.
equivalent ratios *(razones equivalentes)* Ratios that name the same comparison.

What It Means to You

You will use equivalent ratios to solve real-world and mathematical problems.

EXAMPLE

A group of 10 friends is in line to see a movie. The table shows how much different groups will pay in all. Predict how much the group of 10 will pay.

Number in Group	3	5	6	12
Amount Paid ($)	15	25	30	60

$6 < 10 < 12$; therefore, the group will pay between $30 and $60. Use the amount paid by a group of 5.

$2 \cdot 5 = 10$

$2 \cdot \$25 = \$50$

A group of 10 friends will pay $50.

COMMON CORE CC.6.NS.6c

Find and position integers and other rational numbers on a horizontal or vertical number line diagram; find and position pairs of integers and other rational numbers on a coordinate plane.

Key Vocabulary

integer *(entero)* A member of the set of whole numbers and their opposites.
rational number *(número racional)* A number that can be written in the form $\frac{a}{b}$, where a and b are integers and $b \neq 0$.
coordinate plane *(plano cartesiano)* A plane formed by the intersection of a horizontal number line called the x-axis and a vertical number line called the y-axis.

What It Means to You

You will graph an ordered pair of rational numbers in a coordinate plane.

EXAMPLE

Graph and label each point on a coordinate plane.

$$Q\left(4\tfrac{1}{2}, 6\right) \qquad\qquad S(0, 4)$$

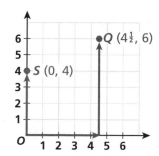

COMMON CORE CC.6.RP.3c

Find a percent of a quantity as a rate per 100 (e.g., 30% of a quantity means 30/100 times the quantity); solve problems involving finding the whole, given a part and the percent.

Key Vocabulary

percent *(porcentaje)* A ratio comparing a number to 100.

What It Means to You

You will find percent of a number and solve real-world problems involving percents.

EXAMPLE

About 67% of a person's total (100%) body weight is water. If Cameron weighs 90 pounds, about how much of his weight is water?

67% of 90

$$\frac{67}{100} \cdot 90$$

$$= \frac{67}{100} \cdot \frac{90}{1}$$

$$= 60.3$$

About 60.3 pounds of Cameron's weight is water.

Key Vocabulary

equivalent ratios *(fracciones equivalents)* Ratios that name the same comparison.

ordered pair *(par ordenado)* A pair of numbers that can be used to locate a point on a coordinate plane.

percent *(porcentaje)* A ratio comparing a number to 100.

rate *(tasa)* A ratio that compares two quantities measured in different units.

ratio *(razón)* A comparison of two quantities by division.

unit rate *(tasa unitaria)* A rate in which the second quantity in the comparison is one unit.

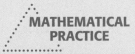

MATHEMATICAL PRACTICE

The Common Core Standards for Mathematical Practice describe varieties of expertise that mathematics educators at all levels should seek to develop in their students. Opportunities to develop these practices are integrated throughout this program.

1. Make sense of problems and persevere in solving them.
2. Reason abstractly and quantitatively.
3. Construct viable arguments and critique the reasoning of others.
4. Model with mathematics.
5. Use appropriate tools strategically.
6. Attend to precision.
7. Look for and make use of structure.
8. Look for and express regularity in repeated reasoning.

Ratios and Rates
Going Deeper

Essential question: *How do you find equivalent ratios and unit rates?*

A **ratio** is a comparison of two numbers by division. The two numbers in a ratio are called *terms*. A ratio can be written in several different ways:

5 dogs to 3 cats   5 to 3   5:3 $\frac{5}{3}$

CC.6.RP.1

1 EXAMPLE Writing Ratios

A The party mix recipe requires _____ cup(s) of pretzels and _____ cup(s) of bagel chips. Write the ratio of pretzels to bagel chips in three different ways.

_____

Party Mix
Makes 8 cups
4 cups pretzels
2 cups bagel chips
1 cup cheese crackers
1 cup peanuts

B The recipe makes a total of _____ cups of party mix. Write the ratio of pretzels to total party mix in three different ways.

_____

TRY THIS!

Write each ratio in three different ways.

1a. bagel chips to peanuts _____

1b. total party mix to pretzels _____

1c. cheese crackers to peanuts _____

REFLECT

1d. What does it mean when the terms in a ratio are equal?

_____

1e. The ratio of floor seats to balcony seats in a theater is 20:1. Does this theater have more floor seats or more balcony seats? How do you know?

_____

1f. At another theater, the ratio of floor seats to balcony seats is 20:19. How do the number of floor seats and the number of balcony seats compare at this theater?

_____

Equivalent ratios are ratios that name the same comparison. Find equivalent ratios by multiplying or dividing both terms of a ratio by the same number.

$$\frac{2}{7} \xrightarrow[\times 2]{\times 2} = \frac{4}{14} \qquad \frac{8}{24} \xrightarrow[\div 4]{\div 4} = \frac{2}{6}$$

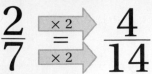

CC.6.RP.3

2 EXPLORE   Equivalent Ratios

You are in charge of making punch for an upcoming school dance. The punch recipe makes 5 cups of punch by mixing 3 cups of cranberry juice with 2 cups of apple juice.

A What is the ratio of cranberry juice to apple juice? _____

Do you think the punch will taste more like cranberry juice or more like apple juice? Explain.

_____

B You must increase the recipe to serve a large number of people. Fill in the boxes to find the ratio of cranberry juice to apple juice when the recipe is doubled and tripled.

$$\frac{3}{2} \xrightarrow[\times 2]{\times 2} = \boxed{} \qquad \frac{3}{2} \xrightarrow[\times 3]{\times 3} = \boxed{}$$

To double the recipe, you need _____ cups of cranberry juice and _____ cups of apple juice. This makes a total of _____ cups of punch.

To triple the recipe, you need _____ cups of cranberry juice and _____ cups of apple juice. This makes a total of _____ cups of punch.

C The ratios you found in **B** are equivalent to $\frac{3}{2}$. Find three other ratios that are equivalent to $\frac{3}{2}$. _____

D How much of each juice would you need to make a total of 40 cups of punch? _____

© Houghton Mifflin Harcourt Publishing Company

TRY THIS!

Complete each pair of equivalent ratios.

2a. $\frac{5}{6} = \frac{\boxed{}}{24}$ **2b.** $\frac{1}{4} = \frac{8}{\boxed{}}$ **2c.** $\frac{30}{6} = \frac{\boxed{}}{3}$

Find three ratios equivalent to the given ratio.

2d. $\frac{6}{8}$ _____   **2e.** $\frac{24}{18}$ _____   **2f.** $\frac{15}{10}$ _____

2g. Why can you multiply or divide both terms of a ratio by the same number without changing the value of the ratio?

_____

_____

CC.6.RP.2

3 EXPLORE **Comparing Prices**

Shana is at the grocery store comparing two brands of juice. Brand A costs $3.84 for a 16-ounce bottle. Brand B costs $4.50 for a 25-ounce bottle.

To compare the costs, Shana must compare prices for equal amounts of juice. How can she do this?

A Complete the tables.

BRAND A	
Ounces	Price ($)
16	3.84
8	1.92
4	
2	
1	

÷ 2, ÷ 2, ÷ 2, ÷ 2 ÷ 2, ÷ 2, ÷ 2, ÷ 2

BRAND B	
Ounces	Price ($)
25	4.50
5	
1	

÷ 5, ÷ 5 ÷ 5, ÷ 5

B Brand A costs $ _____ per ounce. Brand B costs $ _____ per ounce.

C Which brand is the better buy? Why? _____

REFLECT

3a. Describe another method to compare the costs.

_____

_____

TRY THIS!

3b. Abby can buy an 8-pound bag of dog food for $7.40 or a 4-pound bag of the same dog food for $5.38. Which is the better buy? _____

A **rate** is a ratio of two quantities that have different units. A **unit rate** is a rate in which the second quantity is one unit. When the first quantity in a unit rate is an amount of money, the unit rate is sometimes called a *unit price* or *unit cost*.

4 E X A M P L E   Calculating Unit Rates

A **Maria pays $60 for 5 music lessons. What is the cost per lesson?**

Use the information in the problem to write a rate: $\dfrac{\$60}{5 \text{ lessons}}$

To find the unit rate, divide both quantities in the rate by the same number so that the second quantity is 1:

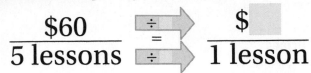

$$\dfrac{\$60}{5 \text{ lessons}} = \dfrac{\$}{1 \text{ lesson}}$$

Maria's music lessons cost $ _____ per lesson.

B **The cost of 3 candles is $19.50. What is the unit price?**

$$\dfrac{\$19.50}{3 \text{ candles}} = \dfrac{\$}{1 \text{ candle}}$$

The unit price is $ _____ per candle.

C **Michael walks 30 meters in 20 seconds. How many meters does Michael walk per second?**

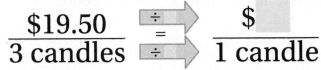

$$\dfrac{30 \text{ meters}}{20 \text{ seconds}} = \dfrac{ \text{ meters}}{1 \text{ second}}$$

Michael walks _____ meters per second.

D **A bakery charges $7 for $\frac{1}{2}$ dozen muffins. What is the price per dozen?**

Use the information in the problem to write a rate: $\dfrac{\$7}{\frac{1}{2} \text{ dozen}}$

In this rate, the second quantity is less than 1. To find the unit rate, *multiply* both quantities by the same number so that the second unit is 1:

$$\dfrac{\$7}{\frac{1}{2} \text{ dozen}} = \dfrac{\$}{1 \text{ dozen}}$$

The muffins cost $ _____ per dozen.

TRY THIS!

4a. There are 156 players on 13 teams. How many players are on each team?
_____ players per team

4b. A package of 36 photographs costs $18. What is the cost per photograph?
$ _____ per photograph

REFLECT

4c. In all of these problems, how is the unit rate related to the rate given in the original problem? _____

5 **E X A M P L E** Problem-Solving with Unit Rates

A In a youth soccer league, each team will have 18 players and 3 coaches. This year, 162 players signed up to play soccer. How many coaches are needed?

Method 1 Find the unit rate. How many players per coach?

$$\frac{18 \text{ players}}{3 \text{ coaches}} \quad \overset{\div}{\underset{\div}{=}} \Rightarrow \quad \frac{\boxed{} \text{ player(s)}}{1 \text{ coach}}$$

There are _____ players per coach.

$$\frac{162 \text{ players}}{\boxed{} \text{ players per coach}} = \boxed{} \text{ coaches}$$

Method 2 Use equivalent ratios.

$$\frac{18 \text{ players}}{3 \text{ coaches}} \quad \overset{\times}{\underset{\times}{=}} \Rightarrow \quad \frac{162 \text{ players}}{\boxed{} \text{ coaches}}$$

The soccer league needs _____ coaches.

B Tim can mow 4 lawns in 6 hours. How many lawns can he mow in 15 hours?

Find the unit rate.

$$\frac{4 \text{ lawns}}{6 \text{ hours}} \quad \overset{\div}{\underset{\div}{=}} \Rightarrow \quad \frac{\boxed{} \text{ lawn(s)}}{1 \text{ hour}}$$

How can you use the unit rate to find how many lawns Tim can mow in 15 hours?

_____

Tim can mow _____ lawns in 15 hours.

TRY THIS!

5a. On Tuesday, Donovan earned $9 for 2 hours of babysitting. On Saturday, he babysat for the same family and earned $31.50. How many hours did he babysit on Saturday? _____ hours

REFLECT

5b. How could you use estimation to check that your answer to **5a** is reasonable?

_____

_____

PRACTICE

The contents of Dean's pencil box are shown. Write each ratio in three different ways.

Dean's Pencil Box
5 pencils
3 pens
12 markers

1. pencils to pens _____

2. markers to total items _____

Write three ratios equivalent to the given ratio.

3. $\frac{12}{28}$ _____

4. $\frac{5}{2}$ _____

5. $\frac{10}{3}$ _____

The sizes and prices of three brands of laundry detergent are shown in the table. Use the table for 6 and 7.

Brand	Size (oz)	Price ($)
A	32	4.80
B	48	5.76
C	128	17.92

6. What is the unit price for each detergent?

Brand A: $ _____ per ounce

Brand B: $ _____ per ounce

Brand C: $ _____ per ounce

7. Which detergent is the best buy? _____

Mason's favorite brand of peanut butter is available in two sizes. Each size and its price are shown in the table. Use the table for 8 and 9.

	Size (oz)	Price ($)
Regular	16	3.36
Family Size	40	7.60

8. What is the unit rate for each size of peanut butter?

Regular: $ _____ per ounce

Family size: $ _____ per ounce

9. Which size is the better buy? _____

For 10 and 11, find the unit rate.

10. Lisa walked 48 blocks in 3 hours.

_____ blocks per hour

11. Gordon can type 1,800 words in 25 minutes.

_____ words per minute

12. The cost of 10 oranges is $1.00. What is the cost of 5 dozen oranges? $ _____

13. A carpenter installed 10 windows in 4 hours. Another carpenter installed 50 windows in 20 hours. Are the two carpenters working at the same rate? Explain.

_____

Using Tables to Explore Equivalent Ratios and Rates

Connection: Comparing Ratios

Essential question: *How can you use tables to find equivalent ratios?*

You can use a multiplication table to find equivalent ratios.

1 EXPLORE | CC.6.RP.3a | **Using a Multiplication Table**

Andrea is making fruit baskets for a school fundraiser. The ratio of oranges to apples in each basket is $\frac{2}{5}$. Name some other ratios that are equivalent to the ratio $\frac{2}{5}$.

Look at the multiplication table below. The rows showing the multiples of 2 and 5 are highlighted. Find the ratio $\frac{2}{5}$ by looking at the values in the two highlighted rows.

×	1	2	3	4	5	6	7	8	9	10
1	1	2	3	4	5	6	7	8	9	10
2	2	4	6	8	10	12	14	16	18	20
3	3	6	9	12	15	18	21	24	27	30
4	4	8	12	16	20	24	28	32	36	40
5	5	10	15	20	25	30	35	40	45	50
6	6	12	18	24	30	36	42	48	54	60

Use the multiplication table to complete this table of equivalent ratios.

Oranges	2		6		10
Apples	5	10		20	

Use the multiplication table to write three equivalent ratios that are not in the table of equivalent ratios. _____

How does the multiplication table show that multiplication can be used to write equivalent ratios?

_____

© Houghton Mifflin Harcourt Publishing Company

1a. Can division be used to write equivalent ratios? Explain by giving an example.

_____

_____

1b. Does the multiplication table given in **1** show all of the ratios that are equivalent to $\frac{2}{5}$? Explain.

_____

_____

CC.6.RP.3a

2 EXAMPLE **Finding Ratios from Tables**

Alex is flying his single-engine plane across the country. While in flight, he engages the autopilot and the plane maintains a constant speed. The table shows the distance that the plane travels with the autopilot engaged for various amounts of time.

Distance (mi)	280		560	700	
Time (h)	2	3			6

A Use the numbers in the first column of the table to write a ratio of distance to time. _____

B How far does the plane travel on autopilot in 1 hour? _____

Use your answer to write a unit rate. _____

C How can your answer to **B** be used to find the distance that the plane travels for any given number of hours?

_____

D Complete the table. What are the equivalent ratios displayed in the table?

$$\frac{280}{2} = \frac{\boxed{}}{3} = \frac{560}{\boxed{}} = \frac{700}{\boxed{}} = \frac{\boxed{}}{6}$$

REFLECT

2. What information given in the problem explains why all of the ratios are equivalent?

_____

3 EXPLORE   Comparing Ratios

Anna's recipe for lemonade calls for 2 cups of lemon juice and 3 cups of water. Bailey's recipe calls for 3 cups of lemon juice and 5 cups of water.

A In Anna's recipe, the ratio of lemon juice to water is _____.
Complete the table with equivalent ratios.

	2·2	2·	2·
Lemon Juice (c)	2	4		
Water (c)	3		9	15
	3·2	3·3	3·5

B In Bailey's recipe, the ratio of lemon juice to water is _____.
Complete the table with equivalent ratios.

	3·3	3·4	3·
Lemon Juice (c)	3	9	12	
Water (c)	5			25
	5·3	5·	5·

C In each table, there is a column in which the amount of water is the same. Circle these columns in the tables.

D Examine these two columns. Whose recipe makes stronger lemonade? How do you know?

_____

_____

E The ratio of lemon juice to water in the stronger recipe is _____ than the ratio of lemon juice to water in the other recipe.

Write inequality symbols to compare the ratios: $\frac{10}{15}$ ☐ $\frac{9}{15}$

$\frac{2}{3}$ ☐ $\frac{3}{5}$

REFLECT

3a. Describe another way to determine which recipe makes stronger lemonade.

_____

_____

_____

3b. **Error Analysis** Marisol said, "Bailey's lemonade is stronger because it has more lemon juice. Bailey's lemonade has 3 cups of lemon juice, and Anna's lemonade has only 2 cups of lemon juice." Explain why Marisol is incorrect.

_____

_____

_____

PRACTICE

1. Use a multiplication table to find three ratios that are equivalent to the ratio $\frac{9}{15}$. _____

2. How could you use multiplication to write a ratio that is equivalent to $\frac{9}{15}$?

_____

3. How could you use division to write a ratio that is equivalent to $\frac{9}{15}$?

_____

Julie's recipe for chicken noodle soup includes 3 pounds of chicken and 2 cups of sliced carrots. She has been asked to make soup for a school fundraiser and will need to increase her recipe to serve more people.

4. In Julie's recipe, the ratio of chicken to carrots is _____.

5. Complete the following table with equivalent ratios.

Chicken (lb)	3	6		
Sliced Carrots (c)	2		8	

6. How many pounds of chicken would Julie use if she used 3 cups of carrots? Explain how you found your answer

_____

_____

_____

Additional Practice

Use a table to find three equivalent ratios.

1. 4 to 7

_____

2. $\frac{10}{3}$

_____

3. 2:5

_____

4. 8 to 9

_____

5. 3 to 15

_____

6. $\frac{30}{90}$

_____

7. 1:3

_____

8. $\frac{7}{2}$

_____

9. Britney does sit-ups every day. The table shows how long it takes her to do different numbers of sit-ups.

Number of Sit-Ups	10	30	50	200	220
Time (min)	2	6	10	40	44

How long do you predict it will take Britney to do 120 sit-ups?

_____

10. The School Supply Store has markers on sale. The table shows some sale prices.

Number of Markers	12	8	6	4	2
Cost ($)	9.00	6.00	4.50	3.00	1.50

How much do you predict you would pay for 10 markers?

_____

Problem Solving

Use the table to answer the questions.

School Outing Student-to-Parent Ratios

Number of Students	8	16	24	32	40	48	56	64	72
Number of Parents	2	4	6	8	10	12	14	16	18

1. Each time some students go on a school outing, their teachers invite students' parents to accompany them. Predict how many parents will accompany 88 students.

_____

2. Next week 112 students will go to the Science Museum. Their teachers invited some of the students' parents to go with them. How many parents do you predict will go with the students to the Science Museum?

_____

Circle the letter of the correct answer.

3. Tanya's class of 28 students will be going to the Nature Center. How many parents do you predict Tanya's teacher will invite to accompany them?

    A 5 parents

    B 7 parents

    C 9 parents

    D 11 parents

4. Some students will be going on an outing to the local police station. Their teachers invited 13 parents to accompany them. How many students do you predict will be going on the outing?

    F 49 students

    G 50 students

    H 51 students

    J 52 students

5. In June, all of the students in the school will be going on their annual picnic. If there are 416 students in the school, what do you predict the number of parents accompanying them on the picnic will be?

    A 52 parents

    B 78 parents

    C 104 parents

    D 156 parents

6. On Tuesday, all of the sixth-grade students will be going to the Space Museum. Their teachers invited 21 parents to accompany them. How many sixth graders do you predict will be going to the Space Museum?

    F 80 sixth graders

    G 82 sixth graders

    H 84 sixth graders

    J 86 sixth graders

7-3

Ordered Pairs
Connection: Graphing Equivalent Ratios and Rates

Essential question: *How can you use tables and graphs to understand ratios?*

CC.6.RP.3a

1 EXPLORE   Graphing Equivalent Ratios

video tutor

The Webster family is taking a train to Washington, D.C. The train travels at a constant speed. The table shows the distance that the train travels in various amounts of time.

Distance (mi)	120	150		240	
Time (h)	2		3		5

A   If the train continues to travel at a constant speed, what value determines the number of miles the train travels?

_____

An **ordered pair** is a pair of numbers (x, y) that gives the location of a point on a coordinate grid.

B   Write the information in the table as ordered pairs. Since the distance depends on the time traveled, use x for time and y for distance.

$(2, 120)\left(, 150\right)\left(3, \right)\left(, 240\right)\left(5, \right)$

Graph the ordered pairs and connect the points.

Describe your graph. _____

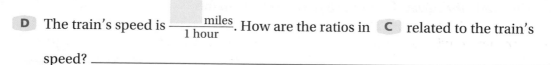

C   For each ordered pair that you graphed, write the ratio of y to x. _____

D   The train's speed is $\dfrac{\text{miles}}{1\text{ hour}}$. How are the ratios in **C** related to the train's

speed? _____

E   The point (3.5, 210) is on the graph but not in the table. The ratio of

y to x is $\dfrac{}{}$. How is this ratio related to the ratios

in **C** and **D** ? _____

So, in 3.5 hours, the train travels _____ miles.

1a. How can you use the graph to find the distance the train travels in 4.5 hours?

_____

_____

1b. If the graph were continued further, would the point (7, 420) be on the

graph? How do you know? _____

TRY THIS!

1c. The school band is selling tickets to the spring concert. Complete the table to show the cost for the purchase of various numbers of tickets.

Cost ($)	8		20		
Tickets	2	4		7	10

1d. What value determines the total cost of the tickets?

_____

1e. Write the information in the table as ordered pairs.

_____

1f. Graph the ordered pairs and connect the points.

1g. Write a ratio that gives the cost of 1 ticket.

_____

1h. Write a ratio that gives the cost of 8 tickets.

_____

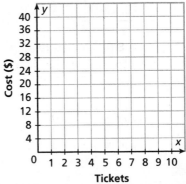

1i. How is the ratio that gives the cost of 8 tickets related to the ratios shown in the table?

_____

Proportions

Connection: Using Equivalent Ratios to Solve Proportions

Essential question: *How can you use equivalent ratios to solve problems?*

video tutor

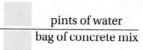

1 EXPLORE   **Using Multiplication to Solve Proportions**

Tom is putting a basketball hoop up along one side of his driveway. The pole needs to be set in concrete. He buys 4 bags of concrete mix at his local lumberyard. Each bag of concrete mix requires 6 pints of water. How many pints of water will Tom need for his 4 bags of concrete mix?

A What is the ratio of pints of water to 1 bag of concrete mix?

$$\frac{\text{pints of water}}{\text{bag of concrete mix}}$$

B Use counters to model the ratio.

C If Tom is using 4 bags of concrete mix, how many groups of the counters model above will you need to model this problem? _____

D Draw a model that represents the ratio of water to concrete mix for the 4 bags of concrete mix that Tom plans to use.

E How many pints of water are represented in your model? _____

F Write equivalent ratios that represent this situation. $\dfrac{6}{1} = \dfrac{}{4}$

G How much water does Tom need for his 4 bags of concrete mix? _____

1. Explain how you used multiplication to find the amount of water Tom needed.

_____

_____

CC.6.RP.3

2 EXPLORE **Using Division to Solve Proportions**

Carmen likes to make her own trail mix. Her recipe calls for 8 cups of peanuts and 2 cups of chocolate chips. She discovers that she only has 4 cups of peanuts in her cupboard. How many cups of chocolate chips does she need for this amount of peanuts?

A What is the ratio of peanuts to chocolate chips in the original recipe?

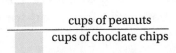
cups of peanuts / cups of choclate chips

B Use counters to model the ratio. Draw your model.

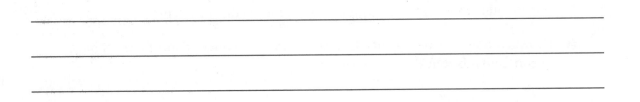

C Explain how to use the model to find the number of cups of chocolate chips for 4 cups of peanuts.

_____

_____

_____

_____

_____

D Write equivalent ratios that represent this situation.

$$\frac{8}{2} = \frac{4}{}$$

E How many cups of chocolate chips will Carmen need if she uses 4 cups of peanuts? _____

REFLECT

2. Explain how you used division to find the amount of chocolate chips Carmen needed.

_____

_____

_____

3 EXAMPLE Solving Proportions Using Equivalent Ratios

Solve each proportion by finding equivalent ratios.

A $\dfrac{3}{5} = \dfrac{n}{20}$

$$\dfrac{3}{5} = \dfrac{n}{20}$$

$$\dfrac{3 \times \rule{1cm}{0.4pt}}{5 \times \rule{1cm}{0.4pt}} = \dfrac{n}{20}$$ *Multiply by* _____ *to get a common denominator.*

$$\dfrac{\rule{1cm}{0.4pt}}{20} = \dfrac{n}{20}$$

Check your answer using a table of equivalent ratios.

	3 · 2	3 ·	3 ·	3 ·
3	6	9		
5	10		20	
	5 · 2	5 · 3	5 · 4	5 · 5

$n = $ _____

B $\dfrac{20}{30} = \dfrac{4}{w}$

$$\dfrac{20}{30} = \dfrac{4}{w}$$

$$\dfrac{20 \div \rule{0.8cm}{0.4pt}}{30 \div \rule{0.8cm}{0.4pt}} = \dfrac{4}{w}$$ *Divide by* _____ *to get 4 in the numerator.*

$$\dfrac{4}{\rule{0.8cm}{0.4pt}} = \dfrac{4}{w}$$

Check your answer using a table of equivalent ratios.

	4 · 2	4 ·	4 ·	4 ·
4	8	12		
6	12		24	
	6 · 2	6 · 3	6 · 4	6 · 5

$w = $ _____

TRY THIS!

Solve each proportion by finding equivalent ratios.

3a. $\dfrac{5}{9} = \dfrac{d}{36}$

3b. $\dfrac{64}{40} = \dfrac{8}{m}$

3c. $\dfrac{z}{7} = \dfrac{45}{35}$

$d = $ _____

$m = $ _____

$z = $ _____

Each year a group of math and science students take a trip to Chicago. For every 4 students on the trip, there must be 1 adult chaperone. This year there are 32 students going on the trip. How many adult chaperones will they need?

1. Use counters to model the situation.

2. Write the ratio of students to one chaperone. _____

3. Write equivalent ratios that represent the situation._____

4. Solve the proportion using equivalent ratios.

_____

5. How many adult chaperones are needed for this year's trip?

_____

Solve each proportion by finding equivalent ratios.

6. $\frac{3}{8} = \frac{t}{48}$

   $t =$ _____

7. $\frac{75}{30} = \frac{5}{s}$

   $s =$ _____

8. $\frac{h}{9} = \frac{27}{81}$

   $h =$ _____

9. $\frac{5}{9} = \frac{d}{36}$

   $d =$ _____

10. $\frac{64}{40} = \frac{8}{m}$

   $m =$ _____

11. $\frac{z}{7} = \frac{45}{35}$

   $z =$ _____

For 12 and 13, write equivalent ratios that represent the situation and solve.

12. Angela pays $120 for 4 piano lessons. How much does she pay for 8 piano lessons?

_____

13. Jesse needs 18 cups of flour to make 78 pancakes. How many pancakes can Jesse make with 6 cups of flour?

_____

Percents
Modeling

Essential question: *How can you write a percent as a fraction or a decimal?*

A **percent** is a ratio that compares a number to 100. The symbol % is used to show a percent.

17% is equivalent to:
- $\frac{17}{100}$
- 17 to 100
- 17:100

62.5% is equivalent to:
- $\frac{62.5}{100}$
- 62.5 to 100
- 62.5:100

1 EXPLORE Modeling Percents

At Javier's middle school, 42% of this year's sixth graders ride a bus to school.

How is 42% written as a ratio comparing 42 to 100? _____

Use the grid to model 42%.

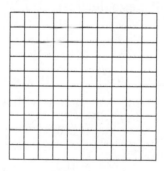

Explain what it means to say that 42% of the sixth graders ride a bus.

_____

TRY THIS!

1a. Use the grids to model 118%.

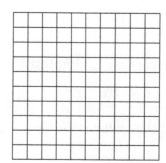 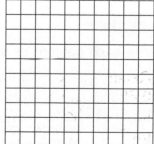

REFLECT

1b. Why are two grids needed to model 118%?

_____

2 EXAMPLE   Write a Percent as a Fraction and a Decimal

A   **Write 15% as a fraction in simplest form.**

Step 1 Write the percent as a fraction with a denominator of 100.

$$15\% = \frac{15}{\boxed{}}$$

Step 2 Simplify the fraction.

What is the GCF of 15 and 100? _____

Divide the numerator and the denominator by the GCF.

$$\frac{15}{100} = \frac{15 \div \boxed{}}{100 \div \boxed{}} = \frac{\boxed{}}{\boxed{}}$$

B   **Write 15% as a decimal.**

Step 1 Write the percent as a fraction with a denominator of 100.

$$15\% = \frac{15}{\boxed{}}$$

Step 2 Write the fraction as a decimal.

$$15\% = \frac{15}{\boxed{}} = \underline{\hspace{2cm}}$$

C   **Write 300% as a fraction in simplest form and as a decimal.**

Fraction Write the percent as a fraction with a denominator of 100. Then simplify.

$$300\% = \frac{\boxed{}}{\boxed{}} = \frac{\boxed{} \div 100}{\boxed{} \div 100} = \frac{\boxed{}}{\boxed{}}$$

Decimal Write the percent as a fraction with a denominator of 100. Then write the fraction as a decimal.

$$300\% = \frac{300}{\boxed{}} = \boxed{}$$

TRY THIS!

Write each percent as a fraction in simplest form and as a decimal.

2a. 10% _____   **2b.** 85% _____   **2c.** 3% _____

2d. 450% _____   **2e.** 38% _____   **2f.** 95% _____

REFLECT

2g. Why is 100% equal to 1? _____

2h. What is a "shortcut" for writing a percent as a decimal? Give an example.

_____

_____

Percents, Decimals, and Fractions
Extension: Compare and Order Fractions, Decimals, and Percents

Essential question: *How do you write fractions and decimals as percents?*

video tutor

CC.6.RP.3c

1 EXPLORE   Fractions and Decimals

The free-throw ratios for three basketball players are shown.

Player 1: $\frac{17}{25}$ Player 2: 0.72   Player 3: $\frac{14}{20}$

A   For each player, shade the grid to represent his free-throw ratio.

Player 1   Player 2   Player 3

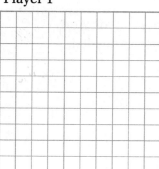   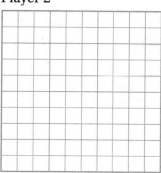   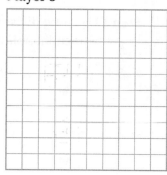

B   Which player has the greatest free-throw ratio? _____

How is this shown on the grids?

_____

C   Write the free-throw ratios in order from least to greatest.

_____

REFLECT

1a.   How did you determine how many squares to shade on each grid?

_____

_____

_____

1b.   Use the models to explain how you can express the free-throw ratios of each player as a percent.

_____

_____

_____

2 EXAMPLE Write Fractions and Decimals as Percents

A Write $\frac{7}{20}$ as a percent.

Method 1 *When the denominator is a factor of 100:*

Write an equivalent fraction with a denominator of 100.

$$\frac{7}{20} = \frac{\boxed{}}{100}$$

Write the percent.

$$\frac{\boxed{}}{100} = \underline{\qquad}\%$$

B Write $\frac{3}{8}$ as a percent.

Method 2 *When the denominator is NOT a factor of 100:*

Step 1 Use long division to divide the numerator by the denominator. Add a decimal point and zeros to the right of the numerator as needed.

$$\frac{3}{8} = 8)\overline{\begin{array}{c} 0.3\boxed{} \\ 3.000 \end{array}}$$

$$
\begin{array}{r}
0.3\boxed{} \\
8)\overline{3.000} \\
-\underline{2\,4} \\
60 \\
-\boxed{} \\
\overline{40} \\
-\boxed{} \\
\overline{0}
\end{array}
$$

Step 2 Write the quotient. Then move the decimal point two places to the right and add a percent symbol.

$$\frac{3}{8} = 0.\boxed{} = \underline{\qquad}\%$$

TRY THIS!

Write each fraction as a decimal and as a percent.

2a. $\frac{3}{10}$ _____ **2b.** $\frac{2}{25}$ _____ **2c.** $\frac{7}{50}$ _____

2d. $\frac{12}{30}$ _____ **2e.** $\frac{1}{8}$ _____ **2f.** $\frac{350}{100}$ _____

REFLECT

2g. Moving the decimal point two places to the right is equivalent to performing what operation? _____

2h. A given fraction's numerator is greater than its denominator. When this fraction is written as a percent, what will be true about the percent?

_____

3 **EXAMPLE** Using a Number Line to Compare

The table shows the scores of six students on a math test. Compare the six scores and place them in order from least to greatest.

Student	Roger	Amber	Ann	David	Katie	Steve
Reported Score	87%	$\frac{72}{80}$	0.88	$\frac{76}{80}$	0.92	91%

Step 1 Rewrite Roger's and Steve's scores as decimals.

$$87\% = \frac{}{100} = \underline{\hspace{2cm}}$$

$$91\% = \frac{}{} = \underline{\hspace{2cm}}$$

Step 2 Rewrite Amber's and David's scores as decimals.

$$\frac{72}{80} = \underline{\hspace{2.5cm}}$$

$$\frac{76}{80} = \underline{\hspace{2.5cm}}$$

Step 3 Graph each decimal on the number line.

0.50 0.55 0.60 0.65 0.70 0.75 0.80 0.85 0.90 0.95 1.00

Step 4 Write the scores in order from least to greatest.

_____

REFLECT

3a. Describe another way to compare the six scores.

_____

_____

_____

_____

3b. How would you read the decimals graphed on the number line to find the scores in order from greatest to least?

_____

Write each fraction as a decimal and as a percent.

1. $\frac{27}{50}$

_____

2. $\frac{250}{100}$

_____

3. $\frac{7}{10}$

_____

4. $\frac{24}{30}$

_____

5. $\frac{3}{5}$

_____

6. $\frac{11}{16}$

_____

7. $\frac{9}{20}$

_____

8. $\frac{1}{25}$

_____

9. $\frac{18}{45}$

_____

10. Justine answered 68 questions correctly on an 80-question test.

    a. What percent of the questions did Justine answer correctly? _____

    b. To find the percent of questions that Justine answered incorrectly, subtract your answer to **a** from 100%: 100% − ▢ = ▢

    What percent of the questions did Justine answer incorrectly? _____

11. Graph each fraction or percent on the number line.

    A. $\frac{4}{5}$ **B.** 20%   **C.** $\frac{1}{2}$ **D.** $\frac{6}{8}$

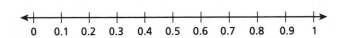

```
<—+——+——+——+——+——+——+——+——+——+——+—>
   0   0.1  0.2  0.3  0.4  0.5  0.6  0.7  0.8  0.9   1
```

12. Last month at Brian's Bookstore, 0.3 of the books sold were mysteries, 25% were travel books, and $\frac{7}{20}$ were children's books. Which type of book was sold the most last month?

_____

13. Angela is shopping for a new dress. One store is having a dress sale with $\frac{1}{3}$ off of the regular price. Another store has 35% off everything in the store. A third store is taking 0.4 off the price of any single item. At which store can Angela get the biggest discount on a dress?

_____

14. In Rene's closet, 38% of the hanging space is taken up by pants, 0.35 is taken up by shirts, and $\frac{2}{5}$ is taken up by sweaters. Put these values in order from least to greatest.

_____

Additional Practice

Write each decimal as a percent.

1. 0.03

2. 0.92

3. 0.18

_____

_____

_____

4. 0.49

5. 0.7

6. 0.09

_____

_____

_____

7. 0.26

8. 0.11

9. 1.0

_____

_____

_____

Write each fraction as a percent.

10. $\frac{2}{5}$

11. $\frac{1}{5}$

12. $\frac{7}{10}$

_____

_____

_____

13. $\frac{1}{20}$

14. $\frac{1}{50}$

15. $\frac{4}{50}$

_____

_____

_____

Compare. Write <, >, or =.

16. 60% _____ $\frac{2}{3}$

17. 0.4 _____ $\frac{2}{5}$

18. 0.5 _____ 5%

19. $\frac{1}{100}$ _____ 0.03

20. $\frac{7}{9}$ _____ 72%

21. $\frac{3}{10}$ _____ 35%

22. Bradley completed $\frac{3}{5}$ of his homework. What percent of his homework does he still need to complete?

_____

23. After reading a book for English class, 100 students were asked whether or not they enjoyed it. Nine twenty-fifths of the students did not like the book. How many students liked the book?

_____

Problem Solving

Write the correct answer.

1. Deserts cover about $\frac{1}{7}$ of all the land on Earth. About what percent of Earth's land is made up of deserts?

   _____

2. The Sahara is the largest desert in the world. It covers about 3% of the total area of Africa. What decimal expresses this percent?

   _____

3. Cactus plants survive in deserts by storing water in their thick stems. In fact, water makes up $\frac{3}{4}$ of the saguaro cactus's total weight. What percent of its weight is water?

   _____

4. Daytime temperatures in the Sahara can reach 130°F! At night, however, the temperature can drop by 62%. What decimal expresses this percent?

   _____

Circle the letter of the correct answer.

5. The desert nation of Saudi Arabia is the world's largest oil producer. About $\frac{1}{4}$ of all the oil imported to the United States is shipped from Saudi Arabia. What percent of our nation's oil is that?

   A 20%

   B 22%

   C 25%

   D 40%

6. About $\frac{2}{5}$ of all the food produced on Earth is grown on irrigated cropland. What percent of the world's food production relies on irrigation? What is the percent written as a decimal?

   F 40%; 40.0

   G 40%; 4.0

   H 40%; 0.4

   J 40%; 0.04

7. About $\frac{3}{25}$ of all the freshwater in the United States is used for drinking, washing, and other domestic purposes. What percent of our fresh water resources is that?

   A 3%

   B 25%

   C 12%

   D $\frac{1}{5}$

8. Factories and other industrial users account for about $\frac{23}{50}$ of the total water usage in the United States. Which of the following show that amount as a percent and decimal?

   F 46% and 0.46

   G 23% and 0.23

   H 50% and 0.5

   J 46% and 4.6

Percent of a Number
Going Deeper

Essential question: *How do you find percent of a number?*

CC.6.RP.3c

1 EXPLORE Finding Percent of a Number

video tutor

A sporting-goods store received a shipment of 400 baseball gloves, and 30% were left-handed. How many left-handed gloves were in the shipment?

A You can draw a diagram to solve this problem.

30% means 30 out of _____. There were _____ left-handed gloves for every 100 baseball gloves.

Complete the diagram to model this situation.

30	

100

400

REFLECT

1a. Describe how the diagram models the shipment of gloves.

_____

_____

_____

1b. How can you use the diagram to find the total number of left-handed gloves in the shipment?

_____

1c. Explain how you could use a diagram to find the number of right-handed gloves in the shipment.

_____

_____

_____

_____

B You can use a bar model to solve this problem. The bar represents 100%, or the entire shipment of 400 gloves. Divide the bar into 10 equal parts and label each part.

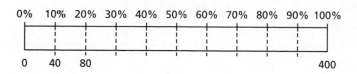

0%   10% 20% 30% 40% 50% 60% 70% 80% 90% 100%

0   40   80   400

Chapter 7　　　　　　　　　　317　　　　　　　　　　Lesson 7

© Houghton Mifflin Harcourt Publishing Company

1d. How did you determine the labels along the bottom of the bar model?

_____

_____

1e. How can you use the bar model to find the number of left-handed gloves?

_____

When finding the percent of a number, convert the percent to a fraction or decimal and then multiply.

CC.6.RP.3c

2 EXAMPLE   **Using a Fraction**

A lacrosse team played 30 games and won 80% of the games. How many games did the team win?

To answer this question, you must find 80% of 30.

Method 1 Use a rate per 100.

Step 1 Write the percent as a rate per 100.

$$80\% = \frac{\boxed{}}{100}$$

Step 2 Multiply by the total number of games.

$$\frac{\boxed{}}{100} \cdot 30 = \frac{\boxed{}}{100} \cdot \frac{30}{\boxed{}} = \frac{\boxed{}}{100} = \boxed{}$$

Method 2 Simplify the fraction.

Step 1 Write the percent as a fraction in simplest form.

$$80\% = \frac{80}{\boxed{}} = \frac{\boxed{}}{\boxed{}}$$

Step 2 Multiply this fraction by the total number of games.

$$\frac{\boxed{}}{\boxed{}} \cdot 30 = \frac{\boxed{}}{\boxed{}} \cdot \frac{30}{\boxed{}} = \frac{\boxed{}}{5} = \boxed{}$$

80% of 30 is _____. The team won _____ games.

REFLECT

2. Explain how Method 1 and Method 2 are similar and how they are different.

_____

_____

3 EXAMPLE   Using a Decimal

Sullivan has read 40% of a 210-page book. How many pages of the book does he have left to read?

Step 1 Write the percent as a decimal: 40% = ▢

Step 2 Multiply this decimal by the total number of pages.

▢ · 210 = ▢

40% of 210 is ▢. Sullivan has read _____ pages so far.

Step 3 Subtract to find the pages he has left to read.

210 − ▢ = ▢

Sullivan has _____ pages left to read.

TRY THIS!

Find the percent of each number.

3a. 20% of 180

_____

3b. 80% of 40

_____

3c. 75% of 480

_____

3d. 20% of 45

_____

3e. 25% of 16

_____

3f. 90% of 80

_____

REFLECT

3g. When might it be easier to write the percent as a fraction rather than as a decimal? Give an example.

_____

_____

_____

_____

3h. What is another way to solve the problem in **3**?

_____

_____

_____

_____

PRACTICE

Find the percent of each number.

1. 5% of 30

_____

2. 80% of 80

_____

3. 95% of 260

_____

4. 20% of 90

_____

5. 32% of 50

_____

6. 2% of 350

_____

7. 25% of 56

_____

8. 3% of 600

_____

9. 7% of 200

_____

10. At a shelter, 15% of the dogs are puppies. There are 60 dogs at the shelter. How many are puppies? _____ puppies

11. Terry has a box that originally held 64 crayons. She is missing 25% of the crayons. How many crayons are missing? _____ crayons

12. In a survey, 230 people were asked their favorite color, and 20% of the people surveyed chose blue. How many people chose blue? _____ people

13. Leah is saving money to buy her sister a graduation gift. She needs $44, and she has saved 25% of this amount so far. How much more money must Leah save? $ _____

14. Ali and her friend handed out nutrition pamphlets at the Health Fair. They were given 560 pamphlets and they handed out 35% of them. How many pamphlets were left at the end of the Health Fair? _____ pamphlets

15. Keenan is training for a bicycle race. His goal is to ride 150 miles each week. By Tuesday of one week, he had ridden 35% of his goal. How many miles did he have left to ride to meet his goal that week? _____ miles

16. Kionda and Jeremy sold 25 boxes of popcorn for a fundraiser. Kionda sold 60% of the boxes. How many boxes did they each sell? Kionda sold _____ boxes and Jeremy sold _____ boxes.

17. Use the circle graph to determine how many hours per day Becky spends on each activity.

School: _____ hours

Eating: _____ hours

Sleep: _____ hours

Homework: _____ hours

Free time: _____ hours

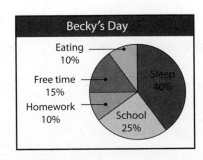

Becky's Day

Eating 10%
Free time 15%
Homework 10%
Sleep 40%
School 25%

© Houghton Mifflin Harcourt Publishing Company

Additional Practice

Find the percent of each number.

1. 25% of 56

2. 10% of 110

3. 5% of 150

4. 90% of 180

5. 125% of 48

6. 225% of 88

7. 2% of 350

8. 285% of 200

9. 150% of 125

10. 46% of 235

11. 78% of 410

12. 0.5% of 64

Find the percent of each number. Check whether your answer is reasonable.

13. 55% of 900

14. 140% of 50

15. 75% of 128

16. 3% of 600

17. 16% of 85

18. 22% of 105

19. 0.7% of 110

20. 95% of 500

21. 3% of 750

22. 162% of 250

23. 18% of 90

24. 23.2% of 125

25. 0.1% of 950

26. 11% of 300

27. 52% of 410

28. 250% of 12

29. The largest frog in the world is the goliath, found in West Africa. This type of frog can grow to be 12 inches long. The smallest frog in the world is about 4% as long as the goliath. What is the approximate length of the smallest frog in the world?

_____

Problem Solving

Write the correct answer.

The world population is estimated to exceed 9 billion by the year 2050. Use the circle graph to solve Exercises 1–3.

1. What is the estimated population of Africa in the year 2050?

   _____

2. Which continent is estimated to have more than 5.31 billion people by the year 2050?

   _____

3. In the year 2002, the world population was estimated at 6 billion people. Based on research from the World Bank, about 20% lived on less than $1 per day. How many people lived on less than $1 per day?

   _____

Estimated 2050 World Population

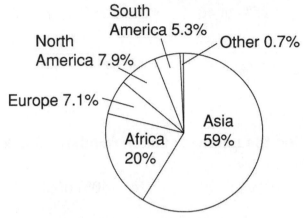

4. What is the combined estimated population for North and South America by the year 2050?

   _____

Circle the letter of the correct answer.

5. The student population at King Middle School is 52% female. The total student population is 1,225 students. How many boys go to King Middle School?

   A 538 boys   C 637 boys

   B 588 boys   D 1,173 boys

6. There are 245 students in the seventh grade. If 40% of them ride the bus to school, how many seventh graders do not ride the bus to school?

   F 98 students   H 185 students

   G 147 students   J 205 students

7. A half-cup of pancake mix has 5% of the total daily allowance of cholesterol. The total daily allowance of cholesterol is 300 mg. How much cholesterol does a half-cup of pancake mix have?

   A 100 mg   C 20 mg

   B 60 mg   D 15 mg

8. Carey needs $45 to buy her mother a birthday present. She has saved 22% of the amount so far. How much more does she need?

   F $35.10   H $23.00

   G $44.01   J $9.90

Solving Percent Problems
Going Deeper

Essential question: *How do you find the whole given a part and the percent?*

You can use an equation to solve percent problems:

$$\boxed{\text{percent}} \cdot \boxed{\text{whole}} = \boxed{\text{part}}$$

A percent problem may ask you to find any of the three pieces of this equation—the percent, the whole, or the part.

CC.6.RP.3c

1 EXAMPLE **Finding the Whole**

A girls' softball team has 3 pitchers. The pitchers make up 20% of the team. How many total players are on the softball team?

_____ % of the total number of players is _____.

Identify the pieces of the percent equation. Use the variable *n* for any piece that is unknown.

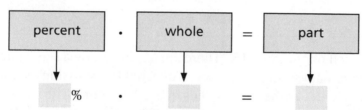

$$\boxed{\text{percent}} \cdot \boxed{\text{whole}} = \boxed{\text{part}}$$

$$\boxed{}\% \cdot \boxed{} = \boxed{}$$

Write the percent as a decimal. _____

Substitute this decimal for the percent and rewrite the equation. _____

Solve the equation.

$$\frac{0.2n}{\boxed{}} = \frac{3}{\boxed{}}$$ *Divide both sides by* _____.

$$n = \boxed{}$$

There are _____ players on the softball team.

REFLECT

1a. What ratio is represented by the percent equation?

_____

TRY THIS!

1b. 12% of what number is 45?   12% of _____ is 45.

1c. 180 is 30% of _____.   **1d.** 25% of _____ is 40.

Complete each sentence.

1. 4% of _____ is 56.

2. 58 is 20% of _____.

3. 35% of _____ is 42.

4. 360 is 24% of _____.

5. 92% of _____ is 115.

6. 9 is 3% of _____.

7. 45 is 60% of _____.

8. 8% of _____ is 2.

Solve each problem.

9. Heidi spent 20 minutes on the treadmill at the gym last Saturday. That was 25% of her total workout. How long, in minutes, was Heidi's workout at the gym Saturday?

10. Alan spent 3 hours building a model for his science project. This was 60% of the total time he worked on the project. How many hours did he work on his project?

11. Reed scored 17 points in his team's last basketball game. This was 34% of the team's total points for the game. How many total points did the team score?

12. The girls make up 70% of the students in the school swing choir. There are 21 girls in the choir. How many total students are in the swing choir?

13. Yolanda is saving for a new cell phone. So far she has saved $54 from her babysitting jobs. She calculated that this is 45% of the amount she needs for the phone. What is the total cost of the new cell phone?

14. There are 6 students on a school advisory committee that is discussing technology needs in the classroom. The students make up 40% of the committee. How many total people are on the committee?

15. Look back at Exercise 12. What percent of the choir is made up of boys? Describe two ways to find the number of boys in the choir.

_____

_____

16. **Error Analysis** Jamie calculated the answer to be 14 for Exercise 1. What error did he make in his calculations?

_____

_____

Additional Practice

1. 50 is 40% of what number?

_____

2. 12 is 25% of what number?

_____

3. 18 is what percent of 60?

_____

4. 12 is what percent of 96?

_____

5. 4% of what number is 25?

_____

6. 80% of what number is 160?

_____

7. What percent of 55 is 22?

_____

8. What percent of 75 is 6?

_____

9. 15 is 30% of what number?

_____

10. 8% of what number is 2?

_____

11. 7 is what percent of 105?

_____

12. 24 is 40% of what number?

_____

13. 10% of what number is 14?

_____

14. 16 is what percent of 200?

_____

15. What percent of 32 is 4?

_____

16. What percent of 150 is 60?

_____

17. 1% of what number is 11?

_____

18. 20% of what number is 14?

_____

19. The sales tax on a $750 computer at J & M Computers is
$48.75. What is the sales tax rate?

_____

20. A hardcover book sells for $24 at The Bookmart. Ben pays a
total of $25.02 for the book. What is the sales tax rate?

_____

Problem Solving

Write the correct answer.

1. At one time during 2001, for every 20 copies of *Harry Potter and the Sorcerer's Stone* that were sold, 13.2 copies of *Harry Potter and the Prisoner of Azkaban* were sold. Express the ratio of copies of *The Prisoner of Azkaban* sold to copies of *The Sorcerer's Stone* sold as a percent.

_____

2. A souvenir mug sells for $8.00 at a hotel gift store. Kendra gives the clerk $9.00 and receives $0.56 in change. What is the sales tax rate?

_____

3. Craig just finished reading 120 pages of his history assignment. If the assignment is 125 pages, what percent has Craig read so far?

_____

4. Hal's Sporting Goods had a 1-day sale. The original price of a mountain bike was $325. On sale, it was $276.25. What is the percent reduction for this sale?

_____

Choose the correct letter for the best answer.

5. China's area is about 3.7 million square miles. It is on the continent of Asia, which has an area of about 17.2 million square miles. About what percent of the Asian continent does China cover?

   A about 10%   C about 17%

   B about 15%   D about 22%

6. After six weeks, the tomato plant that was given extra plant food and water was 26 centimeters tall. The tomato plant that was not given any extra plant food was only 74.5% as tall. How tall was the tomato plant that was not given extra plant food?

   F 1.94 cm   H 34.89 cm

   G 19.37 cm   J 48.5 cm

7. In a survey, 46 people, which was 20% of those surveyed, chose red as their favorite color. How many people were surveyed?

   A 66 people   C 460 people

   B 230 people   D 920 people

8. Of the 77 billion food and drink cans, bottles, and jars Americans throw away each year, about 65% of them are cans. How many food and drink cans, to the nearest billion, do Americans throw away each year?

   F 12 billion   H 50 billion

   G 17 billion   J 65 billion

Problem Solving Connections

COMMON
CORE

CC.6.RP.1
CC.6.RP.2
CC.6.RP.3a, b, c, d

Sweet Success? A youth group is raising money for a ski trip by baking and selling muffins on weekend mornings. The money raised will be distributed evenly among the group members, and the goal is to raise $65 per person. Will the group meet this goal?

1 Making Muffins

Ruth volunteered to make pumpkin muffins for the sale. The ingredients used in Ruth's recipe are shown.

Pumpkin Muffins
4 cups white flour
4 cups wheat flour
4 tsp baking soda
2 tsp salt
4 tsp cinnamon
2 tsp ginger
1 tsp cloves
3 cups brown sugar
6 tsp molasses
1 cup oil
8 eggs
4 cups pumpkin
4 tsp vanilla
3 cups milk

A Write the ratio of total flour to sugar in three different ways.

_____

B Write the ratio of vanilla to molasses. Then write a ratio that is equivalent. Explain how you found the equivalent ratio.

_____

C At the grocery store, Ruth sees that a 15-ounce can of pumpkin costs $1.59 and a 29-ounce can of pumpkin costs $3.05. Which is the better buy?

D Ruth decides to make a larger batch of muffins for the bake sale by increasing the recipe. The increased recipe requires 6 teaspoons of cinnamon. Now Ruth must determine how many eggs she needs.

What is the ratio of cinnamon to eggs in the original recipe? _____

The ratio of cinnamon to eggs in the increased recipe must be _____ to the ratio in the original recipe.

Use the table to help you find the number of eggs that Ruth needs.

Cinnamon (tsp)	4		6
Eggs	8		

Ruth needs _____ eggs.

2 Preparing for the Sale

A Allison has painted a large "Muffin Sale" sign to display at the table. Chris wants to paint more signs.

Allison made purple paint by mixing 3 parts red paint with 4 parts blue paint. Chris has 2 fluid ounces of blue paint. To match Allison's shade of purple, how much red paint should Chris mix with his blue paint?

B The group members price the muffins at $15 per dozen. What is the price per muffin?

3 Sale Results

A The table shows results after several weekends of sales.

Muffins	Dozens Made	Dozens Sold
Pumpkin	18	17
Blueberry	16	15
Chocolate chip	24	24
Banana nut	14	13

What percent of the muffins made were pumpkin muffins?

B Which type of muffin represents $\frac{1}{3}$ of the muffins made? Explain.

C What percent of the muffins that youth group members made did NOT sell? Round your answer to the nearest percent.

D Which type of muffin was most popular? Justify your answer.

4 Answer the Question

A The treasurer of the youth group tracks the muffin sales for several weeks. Help her complete her spreadsheet.

Muffin Sales				
Type of Muffin	Dozens Made	Dozens Sold	Number of Muffins Sold	Income
Pumpkin	18	17		
Blueberry	16	15		
Chocolate chip	24	24		
Banana	14	13		
			Total Income	

B After tallying the group members' receipts for supplies, the treasurer has calculated that it cost the youth group $3.50 to bake a dozen muffins. How much has it cost the group to bake all of the muffins so far?

C To find the group's profit, subtract cost from income. How much profit has the group earned from muffin sales so far?

D The youth group divides the profit evenly between the 15 members. How much does each member now have toward the cost of the trip? Did the group meet its goal?

E Ruth suggests raising the price per muffin by $0.25 in future sales, saying, "If this had been the price from the beginning, we would have met our goal by now." Is Ruth correct? Explain.

Performance Task

CHAPTER 7

COMMON CORE

CC.6.RP.2
CC.6.RP.3a
CC.6.RP.3b
CC.6.RP.3c

⭐ **1.** Adam regularly buys a drink for $4.25 at a juice bar. He has a rewards card that is punched each time he buys a drink. After 5 drink purchases, Adam is awarded a 6th drink for free. With the rewards card, what percent of the regular price for 6 drinks does Adam save? Round your answer to the nearest whole percent.

⭐ **2.** Lloyd found the amount of milk the average person in the U.S. drinks in one year in gallons. He created a table and converted gallons to cups and ounces. Explain how he used equivalent ratios to find the missing value, then calculate the value.

Whole Milk	Low Fat Milk
8 gal	15 gal
128 cups	240 cups
1,024 oz	

⭐⭐ **3.** A gallon of paint costs $32.50 and its label says it covers about 350 square feet.

a. What is the cost of the paint per square foot? Show your work.

b. Kaylee measured the room she wanted to paint and calculated a total area of 825 square feet. If the paint is only available in one-gallon cans, how many cans of paint should she buy? Justify your answer.

c. The sales tax where Kaylee buys her paint is 5%, and the tax is always rounded up to the nearest cent. What is Kaylee's total cost for paint, including tax?

4. Davette wants to buy flannel sheets. She reads that a weight of at least 190 grams per square meter is considered high quality.

a. Davette finds a sheet that she likes, and it has a weight of 920 grams for 5 square meters. Does this sheet satisfy the requirement for high-quality sheets? If not, what should the weight be for 5 square meters? Justify your answer.

b. Davette finds 3 more options for flannel sheets:

Option 1: 1,100 g of flannel in 6 square meters, $45

Option 2: 1,060 g of flannel in 5.5 square meters, $42

Option 3: 1,300 g of flannel in 6.5 square meters, $52

She would like to buy the sheet that meets her requirement for high quality and has the lowest price per square meter. Which option should she buy? Justify your answer.

Name _____ Class _____ Date _____

SELECTED RESPONSE

1. The ratio of boys to girls in a classroom is 15 to 12. What is the ratio of boys to total students in the classroom?

    A. 12:15   **C.** 15:27

    B. 12:27   **D.** 27:15

2. Each day, the cafeteria staff at Brookview Middle School orders 80 pints of white milk and 30 pints of chocolate milk. Which ratio is equivalent to the ratio of white milk to chocolate milk?

    F. 8:11   **H.** 3:8

    G. 8:3   **J.** 3:11

3. A baker makes 5 apple pies for every 3 blueberry pies. Last week the baker made 15 blueberry pies. How many apple pies did the baker make?

    A. 8   **C.** 25

    B. 9   **D.** 40

4. Bagel prices at four different bakeries are shown below. Which is the best buy?

    F. Bakery 1: A dozen bagels costs $7.79.

    G. Bakery 2: 6 bagels cost $4.09.

    H. Bakery 3: Bagels cost $0.75 each.

    J. Bakery 4: 2 bagels cost $1.55.

5. Which is another way to write the ratio 8:3?

    A. 3 to 8   **C.** 8 to 11

    B. $\frac{3}{8}$ **D.** 8 to 3

6. Which is **not** equivalent to $\frac{45}{75}$?

    F. $\frac{9}{15}$ **H.** 60%

    G. $\frac{15}{25}$ **J.** 70%

7. Which shows the ratio "44 to 200" written as a percent, a decimal, and a fraction in simplest form?

    A. 44%, 0.44, $\frac{44}{50}$

    B. 44%, 0.22, $\frac{22}{100}$

    C. 22%, 0.2, $\frac{22}{100}$

    D. 22%, 0.22, $\frac{11}{50}$

8. Out of 20 athletes surveyed, 10 athletes chose soccer as their favorite sport, 6 chose golf, and the others chose football. What percent of the athletes chose football?

    F. 20%

    G. 30%

    H. 40%

    J. 50%

9. A certain shade of orange requires a 3 to 2 ratio of yellow to red paint. You have 6 gallons of red paint. How much yellow paint do you need?

    A. 4 gallons

    B. 5 gallons

    C. 9 gallons

    D. 12 gallons

10. In Miranda's flower garden, 65% of the flowers are tulips. What fraction of Miranda's flowers are tulips?

    F. $\frac{100}{65}$ **H.** $\frac{65}{1}$

    G. $\frac{13}{20}$ **J.** $\frac{7}{40}$

CONSTRUCTED RESPONSE

11. Use the tables to compare the ratios $\frac{7}{8}$ and $\frac{11}{12}$.

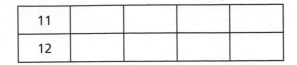

7			
8			

11			
12			

$\dfrac{7}{8}$ ▢ $\dfrac{11}{12}$

12. Orin's Sports store has a 40% off sale on all of its merchandise. How much is the discount on a soccer ball that originally costs $30?

_____

_____

13. A flower shop sells carnations for $18.50 per dozen. The sales tax is 6%.

a. How much is the sales tax on a dozen carnations? Show your work.

_____

_____

b. What will be the total cost of a dozen carnations? Show your work.

_____

_____

14. Samantha correctly answered 38 out of 55 questions on a test. She must score 70% or greater to pass the test. Did she pass? Justify your answer.

_____

_____

15. To earn money, Peter shovels driveways in the winter. He earns $24 in 3 hours.

a. Complete the table.

Hours	0.5	1	3	4	5
Amount Earned ($)			24		

b. Write the information in the table as ordered pairs. Use Hours as the x-coordinates and Amount earned as the y-coordinates.

_____

c. Graph the ordered pairs from **b** and connect the points.

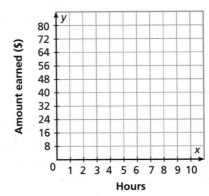

d. What is Peter's unit rate in dollars per hour? How are the table and the graph above related to this unit rate?

_____

_____

_____

_____

e. How can you use the graph to find the amount of money Peter earns in 6 hours?

_____

_____

_____

f. How can you use the unit rate to find the amount of money Peter earns in 6 hours?

_____

Measurement and Geometry

Chapter Focus

You will learn to convert from one unit to another in the customary system and to convert between the customary and metric systems. You will also find the area of rectangles, parallelograms, rhombuses, triangles, trapezoids, and composite figures. Volume is the number of cubic units needed to fill a given space. You will find the volume of prisms including those with fractional side lengths. Nets will be used to find the surface area of figures by finding the area of each face and then adding to find the surface area of the figure.

Chapter at a Glance

COMMON CORE

Lesson		Standards for Mathematical Content
8-1	Converting Customary Units	CC.6.RP.3d
8-2	Converting Metric Units	CC.6.RP.3d
8-3	Area of Rectangles and Parallelograms	CC.6.G.1, CC.6.EE.2c
8-4	Area of Triangles and Trapezoids	CC.6.G.1
8-5	Area of Composite Figures	CC.6.G.1
8-6	Volume of Prisms	CC.6.G.2
8-7	Surface Area	CC.6.G.4
	Problem Solving Connections	
	Performance Task	
	Assessment Readiness	

CHAPTER 8

Unpacking the Standards

Understanding the standards and the vocabulary terms in the standards will help you know exactly what you are expected to learn in this chapter.

CC.6.RP.3d

Use ratio reasoning to convert measurement units; manipulate and transform units appropriately when multiplying or dividing quantities.

Key Vocabulary

ratio *(razón)* A comparison of two quantities by division.

What It Means to You

You will convert between customary and metric measurements using a conversion factor.

EXAMPLE

The Washington Monument is about 185 yards tall. This height is almost equal to the length of two football fields. About how many feet is this?

$$185 \text{ yd} \cdot \frac{3 \text{ ft}}{1 \text{ yd}}$$

$$= \frac{185 \text{ yd}}{1} \cdot \frac{3 \text{ ft}}{1 \text{ yd}}$$

$$= 555 \text{ ft}$$

The Washington Monument is about 555 ft tall.

CC.6.G.4

Represent three-dimensional figures using nets made up of rectangles and triangles, and use the nets to find the surface area of these figures. Apply these techniques in the context of solving real-world and mathematical problems.

Key Vocabulary

net *(plantilla)* An arrangement of two-dimensional figures that can be folded to form a polyhedron.

surface area *(área total)* The sum of the areas of the faces, or surfaces, of a three-dimensional figure.

What It Means to You

You will use nets to find the surface area of three-dimensional figures in real-world and mathematical problems.

EXAMPLE

Julie is wrapping a present for a friend. Find the surface area of the box.

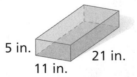

Draw a net to help you see each face of the prism.

Use the formula $A = lw$ to find the area of each face.

A: $A = 11 \times 5 = 55$

B: $A = 21 \times 11 = 231$

C: $A = 21 \times 5 = 105$

D: $A = 21 \times 11 = 231$

E: $A = 21 \times 5 = 105$

F: $A = 11 \times 5 = 55$

$S = 55 + 231 + 105 + 231 + 105 + 55 = 782$

The surface area is 782 in^2.

COMMON CORE **CC.6.G.2**

Find the volume of a right rectangular prism with fractional edge lengths by packing it with unit cubes of the appropriate unit fraction edge lengths, and show that the volume is the same as would be found by multiplying the edge lengths of the prism. Apply the formulas $V = lwh$ and $V = bh$ to find volumes of right rectangular prisms with fractional edge lengths in the context of solving real-world and mathematical problems.

Key Vocabulary

volume *(volumen)* The number of cubic units needed to fill a given space.
rectangular prism *(prisma rectangular)* A polyhedron whose bases are rectangles and whose other faces are rectangles.

What It Means to You

You will find the volume of a right rectangular prism with fractional side lengths to solve real-world and mathematical problems.

EXAMPLE

Robert has a storage locker in the shape of a rectangular prism. The dimensions of the locker are 3 ft, $2\frac{1}{2}$ ft, and $5\frac{1}{2}$ ft. What is the volume of the locker?

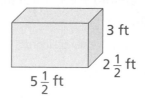

3 ft

$2\frac{1}{2}$ ft

$5\frac{1}{2}$ ft

$V = lwh$

$V = 5\frac{1}{2} \cdot 2\frac{1}{2} \cdot 3$

$V = \frac{11}{2} \cdot \frac{5}{2} \cdot \frac{3}{1}$

$V = \frac{165}{4} = 41\frac{1}{4}$ ft³

The volume of the locker is $41\frac{1}{4}$ ft³.

COMMON CORE **CC.6.G.1**

Find the area of right triangles, other triangles, special quadrilaterals, and polygons by composing into rectangles or decomposing into triangles and other shapes; apply these techniques in the context of solving real-world and mathematical problems.

Key Vocabulary

polygon *(polígono)* A closed plane figure formed by three or more line segments that intersect only at their endpoints.

What It Means to You

You will find the area of triangles to solve both real-world and mathematical problems.

EXAMPLE

The diagram shows the outline of the foundation of the Flatiron Building. What is the area of the foundation?

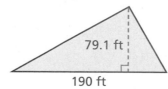

79.1 ft

190 ft

$A = \frac{1}{2}bh$

$A = \frac{1}{2}(190 \cdot 79.1)$

$A = \frac{1}{2}(15,029) = 7,514.5$ ft²

The area of the foundation is $7,514.5$ ft².

CHAPTER 8

Key Vocabulary

conversion factor *(factor de conversión)* A ratio of two equivalent measurements. A conversion factor is equivalent to 1.

net *(plantilla)* An arrangement of two-dimensional figures that can be folded to form a polyhedron.

pyramid *(pirámide)* A polyhedron with a polygon base and triangular sides that all meet at a common vertex.

rhombus *(rombo)* A parallelogram with all sides congruent.

surface area *(área total)* The sum of the areas of the faces, or surfaces, of a three-dimensional figure.

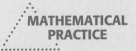

MATHEMATICAL PRACTICE

The Common Core Standards for Mathematical Practice describe varieties of expertise that mathematics educators at all levels should seek to develop in their students. Opportunities to develop these practices are integrated throughout this program.

1. **Make sense of problems and persevere in solving them.**
2. **Reason abstractly and quantitatively.**
3. **Construct viable arguments and critique the reasoning of others.**
4. **Model with mathematics.**
5. **Use appropriate tools strategically.**
6. **Attend to precision.**
7. **Look for and make use of structure.**
8. **Look for and express regularity in repeated reasoning.**

8-1

Converting Customary Units
Going Deeper

Essential question: *How can you convert from one customary unit to another?*

CC.6.RP.3d

1 EXPLORE — Using a Model to Convert Feet to Inches

A Use the diagram to complete each equation.

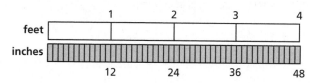

1 foot = 12 inches   2 feet = _____ inches

3 feet = _____ inches   4 feet = _____ inches

B Write each of these ratios in simplest form.

$$\frac{2 \text{ feet}}{\boxed{} \text{ inches}} = \frac{\boxed{} \text{ foot}}{\boxed{} \text{ inches}}$$

$$\frac{3 \text{ feet}}{\boxed{} \text{ inches}} = \frac{\boxed{} \text{ foot}}{\boxed{} \text{ inches}}$$

Since 1 foot = 12 inches, the ratio of feet to inches in any measurement is always $\frac{1}{12}$.

C Any ratio equivalent to $\frac{1}{12}$ can represent a ratio of feet to inches.

$\frac{1}{12} = \frac{\boxed{}}{48}$, so _____ feet = 48 inches.

$\frac{1}{12} = \frac{5}{\boxed{}}$, so _____ feet = _____ inches.

$\frac{1}{12} = \frac{6}{\boxed{}}$, so _____ feet = _____ inches.

REFLECT

1. **Error Analysis** Kim says, "Since a foot is 12 times as long as an inch, to convert feet to inches I need to divide the number of feet by 12." Is Kim right? Explain.

_____

_____

You can use these equivalencies to convert among measures of lengths.

12 inches = 1 foot   3 feet = 1 yard   36 inches = 1 yard

CC.6.RP.3d

2 E X A M P L E   Using Proportions to Convert Measures of Length

Jolene makes candles to sell online. Each candle goes in a glass jar with a ribbon wrapped around it. She uses 9 inches of ribbon on each jar. She has 12 yards of ribbon. What is the greatest number of candles that she can make using the ribbon she has?

What is the unit rate of inches to yards? _____

Use the unit rate to write and solve a proportion to find how many inches are in 12 yards.

$$\frac{36 \text{ inches}}{1 \text{ yard}} = \frac{\boxed{} \text{ inches}}{12 \text{ yards}}$$

Use division to find how many 9-inch pieces of ribbon Jolene can cut.

So, Jolene can make _____ candles using the 12 yards of ribbon that she has.

REFLECT

2a. **What if** Suppose that the division had resulted in a quotient with a remainder. Would this have changed the number of candles that Jolene could make? Explain.

_____

_____

2b. Describe another way that you might solve this problem.

_____

_____

_____

TRY THIS!

Convert each measurement.

2c. 6 feet = _____ inches   **2d.** 9 yards = _____ feet

You can use these equivalencies to convert among measures of capacity.

4 quarts = 1 gallon	2 pints = 1 quart	8 pints = 1 gallon	2 cups = 1 pint
16 cups = 1 gallon	8 fluid ounces = 1 cup	16 fluid ounces = 1 pint	
32 fluid ounces = 1 quart	128 fluid ounces = 1 gallon		

CC.6.RP.3d

3 EXAMPLE Solving Problems Involving Conversions

The table shows the prices of three brands of low-fat salad dressing. Which brand is the best buy? Justify your answer.

Low-Fat Salad Dressing Prices		
Brand	**Size**	**Price**
Country Choice	3 cups	$2.40
Nature's Best	1 pint	$1.92
Garden Fresh	12 fluid ounces	$1.32

Convert the sizes of the first two brands to fluid ounces so that all three items use the same unit of measurement.

What is the unit rate of fluid ounces to cups? _____

Use this unit rate to write and solve a proportion to find how many fluid ounces are in 3 cups.

$$\frac{8 \text{ fluid ounces}}{1 \text{ cup}} = \frac{\text{fluid ounces}}{3 \text{ cups}}$$

3 cups = _____ fluid ounces.

1 pint = _____ fluid ounces.

Use division to find the price per fluid ounce for each of the three brands.

Country Choice: $2.40 ÷ _____ fluid ounces = _____ per fluid ounce

Nature's Best: $1.92 ÷ _____ fluid ounces = _____ per fluid ounce

Garden Fresh: $1.32 ÷ _____ fluid ounces = _____ per fluid ounce

Which brand is the best buy? Why?

_____

TRY THIS!

Convert each measurement.

3a.   16 pints = _____ quarts

3b.   3 gallons = _____ cups

3c.   64 fluid ounces = _____ pints

3d.   192 fluid ounces = _____ quarts

There are 16 ounces (oz) in 1 pound (lb). Find each measurement in pounds.

1. 64 oz = _____ lb   **2.** 96 oz = _____ lb   **3.** 112 oz = _____ lb

There are 2,000 pounds (lb) in 1 ton (T). Find each measurement in tons.

4. 4,000 lb = _____ T   **5.** 8,000 lb = _____ T   **6.** 20,000 lb = _____ T

7. Estavan owns a sawmill. Today he is cutting long boards into 4-foot pieces. He has boards of the following lengths: 122 inches, 146 inches, and 160 inches. What is the greatest number of 4-foot pieces that he can cut from these three boards? Explain.

_____

_____

8. The table below shows the prices of three brands of liquid hand soap. Which brand is the best buy? Justify your answer.

Liquid Hand Soap Prices		
Brand	**Size**	**Price**
Nature's Own	2 quarts	$6.40
Ultra-Clean	8 fluid ounces	$1.20
Garden Scents	1 pint	$1.92

_____

_____

9. The table below shows the distances that three animals can travel in different amounts of time. Which animal is the fastest? Justify your answer.

Animal	Distance	Time
Ant	94 inches	1 minute
Roach	35 yards	1 minute
Snail	160 feet	1 hour

_____

_____

Converting Metric Units
Extension: Converting Between Customary and Metric

Essential question: *How can you use ratios to convert measurements?*

Measurement is a mathematical tool that people use every day. Measurements are used when determining the length, weight, or capacity of an object.

There are several different systems of measurement. The two most common systems are the *customary system* and the *metric system*.

The table below shows equivalencies between the customary and metric systems. You can use these equivalencies to convert a measurement in one system to a measurement in the other system.

Length	Weight/Mass	Capacity
1 inch = 2.54 centimeters 1 foot ≈ 0.305 meters 1 yard ≈ 0.914 meters 1 mile ≈ 1.61 kilometers	1 ounce ≈ 28.4 grams 1 pound ≈ 0.454 kilograms	1 fluid ounce ≈ 29.6 milliliters 1 quart ≈ 0.946 liter 1 gallon ≈ 3.79 liters

Most conversions are approximate, as indicated by the symbol ≈.

CC.6.RP.3d

1 EXPLORE Converting Inches to Centimeters

The length of a sheet of a paper is 11 inches. What is this length in centimeters?

You can use a diagram to solve this problem. Each block represents 1 inch.

1 inch = _____ centimeter(s)

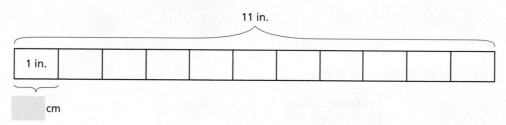

11 in.

1 in.

cm

How does the diagram help you solve the problem?

_____

11 inches = _____ centimeters

TRY THIS!

1. Draw a diagram to find approximately how many grams are equivalent to 6 ounces.

6 ounces ≈ _____ grams

© Houghton Mifflin Harcourt Publishing Company

Another way to convert measurements is by using a ratio called a *conversion factor*. A **conversion factor** is a ratio of two equivalent measurements. Since the two measurements in a conversion factor are equivalent, a conversion factor is a ratio equivalent to 1.

CC.6.RP.3d

2 E X A M P L E   Using Conversion Factors

A Vicki put 22 gallons of gasoline in her car. About how many liters of gasoline did she put in her car?

Step 1 Find the conversion factor.

_____ liter(s) ≈ 1 gallon

Write as a ratio: $\dfrac{\boxed{}\text{ liter(s)}}{1\text{ gallon}}$

Step 2 Convert the given measurement.

$$\boxed{\text{gallons}} \cdot \boxed{\text{conversion factor}} = \boxed{\text{liters}}$$

$$\boxed{}\text{ gallons} \cdot \dfrac{\boxed{}\text{ liter(s)}}{1\text{ gallon}} \approx \boxed{}\text{ liters}$$

Vicki put about _____ liters of gasoline in her car.

B While lifting weights, John adds 11.35 kilograms to his bar. About how many pounds did he add to his bar?

Step 1 Find the conversion factor.

1 pound ≈ _____ kilogram(s)

Write as a ratio: $\dfrac{1\text{ pound}}{\boxed{}\text{ kilogram(s)}}$

Step 2 Convert the given measurement.

$$\boxed{\text{kilograms}} \cdot \boxed{\text{conversion factor}} = \boxed{\text{pounds}}$$

$$\boxed{}\text{ kilograms} \cdot \dfrac{1\text{ pound}}{\boxed{}\text{ kilogram(s)}} \approx \boxed{}\text{ pounds}$$

John has added about _____ pounds to his bar.

TRY THIS!

2a. 6 quarts ≈ _____ liters

2b. 14 feet ≈ _____ meters

2c. 255.6 grams ≈ _____ ounces

2d. 7 liters ≈ _____ quarts

© Houghton Mifflin Harcourt Publishing Company

3 EXAMPLE Converting Units

Yolanda's office is 12 feet long by 8 feet wide. She plans to purchase carpet for the entire office. The carpet costs $15 per square meter. What will be the total cost of the new carpet?

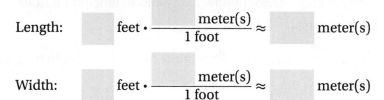

8 feet

12 feet

First find the area of the office in square meters.

Step 1 Convert each measurement to meters.

Length: ⬜ feet · $\dfrac{\text{meter(s)}}{1 \text{ foot}}$ ≈ ⬜ meter(s)

Width: ⬜ feet · $\dfrac{\text{meter(s)}}{1 \text{ foot}}$ ≈ ⬜ meter(s)

Step 2 Find the area.

Area = length · width

= ⬜ · ⬜

= ⬜ square meters

Now find the total cost of the carpet.

square meters · cost per square meter = total cost

⬜ · ⬜ = $ ⬜

REFLECT

3a. **Error Analysis** Leo found the area of Yolanda's office in square meters as shown. Explain why Leo's answer is incorrect.

> Area = 12 · 8 = 96 square feet
>
> 96 square feet · $\dfrac{0.305 \text{ meter}}{1 \text{ foot}}$ ≈ 29.28 square meters

_____

_____

TRY THIS!

3b. A flower bed is 6 feet wide and 10 feet long. What is the area of the flower bed in square meters? Round your answer to the nearest hundredth.

_____ square meters

1. A ruler is 12 inches long. What is the length of this ruler in centimeters?
_____ centimeters

2. A bottle contains 4 fluid ounces of medicine. About how many milliliters of medicine are in the bottle? _____ milliliters

3. Miguel rode 19 miles on his bicycle. About how many kilometers did he ride?
_____ kilometers

4. A gas can contains 2.5 gallons of gas. About how many liters of gas are in the gas can?
_____ liters

5. A kitten weighs 4 pounds. About how many kilograms does the kitten weigh?
_____ kilograms

Convert each measurement.

6. 20 yards ≈ _____ meters

7. 12 ounces ≈ _____ grams

8. 5 quarts ≈ _____ liters

9. 30 inches ≈ _____ centimeters

10. 42 feet ≈ _____ meters

11. 7 gallons ≈ _____ liters

12. 5 miles ≈ _____ kilometers

13. 400 meters ≈ _____ yards

14. 165 centimeters ≈ _____ inches

15. 137.25 meters ≈ _____ feet

16. 10 liters ≈ _____ gallons

17. 10,000 kilometers ≈ _____ miles

18. A countertop is 16 feet long and 3 feet wide.

   a. What is the area of the countertop in square meters? _____ square meters

   b. Tile costs $28 per square meter. How much will it cost to cover the countertop with new tile? $ _____

19. **Reasoning** The length of a particular object is x inches.

   a. Will this object's length in centimeters be greater than x or less than x? Explain.

   _____

   _____

   b. Will this object's length in meters be greater than x or less than x? Explain.

   _____

   _____

Area of Rectangles and Parallelograms
Going Deeper: Parallelograms

Essential question: *How do you find the areas of parallelograms and rhombuses?*

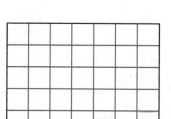

video tutor

CC.6.G.1

1 EXPLORE Modeling Areas of Rectangles

Find the area of the rectangle shown at the right. Each square in the grid is one square unit.

A Since the area of a figure is the amount of surface it covers, count the squares inside the rectangle.

Area = _____ square units

B What is the length of the base? _____ units
What is the length of the height? _____ units
Find the product of these two measures. _____ square units

Compare the product with the result in **A**. How do they compare? _____

For all rectangles, the area can be found by multiplying the base and the height. The formula for the area of a rectangle is $A = bh$.

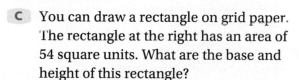

h $A = bh$ b

C You can draw a rectangle on grid paper. The rectangle at the right has an area of 54 square units. What are the base and height of this rectangle?

base: _____ height: _____

On grid paper, draw other rectangles that have an area of 54 square units. Shade only whole squares so that the base and height of your rectangles are whole numbers. Label the base and height of each rectangle, and verify that $A = bh$.

How many *different* rectangles with an area of 54 square units can be formed? _____

TRY THIS!

Find the area of each rectangle.

1a. $b = 9$ ft, $h = 5$ ft $A =$ _____   **1b.** $b = 20$ yd, $h = 12$ yd $A =$ _____

2 E X P L O R E Area of a Parallelogram

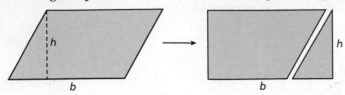

A Draw a large parallelogram on grid paper. Cut out your parallelogram.

B Cut your parallelogram on the dashed line as shown. Then move the triangular piece to the other side of the parallelogram.

C What figure have you formed? _____

Does this figure have the same area as the parallelogram? _____

What is the formula for the area of this figure? $A =$ _____

D What is the formula for the area of a parallelogram? $A =$ _____

> **TRY THIS!**

Find the area of each parallelogram.

2a.

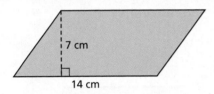

7 cm

14 cm

$A =$ _____

2b.

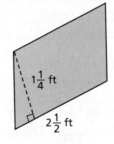

$1\frac{1}{4}$ ft

$2\frac{1}{2}$ ft

$A =$ _____

> **REFLECT**

2c. Why is the formula for the area of a parallelogram the same as the formula for the area of a rectangle?

_____

Area of a Parallelogram

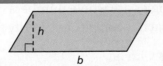

$A = bh$

h

b

Additional Practice

Estimate the area of each figure.

1.

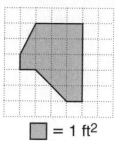

☐ = 1 ft²

_____

2.

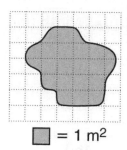

☐ = 1 m²

_____

Find the area of each rectangle.

3.

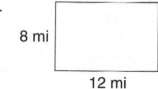

7 yd

9 yd

_____

4.

8 mi

12 mi

_____

Find the area of each parallelogram.

5.

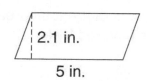

2.1 in.

5 in.

_____

6.

18 ft

16 ft

_____

7. Mariah is planting a rectangular rose garden. In the center of the garden, she puts a smaller rectangular patch of grass. The grass is 2 ft by 3 ft. What is the area of the rose garden?

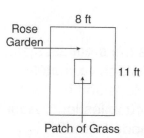

Rose Garden

8 ft

11 ft

Patch of Grass

_____

8. A section of a stained-glass window is shaped like a parallelogram. Its base is 6.5 inches, and its height is 4 inches. How much glass is needed to cover the section completely?

_____

9. Your rectangular yard is 10 feet wide and 26 feet long. How many square feet of grass do you need to plant if you want to cover the entire yard?

_____

Problem Solving

Use the table to answer each question.

State Information

State	Approx. Width (mi)	Approx. length (mi)	Water Area (mi^2)
Colorado	280	380	376
Kansas	210	400	462
New Mexico	343	370	234
North Dakota	211	340	1,724
Pennsylvania	160	283	1,239

1. New Mexico is the 5th-largest state in the United States. What is its approximate total area?

_____

2. Kansas is the 15th-largest state in the United States. What is its approximate total area?

_____

3. What is the difference between North Dakota's land area and water area?

_____

4. What is Pennsylvania's approximate land area?

_____

Circle the letter of the correct answer.

5. What is the difference between Colorado's land area and Pennsylvania's land area?

   A   106,400 mi^2

   B   61,120 mi^2

   C   60,120 mi^2

   D   45,280 mi^2

6. About what percent of the total area of Pennsylvania is covered by land?

   F   about 3%

   G   about 30%

   H   about 67%

   J   about 97%

7. Rhode Island is the smallest state. Its total land area is approximately 1,200 mi^2. Rhode Island is approximately 40 miles long. About how wide is Rhode Island?

   A   about 20 mi

   B   about 40 mi

   C   about 50 mi

   D   about 30 mi

8. The entire United States covers 3,794,085 square miles of North America. About how much of that area is not made up of the 5 states in the chart?

   F   2,537,470 mi^2

   G   3,359,755 mi^2

   H   3,686,525 mi^2

   J   3,1310,818 mi^2

Area of Triangles and Trapezoids
Going Deeper

Essential question: *How do you find the area of triangles and trapezoids?*

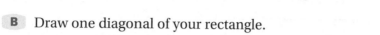

1 EXPLORE — Area of a Right Triangle

video tutor

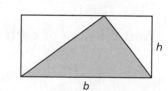

A Draw a large rectangle on grid paper.

What is the formula for the area of a rectangle? $A =$ _____

B Draw one diagonal of your rectangle.

The diagonal divides the rectangle into _____.
Each one represents _____ of the rectangle.

Use this information and the formula for area of a rectangle to

write a formula for the area of a right triangle. $A =$ _____

 REFLECT

1. In the formula for the area of a right triangle, what do b and h represent?

_____

2 EXPLORE — Area of a Triangle

A Draw a large triangle on grid paper. Do not draw a right triangle.

B Cut out your triangle. Then trace around it to make a copy of your triangle. Cut out the copy.

C Cut one of your triangles into two pieces by cutting through one angle directly across to the opposite side. Now you have three triangles — one large triangle and two smaller triangles.

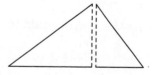

When added together, the areas of the two smaller triangles equal the _____ of the large triangle.

D Arrange the three triangles into a rectangle. What fraction

of the rectangle does the large triangle represent? _____

The area of the rectangle is $A = bh$. What is the area of

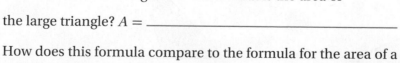

the large triangle? $A =$ _____

How does this formula compare to the formula for the area of a right triangle that you found in **1**?

_____

© Houghton Mifflin Harcourt Publishing Company

2. In the formula for the area of a triangle, what do *b* and *h* represent?

_____

_____

Area of a Triangle

$$A = \frac{1}{2}bh$$

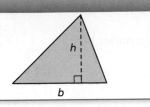

CC.6.G.1

3 EXAMPLE Finding the Area of a Triangle

Find the area of each triangle.

A

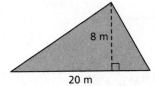

8 m

20 m

$b =$ _____ meters

$h =$ _____ meters

Use the formula to find the area. $A = \frac{1}{2}bh$

$$= \frac{1}{2}\left(\boxed{}\ \text{meters}\right)\left(\boxed{}\ \text{meters}\right)$$

$$= \boxed{}\ \text{square meters}$$

B

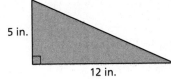

5 in.

12 in.

$b =$ _____ inches

$h =$ _____ inches

Use the formula to find the area. $A = \frac{1}{2}bh$

$$= \frac{1}{2}\left(\boxed{}\ \text{inches}\right)\left(\boxed{}\ \text{inches}\right)$$

$$= \boxed{}\ \text{square inches}$$

TRY THIS!

Find the area of each triangle.

3a.

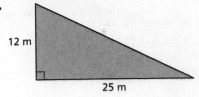

12 m

25 m

3b.

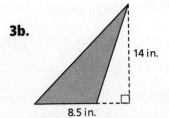

14 in.

8.5 in.

$A =$ _____

$A =$ _____

4 **EXAMPLE** Problem Solving Using Areas of Triangles

The Hudson High School wrestling team just won the state tournament and has been awarded a triangular pennant to hang on the wall in the school gymnasium. What is the area of the pennant?

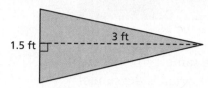

$b =$ _____ feet

$h =$ _____ feet

Use the formula to find the area.

$A = \frac{1}{2}bh$

$= \frac{1}{2}\left(\boxed{} \text{ feet}\right)\left(\boxed{} \text{ feet}\right)$

$= \boxed{}$ square feet

TRY THIS!

4a. Renee is sewing a quilt whose pattern contains right triangles. What is the area of one triangular quilt piece?

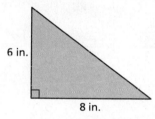

$A =$ _____

4b. William is making a model of a dinosaur. The dinosaur has triangular plates along its back. What is the area of each model plate?

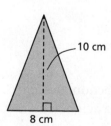

$A =$ _____

REFLECT

4c. When can you use two side lengths to find the area of a triangle? In this situation, does it matter which side is the base and which side is the height?

_____

_____

To find the formula for the area of a trapezoid, notice that two copies of the same trapezoid fit together to form a parallelogram. Therefore, the area of the trapezoid is $\frac{1}{2}$ the area of the parallelogram.

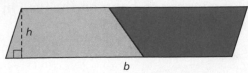

The height of the parallelogram is the same as the height of the trapezoid. The base of the parallelogram is the sum of the two bases of the trapezoid.

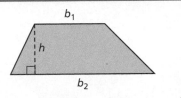

$$A = \quad b \quad \cdot h$$
$$A = \overbrace{(b_1 + b_2)} \cdot h$$

Area of a Trapezoid

$$A = \frac{1}{2}h(b_1 + b_2)$$

b_1

h

b_2

CC.6.G.1

5 EXAMPLE Finding the Area of a Trapezoid

A section of a deck is in the shape of a trapezoid. What is the area of this section of the deck?

17 ft

16 ft

39 ft

$b_1 =$ _____ $b_2 =$ _____ $h =$ _____

Use the formula for area of a trapezoid.

$A = \frac{1}{2}h(b_1 + b_2)$

$= \frac{1}{2} \cdot \boxed{} \left(\boxed{} + \boxed{} \right)$

$= \frac{1}{2} \cdot \boxed{} \left(\boxed{} \right)$ *Add inside the parentheses.*

$= 8 \cdot \boxed{}$ *Multiply $\frac{1}{2}$ and 16.*

$= \boxed{}$ square feet   *Multiply.*

TRY THIS!

5a. Another section of the deck is also shaped as a trapezoid. For this section, the length of one base is 27 feet, and the length of the other base is 34 feet. The height is 12 feet. What is the area of this section of the deck? $A =$ _____ ft^2

Find the area of each trapezoid.

5b. $b_1 = 12$ meters
$b_2 = 15$ meters
$h = 13$ meters
$A =$ _____ m^2

5c. $b_1 = 16$ ft
$b_2 = 30$ ft
$h = 24$ ft
$A =$ _____ ft^2

5d. Does it matter which of the trapezoid's bases is substituted for b_1 and which is substituted for b_2? Why or why not?

_____

_____

5e. Quanah says that to find the area of a trapezoid, you multiply the height by the top base and the height by the bottom base, then add the two numbers together and divide the sum by 2. Is Quanah correct? Explain.

_____

_____

_____

_____

PRACTICE

Find the area of each triangle.

1.

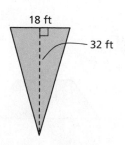

10 cm

15 cm

$A = $ _____

2.

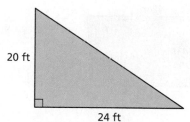

20 ft

24 ft

$A = $ _____

3.

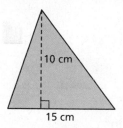

18 ft

32 ft

$A = $ _____

4.

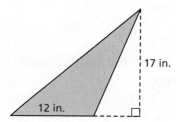

17 in.

12 in.

$A = $ _____

5. $b = 8\frac{1}{2}$ inches; $h = 15$ inches

$A = $ _____

6. $b = 15\frac{1}{4}$ inches; $h = 18$ inches

$A = $ _____

7. $b = 132$ meters; $h = 72$ meters

$A =$ _____

8. $b = 44$ feet; $h = 48$ feet

$A =$ _____

9. What is the area of the triangular plot of land?

$A =$ _____

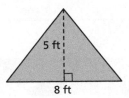
20 km

30 km

10. The sixth grade art students are making a mosaic using tiles in the shape of right triangles. Each tile has leg measures 3 centimeters and 5 centimeters. What is the area of one tile? $A =$ _____

11. A triangular piece of fabric has an area of 45 square inches. The height of the triangle is 15 inches. What is the length of the triangle's base?

$b =$ _____

12. The front part of a tent is 8 feet wide and 5 feet tall. What is the area of this part of the tent? $A =$ _____

5 ft

8 ft

Find the area of each trapezoid.

13.

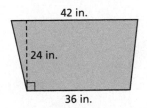
42 in.

24 in.

36 in.

$A =$ _____ in^2

14.

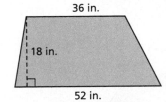
36 in.

18 in.

52 in.

$A =$ _____ in^2

15. $b_1 = 9$ meters

$b_2 = 15$ meters

$h = 8$ meters

$A =$ _____ m^2

16. $b_1 = 11$ meters

$b_2 = 14$ meters

$h = 10$ meters

$A =$ _____ m^2

17. Find the area of the figure. Explain how you found your answer.

_____

_____

_____

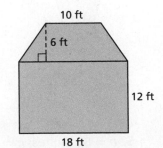
10 ft

6 ft

12 ft

18 ft

8-4

Additional Practice

Find the area of each triangle.

1.
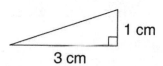
4 yd
25 yd

_____

2.

4 ft
3.5 ft

_____

3.
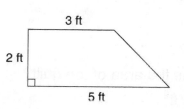
1 cm
3 cm

_____

4.
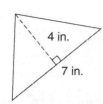
4 in.
7 in.

_____

Find the area of each trapezoid.

5.
3 ft
2 ft
5 ft

_____

6.
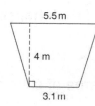
5.5 m
4 m
3.1 m

_____

7.
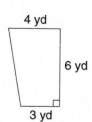
4 yd
6 yd
3 yd

_____

8.
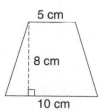
5 cm
8 cm
10 cm

_____

9. The front part of a tent is 8 feet long and 5 feet tall. What is the area of the front part of the tent?

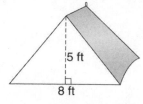
5 ft
8 ft

_____

Problem Solving

Use the quilt design to answer the questions.

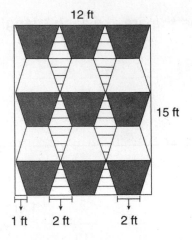

1. What are the lengths of the bases of each trapezoid?

   _____

2. What is the height of each trapezoid?

   _____

3. What is the area of each trapezoid?

   _____

Circle the letter of the correct answer.

4. What is the length of the base of each striped triangle?

   A 1 ft

   B 2 ft

   C 3 ft

   D 4 ft

5. What is the height of each striped triangle?

   F 1 ft

   G 2 ft

   H 3 ft

   J 5 ft

6. What is the area of each striped triangle?

   A 3 ft^2

   B 1 ft^2

   C $\frac{3}{4}$ ft^2

   D $\frac{1}{4}$ ft^2

7. What is the area of the quilt?

   F 36 ft^2

   G 90 ft^2

   H 96 ft^2

   J 180 ft^2

© Houghton Mifflin Harcourt Publishing Company

Area of Composite Figures
Going Deeper

Essential question: *How can you find the area of a polygon by breaking it into simpler shapes?*

8-5

CC.6.G.1

1 EXPLORE **Area Using Tangrams**

The area of the small square is 1 square unit. Find the area of each of the other tangram pieces.

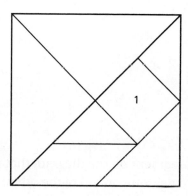

A Place one large triangle on top of the other large triangle. What is true about these two triangles? What does this mean about the areas of these two triangles?

_____

B What is true about the areas of the two small triangles?

_____

C Place the two small triangles on top of the square. Remember that the area of

the square is 1. What is the area of each small triangle? _____ Write this area on the diagram.

D Arrange the square and one of the small triangles as shown.

What is the combined area? _____

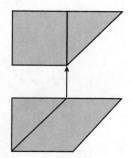

Now place the parallelogram and the other small triangle on top of the combined square and triangle. What is true about the combined area of the parallelogram and one small triangle?

_____

The two small triangles have _____ area. Therefore, the area of the parallelogram is the same as the area of the _____.

Write the area of the parallelogram on the diagram.

1. Complete the rest of the diagram by filling in the remaining areas. Explain how you found your answers.

_____

_____

_____

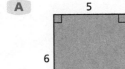

CC.6.G.1

2 EXAMPLE Finding the Area of a Polygon

Find the area of each polygon.

A

```
        5
     ┌──────┐
     │      │ 3
  6  │      └────┐
     │           │
     └───────────┘
          8
```

Step 1 Draw a horizontal line segment on the diagram that divides the polygon into two rectangles, one on top of the other.

What is the length of this segment? _____ Label this length on the diagram.

Step 2 Find the area of the smaller (top) rectangle.

$A = bh = $ ▢ $\cdot$ ▢ $= $ ▢ square units

Step 3 Find the area of the larger (bottom) rectangle.

The base of the larger rectangle is _____.

The height is 6 − ▢ = ▢ .

$A = bh = $ ▢ $\cdot$ ▢ $= $ ▢ square units

Step 4 Add the areas from Steps 2 and 3 to find the total area.

$A = $ ▢ $+$ ▢ $= $ ▢ square units

REFLECT

2a. Redraw the original polygon. Divide the polygon into two rectangles in a different way and use these two rectangles to find the area.

2b. Does the way you divide the original polygon affect the final answer? _____

© Houghton Mifflin Harcourt Publishing Company

B

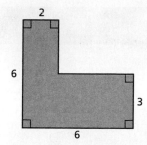

Step 1 On the diagram, form a square with a "missing piece": Extend the top side of the polygon to the right and extend the right side of the polygon up.

What is the side length of this square? _____

The area of the square is [ ] • [ ] = [ ] square units.

Step 2 Find the area of the rectangular "missing piece".

$b = 6 - 2 =$ [ ] $h = 6 -$ [ ] = [ ]

$A = bh =$ [ ] • [ ] = [ ] square units

Step 3 Subtract the area in Step 2 from the area in Step 1.

$A =$ [ ] $-$ [ ] = [ ] square units

C

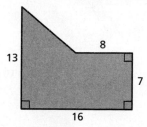

Step 1 Draw a horizontal line segment on the diagram that divides the polygon into a rectangle and a triangle.

Step 2 Find the area of the rectangle.

$A = bh =$ [ ] • [ ] = [ ] square units

Step 3 Find the area of the triangle.

$b = 16 -$ [ ] = [ ] $h = 13 -$ [ ] = [ ]

$A = \frac{1}{2}bh = \frac{1}{2} \cdot$ [ ] • [ ] = [ ] square units

Step 4 Add the areas from Steps 2 and 3 to find the total area.

$A =$ [ ] $+$ [ ] = [ ] square units

TRY THIS!

Find the area of each polygon.

2c.

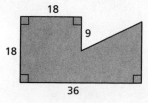

$A =$ _____ square units

2d.

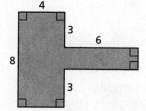

$A =$ _____ square units

Find the area of each polygon.

1.

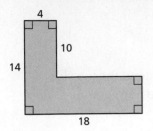

$A =$ _____ square units

2.

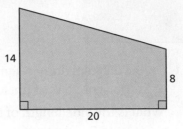

$A =$ _____ square units

3.

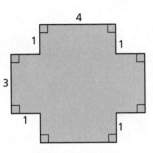

$A =$ _____ square units

4.

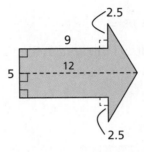

$A =$ _____ square units

5. In Hal's backyard, there is a patio, a walkway, and a garden.

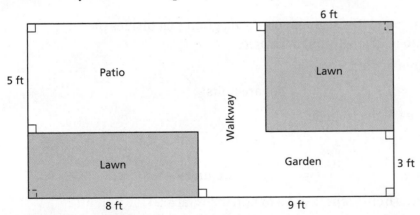

a. Show how to find the total area of the patio, walkway, and garden by adding areas of rectangles.

b. Show how to find the total area of the patio, walkway, and garden by subtracting areas of rectangles.

8-5

Additional Practice

Find the area of each polygon.

1.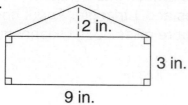

2.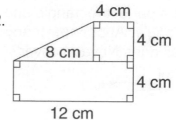

_____

3.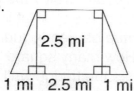

4.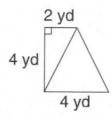

_____

5.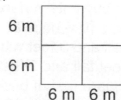

6.

_____

7. Three paintings are shaped like an 8-foot square, a 7-foot by 4-foot rectangle, and a triangle with a 6-foot base and a height of 7 feet. If those paintings are hung together on the outside of a building, how much of the building's wall will they cover altogether?

_____

8. Two diagonals divide a square carpet into 4 congruent triangles. The base of each triangle is 5 feet and the height is 2.5 feet. What is the area of the entire carpet?

_____

Problem Solving

Write the correct answer.

1. The shape of Nevada can almost be divided into a perfect rectangle and a perfect triangle. About how many square miles does Nevada cover?

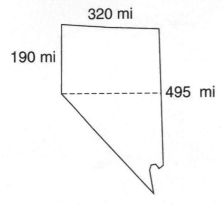

320 mi

190 mi

495 mi

2. The shape of Oklahoma can almost be divided into 2 perfect rectangles and 1 triangle. About how many square miles does Oklahoma cover?

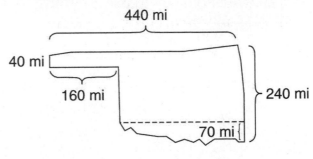

440 mi

40 mi

160 mi

240 mi

70 mi

_____

3. The front side of an apartment building is a rectangle 60 feet tall and 25 feet wide. Bricks cover its surface, except for a door and 10 windows. The door is 7 feet tall and 3 feet wide. Each window is 4 feet tall and 2 feet wide. How many square feet of bricks cover the front side of the building?

_____

4. Each side of a square garden is 12 meters long. A hedge wall 1 meter wide surrounds the garden. What is the area of the entire garden including the hedge wall? How many square meters of land does the hedge wall cover alone?

_____

Circle the letter of the correct answer.

5. A figure is formed by a square and a triangle. Its total area is 32.5 m². The area of the triangle is 7.5 m². What is the length of each side of the square?

   A 5 meters   C 15 meters

   B 25 meters   D 16.25 meters

6. A rectangle is formed by two congruent right triangles. The area of each triangle is 6 in². If each side of the rectangle is a whole number of inches, which of these could not be its perimeter?

   F 26 inches   H 24 inches

   G 16 inches   J 14 inches

Volume of Prisms
Going Deeper

Essential question: *How do you find the volume of a rectangular prism?*

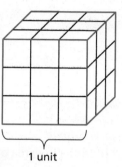

video tutor

CC.6.G.2

1 EXPLORE Volume of a Prism

A cube with edge length 1 unit and volume 1 cubic unit is filled with smaller cubes as shown.

A How many small cubes are there? _____

How does the combined volume of the small cubes compare to the volume of the large cube?

_____

1 unit

Number of small cubes	·	Volume of one small cube	=	Volume of large cube

⬇   ⬇   ⬇

☐ · **?** = ☐

What is the volume of one small cube? _____ cubic unit(s)

B Each edge of the large cube contains _____ small cubes.

Number of small cubes per edge	·	Edge length of one small cube	=	Edge length of large cube

⬇   ⬇   ⬇

☐ · **?** = ☐

What is the edge length of one small cube? _____ unit(s)

C Combine your results from **A** and **B** to complete the following sentence.

Each small cube has edge length _____ unit(s) and volume _____ cubic unit(s).

D Remember that the formula for volume of a cube with edge length ℓ is $V = \ell \cdot \ell \cdot \ell$, or $V = \ell^3$.

Show how to find the volume of one small cube using this formula.

$V =$ _____ $=$ _____

E Several of the small cubes are arranged into a medium-sized cube as shown.

Show two different ways to find the volume of the medium-sized cube.

Volume of a Rectangular Prism

$V = \ell wh$, or $V = Bh$
(where B represents the area of
the prism's base; $B = \ell w$.)

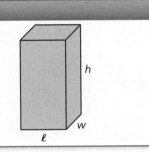

© Houghton Mifflin Harcourt Publishing Company

CC.6.G.2

2 EXAMPLE Finding Volume

Find the volume of the rectangular prism.

$\ell =$ _____ meters $w =$ _____ meters $h =$ _____ meters

$V = \ell\, wh$

= ▢ · ▢ · ▢

= ▢ · ▢ · ▢   *Write each mixed number as an improper fraction.*

= ▢   *Multiply.*

= ▢ cubic meters   *Write as a mixed number in simplest form.*

$4\frac{1}{2}$ m

$2\frac{1}{4}$ m

3 m

REFLECT

2a. Show how to use the formula $V = Bh$ to find the volume.

TRY THIS!

Find the volume of each rectangular prism.

2b.

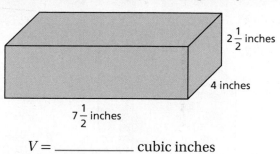

$2\frac{1}{2}$ inches

4 inches

$7\frac{1}{2}$ inches

$V =$ _____ cubic inches

2c. length $= 5\frac{1}{4}$ inches

width $= 3\frac{1}{2}$ inches

height $= 3$ inches

$V =$ _____ cubic inches

CC.6.G.2

3 EXAMPLE **Problem-Solving by Finding Volume**

A rectangular city swimming pool is 25 meters long, $17\frac{1}{2}$ meters wide, and has an average depth of $1\frac{1}{2}$ meters. What is the volume of the pool?

Label the rectangular prism to represent the pool.

$\ell =$ _____ meters $w =$ _____ meters $h =$ _____ meters

$V = \ell wh$

$= \boxed{} \cdot \boxed{} \cdot \boxed{}$

$= \boxed{} \cdot \boxed{} \cdot \boxed{}$ *Write each mixed number as an improper fraction.*

$= \boxed{}$ *Multiply.*

$= \boxed{}$ cubic meters   *Write as a mixed number in simplest form.*

TRY THIS!

3a. Miguel has a turtle aquarium that measures $18\frac{1}{2}$ inches by $12\frac{1}{2}$ inches by 4 inches. What is the volume of the aquarium?

$V =$ _____ cubic inches

REFLECT

3b. How can you use estimation to check the reasonableness of your answer to **3a**?

_____

_____

Find the volume of each rectangular prism.

1.

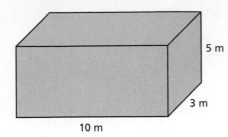

$V =$ _____ cubic meters

2.

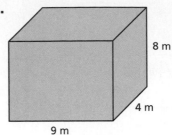

$V =$ _____ cubic meters

3.

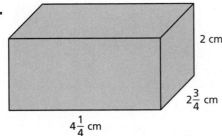

$V =$ _____ cubic centimeters

4.

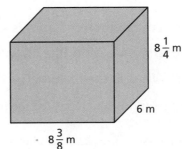

$V =$ _____ cubic meters

5.

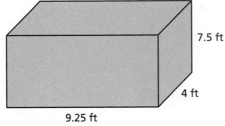

$V =$ _____ cubic feet

6.

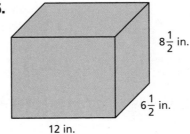

$V =$ _____ cubic inches

7. A block of wood measures 4.5 centimeters by 3.5 centimeters by 7 centimeters. What is the volume of the block of wood?

$V =$ _____ cubic centimeters

8. A restaurant buys a freezer in the shape of a rectangular prism. The dimensions of the freezer are shown. What is the volume of the freezer?

$V =$ _____ cubic inches

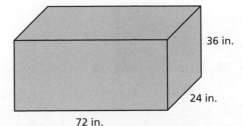

9. Conjecture The length, width, and height of a rectangular prism are doubled. How many times greater is the volume compared to the original prism?

Additional Practice

Find the volume of each rectangular prism.

1. 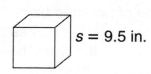 s = 9.5 in.

2. 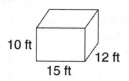 10 ft 12 ft 15 ft

3. 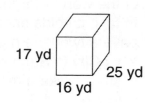 17 yd 25 yd 16 yd

_____

4. 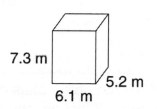 7.3 m 5.2 m 6.1 m

5. 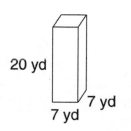 20 yd 7 yd 7 yd

6. 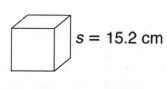 s = 15.2 cm

_____

7. Tim made a toy chest for his little sister's square building blocks. If 6 layers of blocks can fit in the box, and each layer has 15 blocks, how many building blocks can the toy chest hold in all?

_____

8. A rectangular prism's base is 8 feet long. It is $2\frac{1}{2}$ times taller than it is long and $\frac{1}{2}$ as wide as it is tall. What is the volume of that prism?

_____

9. Fawn built a sandbox that is 6 feet long, 5 feet wide, and $\frac{1}{2}$ foot tall. How many cubic feet of sand does she need to fill the box?

_____

10. Unfinished lumber is sold in units called board feet. A board foot is the volume of lumber contained in a board 1 inch thick, 1 foot wide, and 1 foot long. How many cubic inches of wood are in 1 board foot?

_____

Problem Solving

Write the correct answer.

1. At 726 feet tall, Hoover Dam is one of the world's largest concrete dams. In fact, it holds enough concrete to pave a two-lane highway from New York City to San Francisco! The dam is shaped like a rectangular prism with a base 1,224 feet long and 660 feet wide. About how much concrete forms Hoover Dam?

_____

_____

2. The Vietnam Veterans Memorial in Washington, D.C., is a 493.5-foot-long wall made of polished black granite engraved with the names of soldiers who died in the war. The wall is 0.25 feet thick and has an average height of 9 feet. About how many cubic feet of black granite was used in the Vietnam Veterans Memorial?

_____

_____

3. Nikita built a dollhouse in the shape of a rectangular prism. The base of the dollhouse has an area of 12 square feet. If the volume of the dollhouse is 48 ft^3, what is the height of the dollhouse?

_____

_____

4. A box can hold 175 cubic inches of cereal. If the box is 7 inches long and 2.5 inches wide, how tall is it?

_____

_____

Circle the letter of the correct answer.

5. A box can hold 175 cubic inches of cereal. If the box is 7 inches long and 2.5 inches wide, how tall is it?

  A 25 in.

  B 10 in.

  C 17.5 in.

  D 9.5 in.

6. The world's largest chocolate bar is a huge rectangular prism weighing more than a ton! The bar is 9 feet long, 4 feet tall, and 1 foot wide. How many cubic feet of chocolate does it have?

  F 13 ft^3

  G 14 ft^3

  H 36 ft^3

  J 72 ft^3

Surface Area
Going Deeper

Essential question: *How can you use nets to find surface areas?*

A **net** is a two-dimensional pattern of shapes that can be folded into a three-dimensional figure. The shapes in the net become the faces of the three-dimensional figure.

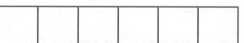
video tutor

CC.6.G.4

1 EXPLORE Nets of a Cube

A Copy the following nets on graph paper and cut them out along the blue lines.

Net A
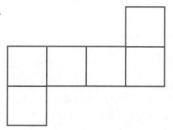

Net B
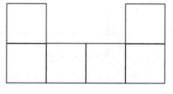

One of these nets can be folded along the black lines to make a cube. Which net will NOT make a cube? _____

B See if you can find another net that can be folded into a cube.

Draw a net that you think will make a cube on your graph paper, and then cut it out. Can you fold it into a cube?

C Compare your results with several of your classmates. How many different nets for a cube did you and your classmates find?

_____

REFLECT

How do you know that each net cannot be folded into a cube without actually cutting and folding it?

1a.

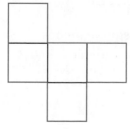

1b.

_____   _____

_____   _____

1c. What shapes will appear in a net for a rectangular prism that is not a cube? How many of these shapes will there be?

_____

The **surface area** of a three-dimensional figure is the sum of the areas of its faces. A net can be helpful when finding surface area.

CC.6.G.4

2 EXPLORE Surface Area of a Rectangular Prism

The gift wrap department of a store has specially sized boxes to wrap sweaters. Use the box's dimensions to label the dimensions of the net. Then find the surface area of the box.

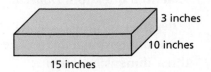

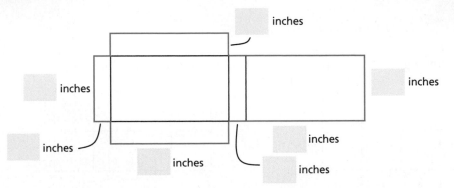

Complete the table to find the surface area.

Face	Base (in.)	Height (in.)	Area (in^2)
Top	15	10	150
Bottom			
Front			
Back			
Right			
Left			
		Total	

The surface area of the sweater box is _____ square inches.

REFLECT

2a. How did you find the area of each face?

_____

2b. If the box had been a cube, how would finding the surface area have been easier?

_____

_____

A **pyramid** is a three-dimensional figure whose base is a polygon and whose other faces are all triangles. A pyramid is named by its base. A pyramid whose base is a triangle is a triangular pyramid. A pyramid whose base is a square is a square pyramid, and so on.

CC.6.G.4

3 EXPLORE   Surface Area of a Pyramid

Find the surface area of the pyramid.

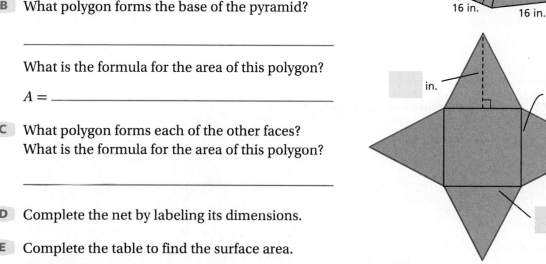

A How many faces does the pyramid have? _____

B What polygon forms the base of the pyramid?

_____

What is the formula for the area of this polygon?

$A =$ _____

C What polygon forms each of the other faces? What is the formula for the area of this polygon?

_____

D Complete the net by labeling its dimensions.

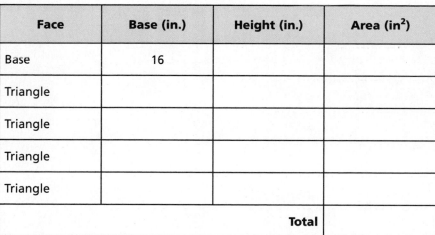

E Complete the table to find the surface area.

Face	Base (in.)	Height (in.)	Area (in²)
Base	16		
Triangle			
Triangle			
Triangle			
Triangle			
		Total	

The surface area of the pyramid is _____ square inches.

REFLECT

3a. What would have been a quicker way to find the combined areas of the triangles?

_____

3b. Surface area is measured in square units. Why are square units used when working with a three-dimensional figure?

_____

PRACTICE

Identify the three-dimensional figure formed by each net.

1.

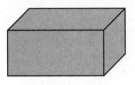

_____

2.

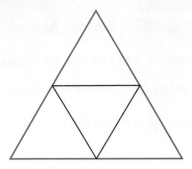

_____

Draw a net for each three-dimensional figure.

3.

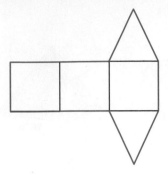

4.

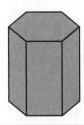

Find the surface area of each figure.

5.

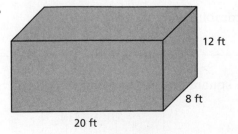

12 ft

8 ft

20 ft

_____ square feet

6.

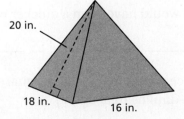

20 in.

18 in.

16 in.

_____ square inches

© Houghton Mifflin Harcourt Publishing Company

Additional Practice

Find the surface area S of each prism.

1.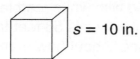

   s = 10 in.

2.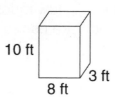

   10 ft   3 ft
      8 ft

_____   _____

Find the surface area S of each pyramid.

3.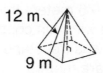

   12 m
   9 m

4.

   16 m
   6 m

_____   _____

5. A rectangular box has no top. It is 6 inches long, 4 inches wide, and 5 inches tall. What is the surface area of the box?

_____

6. The surface area of a rectangular prism is 48 square feet. The area of its front is 4 square feet, and the area of one side is 10 square feet. What is the area of the top of the prism?

_____

Problem Solving

Write the correct answer.

1. Tara made fuzzy cubes to hang in her car. Each side of the 2 cubes is 4 inches long. How much fuzzy material did Tara use to make both cubes?

2. The top of the Washington Monument is a square pyramid covered with white marble. Each triangular face is 58 feet tall and 34 feet wide. About how many square feet of marble covers the top of the monument? (The base is hollow.)

3. The Parthenon, a famous temple in Greece, is surrounded by large stone columns. Each column is 10.4 meters tall and has a diameter of 1.9 meters. To the nearest whole square meter, what is the surface area of each column (not including the top and bottom)?

4. The tablet that the Statue of Liberty holds is 7.2 meters long, 4.1 meters wide, and 0.6 meters thick. The tablet is covered with thin copper sheeting. If the tablet was freestanding, how many square meters of copper covers the statue's tablet?

Circle the letter of the correct answer.

5. The largest Egyptian pyramid is called the Great Pyramid of Khufu. It has a 756-foot square base and a slant height of 481 feet. What is the total surface area of the faces of the Pyramid of Khufu?

   A 727,272 ft^2

   B 727,722 ft^2

   C 727,727 ft^2

   D 772,272 ft^2

6. A glass triangular prism for a telescope is 5.5 inches tall. Each side of the triangular base is 4 inches long, with a 3-inch height. How much glass covers the surface of the prism?

   F 6 in^2

   G 12 in^2

   H 39 in^2

   J 78 in^2

Problem Solving Connections

Something's Fishy As a birthday surprise for their son Wyatt, Mr. and Mrs. Watson plan to purchase a large aquarium, its accessories, and all of Wyatt's favorite species of tropical fish. Once they have decided on an aquarium, Mr. Watson will build a stand for it, and then they will decide how many fish to buy.

COMMON
CORE

CC.6.G.1
CC.6.G.2
CC.6.G.3
CC.6.G.4

1 Volume

After looking at several different aquariums, Mr. and Mrs. Watson have decided to purchase either tank A or tank B.

A Find the volume of tank A.

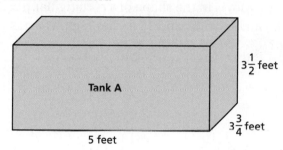

Tank A

$3\frac{1}{2}$ feet

$3\frac{3}{4}$ feet

5 feet

B Find the volume of tank B.

Tank B

3 feet

$3\frac{3}{4}$ feet

$5\frac{1}{2}$ feet

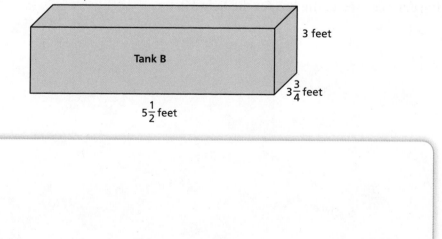

C The Watsons decide to purchase the tank with the greater volume. Which tank is this? How much greater is its volume than that of the other tank?

D A box of fish food is 2.25 inches long, 1.5 inches wide, and 4 inches tall. What is the volume of the box of fish food?

E The filter system for the aquarium is in the shape of a rectangular prism. It measures $8\frac{1}{2}$ inches long, $8\frac{1}{2}$ inches wide, and 15 inches high. What is the volume of the filter system?

2 Surface Area

Mrs. Watson is wrapping the accessories for the aquarium. She will find the surface area of each box to determine how much gift wrap she needs.

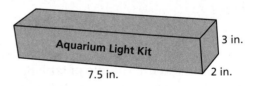

Aquarium Light Kit
3 in.
7.5 in.
2 in.

A Find the surface area of the box for the light kit.

B Find the surface area of the box for the heater.

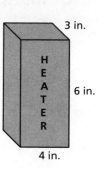

3 in.

HEATER

6 in.

4 in.

3 Area and Perimeter

A A rectangular backdrop for the aquarium measures 5 feet by 3.5 feet. What is the area that the back drop will cover?

B Mr. Watson has a solid rectangular piece of birch plywood for the top of the aquarium stand. The plywood is 6 feet long and $4\frac{3}{4}$ feet wide. He plans to attach decorative trim around the front and side edges. How much trim does he need?

C Mr. Watson removes a rectangle from the top back edge of the stand, as shown, to allow space for electrical cords. Will the aquarium still fit on the stand in front of this space? Explain.

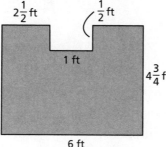

$2\frac{1}{2}$ ft $\frac{1}{2}$ ft

1 ft

$4\frac{3}{4}$ ft

6 ft

D What is the area of the top of the stand? Explain how you found your answer.

E Find the area of the top of the stand using a different method than the one you used in **D** .

4 Answer the Question

A One gallon of water fills 231 cubic inches of space. About how many gallons of water are needed to fill the aquarium? (*Hint*: There are 1,728 cubic inches in a cubic foot.)

B It is recommended that there be at least 12 gallons of water in the aquarium for each fish. Using this rule, what is the maximum number of fish the Watsons could purchase for the aquarium?

C If the Watsons had purchased the smaller tank, what would be the maximum number of fish they could purchase?

Performance Task

COMMON CORE

6.RP.3d
6.G.1
6.G.2
6.G.4

⭐ **1.** Ahmed and Karina are making scenery of the great pyramids out of cardboard for a school play. The diagram shows the measurements of the piece of scenery.

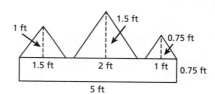

How many square feet of cardboard is in the completed piece? Show your work.

⭐ **2.** How many $1\frac{1}{3}$ cup servings are in 2 gallons of lemonade? Show your work.

⭐⭐ **3.** Miranda designs a purse in the shape of a triangular prism. The dimensions of the purse are shown in the diagram.

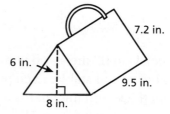

  a. Draw a net of the triangular prism and label the dimensions. Do not include the handle in your net.

© Houghton Mifflin Harcourt Publishing Company

b. In square inches, how much leather does Miranda need to cover the purse, not including the handle? Show your work.

c. What is the volume of the purse? Show your work.

4. Li is making a stand to display a sculpture made in art class. The stand will measure 45 cm wide, 25 cm long, and 1.2 m high.

   a. What is the volume of the stand? Write your answer in cubic centimeters.

   b. Li needs to fill the stand with sand so that it's heavy and stable. Each piece of wood is 1 cm thick, and the boards are put together as shown in the figure. How many cubic centimeters of sand does she need? Explain how you found your answer.

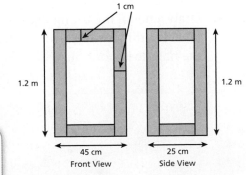

Name _____ Class _____ Date _____

SELECTED RESPONSE

1. New tiles are being laid in the school hallway. The tiles measure 1 foot by 1 foot. The hallway is 75 feet long and 9 feet wide. How many tiles will be needed to cover the floor of the hallway?

A. 84 tiles   **C.** 675 tiles

B. 168 tiles   **D.** 6,075 tiles

2. A triangular street sign has a base of 30 inches and a height of 24 inches.

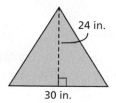

What is the area of the street sign?

F. 54 square inches

G. 114 square inches

H. 360 square inches

J. 720 square inches

3. Martha is putting a wallpaper border along the tops of the four walls in her bedroom. The room is a rectangle that measures 12 feet by 10 feet. One package of wallpaper border is 9 feet long. How many packages does Martha need?

A. 2 packages   **C.** 5 packages

B. 4 packages   **D.** 14 packages

4. A regular polygon has a perimeter of 48 feet. Each side of the polygon measures 6 feet. What is the name of this polygon?

F. triangle   **H.** hexagon

G. square   **J.** octagon

5. A triangular pennant has a base of 12 inches and a height of 18 inches. What is the area of the pennant?

A. 30 square inches

B. 66 square inches

C. 108 square inches

D. 216 square inches

6. Which statement about the square and the rectangle is correct?

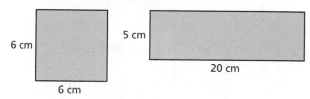

F. They have the same perimeter and the same area.

G. They have the same perimeter but different areas.

H. They have different perimeters but the same area.

J. They have different perimeters and different areas.

7. Katrina is making a wall hanging in the shape of a trapezoid.

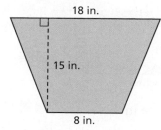

What is the area of Katrina's wall hanging?

A. 144 square inches

B. 195 square inches

C. 270 square inches

D. 390 square inches

8. The length of a poster is 16 inches.

What is the length of this poster in centimeters?

Length
1 inch = 2.54 centimeters

F. 6.30 centimeters

G. 13.46 centimeters

H. 18.54 centimeters

J. 40.64 centimeters

9. What three-dimensional figure will be formed from the net?

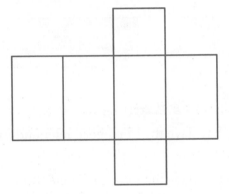

A. triangular prism

B. square pyramid

C. rectangular prism

D. triangular pyramid

10. What is the surface area of the rectangular prism?

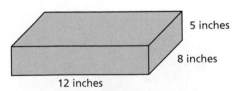

5 inches

8 inches

12 inches

F. 192 square inches

G. 272 square inches

H. 392 square inches

J. 480 square inches

CONSTRUCTED RESPONSE

11. The volume of a rectangular prism is 810 cubic centimeters. The length is 18 centimeters and the width is 9 centimeters. What is the height? Explain how you found your answer.

_____

_____

12. Paula's dog, Toby, weighs 95 pounds.

Weight/Mass
1 pound ≈ 0.454 kilogram

a. To find Toby's weight in kilograms, what conversion factor should you use?

_____

b. Explain why multiplying a quantity by a conversion factor does not change the quantity's value.

_____

_____

_____

c. Find Toby's weight in kilograms.

_____

13. Draw a net of a triangular pyramid.

Integers and the Coordinate Plane

Chapter Focus

You will graph integers and their opposites and find and compare absolute values. You will also compare and order positive and negative integers and rational numbers. The coordinate plane will be extended to include all four quadrants. You will locate and name points in the coordinate plane, solve problems by drawing polygons in the coordinate plane, and identify the reflection of a point across one or both axes in the coordinate plane.

Chapter at a Glance

COMMON
CORE

Lesson	Standards for Mathematical Content
9-1 Integers and Absolute Value	**CC.6.NS.5, CC.6.NS.6a**
9-2 Comparing and Ordering Integers	**CC.6.NS.7a, CC.6.NS.7b**
9-3 The Coordinate Plane	**CC.6.NS.6b, CC.6.NS.8**
9-4 Polygons in the Coordinate Plane	**CC.6.NS.8, CC.6.G.3**
9-5 Transformations in the Coordinate Plane	**CC.6.NS.6b**
Problem Solving Connections	
Performance Task	
Assessment Readiness	

CHAPTER 9

Unpacking the Standards

Understanding the standards and the vocabulary terms in the standards will help you know exactly what you are expected to learn in this chapter.

COMMON CORE **CC.6.NS.6c**

Find and position integers and other rational numbers on a horizontal or vertical number line diagram; find and position pairs of integers and other rational numbers on a coordinate plane.

Key Vocabulary

integer *(entero)* A member of the set of whole numbers and their opposites.

rational number *(número racional)* A number that can be written in the form $\frac{a}{b}$, where a and b are integers and $b \neq 0$.

What It Means to You

You will graph an ordered pair of rational numbers in a coordinate plane.

EXAMPLE

Graph each point on a coordinate plane.

$$P(-3,-2) \qquad R(0,4) \qquad M(3,-4)$$

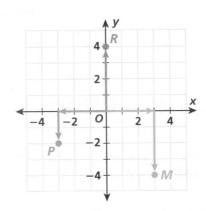

COMMON CORE **CC.6.NS.7a**

Interpret statements of inequality as statements about the relative position of two numbers on a number line diagram.

Key Vocabulary

inequality *(desigualdad)* A mathematical sentence that shows the relationship between quantities that are not equal.

What It Means to You

You will learn the relative positions on a number line of two unequal numbers.

EXAMPLE

At a golf tournament, David scored +6, Celia scored −16, and Xavier scored −4. One of these three players was the winner of the tournament. Who won the tournament?

The winner will be the player with the lowest score. Draw a number line and graph each player's score.

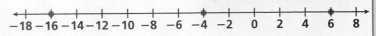

Celia's score, −16, is the farthest to the left, so it is the lowest score. Celia won the tournament.

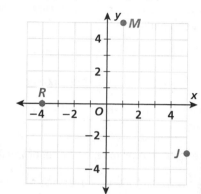

CC.6.NS.6b

Understand signs of numbers in ordered pairs as indicating locations in quadrants of the coordinate plane; recognize that when two ordered pairs differ only by signs, the locations of the points are related by reflections across one or both axes.

Key Vocabulary

quadrant *(cuadrante)* The *x*- and *y*-axes divide the coordinate plane into four regions. Each region is called a quadrant.

coordinate plane *(plano cartesiano)* A plane formed by the intersection of a horizontal number line called the *x*-axis and a vertical number line called the *y*-axis.

ordered pair *(par ordenado)* A pair of numbers that can be used to locate a point on a coordinate plane.

reflection *(reflexión)* A transformation of a figure that flips the figure across a line.

axes *(ejes)* The two perpendicular lines of a coordinate plane that intersect at the origin.

What It Means to You

You will learn to graph ordered pairs of positive and negative numbers on the coordinate plane and identify the quadrant in which a point is located.

EXAMPLE

Name the quadrant where each point is located.

$M(1, 5)$ $J(5, -3)$ $R(-4, 0)$

$M(1, 5)$	Quadrant I
$J(5, -3)$	Quadrant IV
$R(-4, 0)$	*x*-axis, no quadrant

CC.6.G.3

Draw polygons in the coordinate plane given coordinates for the vertices; use coordinates to find the length of a side joining points with the same first coordinate or the same second coordinate. Apply these techniques in the context of solving real-world and mathematical problems.

Key Vocabulary

polygon *(polígono)* A closed plane figure formed by three or more line segments that intersect only at their endpoints.

coordinates *(coordenadas)* The numbers of an ordered pair that locate a point on a coordinate graph.

What It Means to You

You will graph polygons in the coordinate plane, given coordinates for the vertices.

EXAMPLE

Graph the triangle with vertices $F(-1\frac{1}{2}, -2)$,

$G(1, 3)$, and $H(3\frac{1}{2}, -2)$.

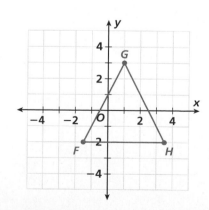

Key Vocabulary

absolute value *(valor absoluto)* The distance of a number from zero on a number line; shown by | |.

axes *(ejes)* The two perpendicular lines of a coordinate plane that intersect at the origin.

coordinates *(coordinadas)* The numbers of an ordered pair that locate a point on a coordinate graph.

coordinate plane *(plano cartesiano)* A plane formed by the intersection of a horizontal number line called the *x*-axis and a vertical number line called the *y*-axis.

heptagon *(heptágono)* A seven-sided polygon.

hexagon *(hexágono)* A six-sided polygon.

inequality *(desigualdad)* A mathematical sentence that shows the relationship between quantities that are not equal.

integer *(entero)* A member of the set of whole numbers and their opposites.

negative number *(número negativo)* A number less than zero.

octagon *(octágono)* An eight-sided polygon.

opposites *(opuestos)* Two numbers that are an equal distance from zero on a number line.

origin *(origen)* The point where the *x*-axis and *y*-axis intersect on the coordinate plane; (0, 0).

pentagon *(pentágono)* A five-sided polygon.

positive number *(número positivo)* A number greater than zero.

quadrant *(cuadrante)* The *x*- and *y*-axes divide the coordinate plane into four regions. Each region is called a quadrant.

x-axis *(eje x)* The horizontal axis on a coordinate plane.

x-coordinate *(coordenada x)* The first number in an ordered pair; it tells the distance to move right or left from the origin, (0, 0).

y-axis *(eje y)* The vertical axis on a coordinate plane.

y-coordinate *(coordenada y)* The second number in an ordered pair; it tells the distance to move up or down from the origin, (0, 0).

CHAPTER 9

Integers and Absolute Value
Extension: Comparing Absolute Values

Essential question: *How do you graph integers and find absolute value?*

video tutor

Positive numbers are numbers greater than 0. They are located to the right of 0 on a number line. Positive numbers can be written with or without a plus sign; for example, 3 is the same as +3.

Negative numbers are numbers less than 0. They are located to the left of 0 on a number line. Negative numbers must always be written with a negative sign.

The number 0 is neither positive nor negative.

CC.6.NS.5

1 EXAMPLE Positive and Negative Numbers

The elevation of a location describes its height above or below sea level, which has elevation 0. Elevations below sea level are represented by negative numbers, and elevations above sea level are represented by positive numbers.

The table shows the elevations of several locations in a state park.

A Graph the locations on the number line according to their elevations.

Location	Little Butte A	Cradle Creek B	Dinosaur Valley C	Mesa Ridge D	Juniper Trail E
Elevation (ft)	5	−5	−8.5	8	−3

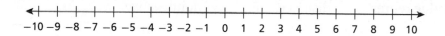

B What point on the number line represents sea level? _____

C Which location is closest to sea level? How do you know?

_____

D Is the location in **C** above or below sea level? _____

E Which two locations are the same distance from sea level? Are these locations above or below sea level?

_____

F Which location has the least elevation? How do you know?

_____

Two numbers are **opposites** if, on a number line, they are the same distance from 0 but on different sides of 0. For example, 5 and –5 are opposites; 2.15 and –2.15 are also opposites. 0 is its own opposite.

Integers are the set of all whole numbers and their opposites.

2 EXPLORE CC.6.NS.6a   Opposites

On graph paper, use a ruler or straightedge to draw a number line. Label the number line with each integer from –10 to 10. Fold your number line in half so that the crease goes through 0. Numbers that line up after folding the number line are opposites.

A Use your number line to find the opposites of 7, –4, 1, and 9. _____

B How does your number line show that 0 is its own opposite?

_____

C What is the opposite of 8.5? _____

D What is the opposite of the opposite of 3? _____

The **absolute value** of a number is the number's distance from 0 on the number line. For example, the absolute value of -3 is 3 because -3 is 3 units from 0. The absolute value of -3 is written $|-3|$.

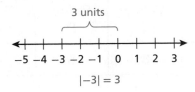

$$|-3| = 3$$

Because absolute value represents a distance, it is always nonnegative.

3 EXAMPLE CC.6.NS.7c   Finding Absolute Value

Graph the following numbers on the number line. Then use your number line to find each absolute value.

$$-7 \qquad 5 \qquad 7 \qquad -2 \qquad 4 \qquad -4$$

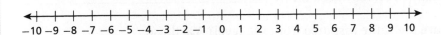

A $|-7| = $ _____ **B** $|5| = $ _____ **C** $|7| = $ _____

D $|-2| = $ _____ **E** $|4| = $ _____ **F** $|-4| = $ _____

3a. Which pairs of numbers in ❸ have the same absolute value? How are these numbers related?

_____

3b. Do you think a number's absolute value can be 0? If so, which number(s) have an absolute value of 0? If not, explain.

_____

In real-world situations, absolute values are often used instead of negative numbers. For example, if Susan charges a total of $25 on her credit card, we can say that Susan has a balance of −$25. However, we usually say that Susan owes $25.

CC.6.NS.7d

4 EXPLORE   **Comparing Absolute Values**

Maria, Susan, George, and Antonio received their credit card statements. The amounts owed are shown.

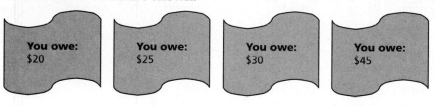

| You owe: $20 | You owe: $25 | You owe: $30 | You owe: $45 |

_____ _____ _____ _____

Answer the following questions. When you have finished, you will have enough clues to match each statement with the correct person.

Remember: When someone owes a positive amount of money, this means that he or she has a *negative* balance.

A Maria's credit card balance is less than −$30. Does Maria owe more than $30 or less than $30? _____

B Susan's credit card balance is greater than −$25. Does Susan owe more than $25 or less than $25? _____

C George's credit card balance is $5 less than Susan's balance. Does George owe more than Susan or less than Susan? _____

D Antonio owes $15 less than Maria owes. This means that Antonio's balance is _____ than Maria's balance.

E Write each person's name underneath his or her credit card statement.

REFLECT

4. Use absolute value to describe the relationship between a negative credit card balance and the amount owed.

_____

PRACTICE

1. The table shows winter temperatures of several world cities. Graph the cities on the number line according to their temperatures.

City	Anchorage, AK, USA *F*	Fargo, ND, USA *G*	Oslo, Norway *H*	St. Petersburg, Russia *I*	Helsinki, Finland *J*	Budapest, Hungary *K*
Temperature (°F)	−4	9	−6	−10	7	6

2a. Graph and label the following points on the number line.

A. −2   **B.** 9.5   **C.** −8   **D.** −9.5   **E.** 5   **F.** 8

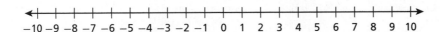

b. Which points represent integers? _____

c. Which pairs of points represent opposites? _____

Write the absolute value of each integer.

3. $|9| =$ _____   4. $|−89| =$ _____   5. $|64| =$ _____

6. $|−105| =$ _____   7. $|−12| =$ _____   8. $|50| =$ _____

9. If a number is _____, then the number is equal to its absolute value. If a number is _____, then the number is less than its absolute value.

10. Negative numbers are less than positive numbers. Does this mean that the absolute value of a negative number must be less than the absolute value of a positive number? Explain.

_____

_____

Additional Practice

Name a positive or negative number to represent each situation.

1. depositing $85 in a bank account

_____

2. riding an elevator down 3 floors

_____

3. the foundation of a house sinking 5 inches

_____

4. a temperature of 98° above zero

_____

Graph each integer and its opposite on the number line.

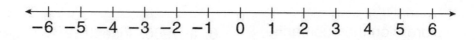

5. –2

_____

6. +3

_____

7. –5

_____

8. +1

_____

Use the number line from the previous exercises to find the absolute value of each integer.

9. –3

_____

10. 4

_____

11. –6

_____

12. –4

_____

13. The highest point in the state of Louisiana is Driskall Mountain. It rises 535 feet above sea level. Write the elevation of Driskall Mountain as an integer.

_____

14. The lowest point in the state of Louisiana is New Orleans. This city's elevation is 8 feet below sea level. Write the elevation of New Orleans as an integer.

_____

Problem Solving

Write the correct answer.

1. The element mercury is used in thermometers because it expands as it is heated. Mercury melts at 38°F below zero. Write this temperature as an integer.

_____

2. Denver, Colorado, earned the nickname "Mile High City" because of its elevation of 5,280 feet above sea level. Write Denver's elevation as an integer in feet and miles.

_____

3. The lowest temperature recorded in San Francisco was 20°F. Buffalo's lowest recorded temperature was the opposite of San Francisco's. What was Buffalo's record temperature?

_____

4. Antarctica holds the record for the lowest temperature recorded on Earth. That temperature in degrees Fahrenheit is –128 degrees below zero. What is Earth's lowest recorded temperature written as an integer?

_____

5. In 1960, explorers on the submarine _Trieste 2_ set the world record for the deepest dive. The ship reached 35,798 feet below sea level. Write this depth as an integer.

_____

6. In 1960, Joseph W. Kittinger, Jr., set the record for the highest parachute jump. He jumped from an air balloon at 102,800 feet above sea level. Write this altitude as an integer.

_____

Circle the letter of the correct answer.

7. Which situation cannot be represented by the integer –10?

   A an elevation of 10 feet below sea level

   B a temperature increase of 10°F

   C a golf score of 10 under par

   D a bank withdrawal of $10

8. Paper was invented in China one thousand, nine hundred years ago. Which integer represents this date?

   F 1,900

   G 900

   H –1,900

   J –1,000

9. The elevation of the Dead Sea is about 1,310 feet below sea level. Which integer represents this elevation?

   A –1,310

   B –131

   C 131

   D 1,310

10. The quarterback had a 10-yard loss and then a 25-yard gain. Which integer represents a 25-yard gain?

   F –25

   G –10

   H 25

   J 10

9-2

Comparing and Ordering Integers
Going Deeper

Essential question: *How do you compare and order positive and negative numbers?*

video tutor

CC.6.NS.7a

1 EXPLORE   **Comparing Positive and Negative Integers**

The Westfield soccer league ranks its teams using a number called the "win/loss combined record." A team with more wins than losses will have a positive combined record, and a team with fewer wins than losses will have a negative combined record. The table shows the total win/loss combined record for each team at the end of the season.

Team	Sharks A	Jaguars B	Badgers C	Tigers D	Cougars E	Hawks F	Wolves G
Win/Loss Combined Record	−4	3	−7	−8	−1	−5	7

A   On the number line, graph a point for each team according to its win/loss combined record.

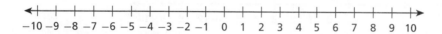

B   Which team had the best record in the league? How do you know?

_____

_____

C   Which team had the worst record? How do you know?

_____

_____

REFLECT

1.   How would you evaluate the Westfield league as a whole? Explain.

_____

_____

_____

© Houghton Mifflin Harcourt Publishing Company

When you read a number line from left to right, the numbers are in order from least to greatest.

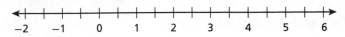

2 **E X P L O R E** Ordering Rational Numbers

Graph the following rational numbers on the number line:

1.6   3.8   4.9   2.0   5.3   −1.2

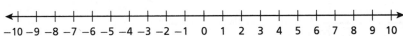

To list the numbers in order from least to greatest, read the numbers on the number line from left to right.

_____

A Which number is third least? _____

B Which number is second greatest? _____

TRY THIS!

Graph each set of numbers on a number line. Then list the numbers in order from least to greatest.

2a. 5.6   −8   3.1   −4   7   −2

```
←+—+—+—+—+—+—+—+—+—+—+—+—+—+—+—+—+—+—+—+—+→
 −10 −9 −8 −7 −6 −5 −4 −3 −2 −1  0  1  2  3  4  5  6  7  8  9  10
```

_____

2b. −14   12   −7   11   18   −2   1   5   −8

```
←+—+—+—+—+—+—+—+—+—+—+—+—+—+→
 −20  −16   −12  −8   −4    0    4    8   12   16   20
```

_____

REFLECT

2c. In a given list of numbers, the greatest number is negative. What can you say about the numbers in this list?

_____

An **inequality** is a statement that two quantities are not equal. The symbols < and > are used to write inequalities.

- The symbol > means "is greater than."
- The symbol < means "is less than."

You can use a number line to help write an inequality.

3 EXAMPLE Writing Inequalities

**On December 18, the high temperature in Portland, Oregon, was 42 °F.
On January 18, the high temperature was 28 °F. Which day was warmer?**

Graph 42 and 28 on the number line.

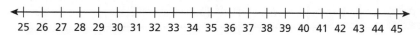

25 26 27 28 29 30 31 32 33 34 35 36 37 38 39 40 41 42 43 44 45

A 42 is to the right of 28 on the number line.

This means that 42 is greater than / less than 28.

Use < or > to complete the inequality: 42 [ ] 28.

B 28 is to the left of 42 on the number line.

This means that 28 is greater than / less than 42.

Use < or > to complete the inequality: 28 [ ] 42.

The temperature was warmer on _____.

C In **A** and **B**, you wrote two inequalities to compare 42 and 28.
Write two inequalities to compare −6 and 7. _____

D Write two inequalities to compare −9 and −4. _____

TRY THIS!

Compare. Write > or <. Use the number line to help you, if necessary.

3a. −10 [ ] −2   **3b.** −6 [ ] 6   **3c.** −7.1 [ ] −8.3

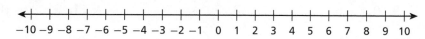

−10 −9 −8 −7 −6 −5 −4 −3 −2 −1 0 1 2 3 4 5 6 7 8 9 10

3d. Write two inequalities to compare −2 and −18. _____

3e. Write two inequalities to compare 39 and −39. _____

REFLECT

3f. Negative numbers are _____ than positive numbers.

3g. 0 is _____ than all negative numbers.

3h. What is the greatest negative integer? _____

3i. Is there a greatest positive integer? If so, what is it? If not, why not?

_____

_____

3j. What is the least nonnegative number? _____

403

1a. On the number line, graph a point for each of the following cities according to their temperatures.

City	A	B	C	D	E
Temperature (°F)	−9	10	−2	0	4

b. Which city was coldest? _____

c. Which city was warmest? _____

List the numbers in order from least to greatest.

2. 4, −6, 0, 8, −9, 1, −3

_____

3. 31, 5, 7, −0.1, 1, 1.5, −9

_____

4. −80, 88, 96, −14, 75, 59, −32

_____

5. −65, 34, 7.6, −13, 55, 62.5, −7.6

_____

6. Write two inequalities to compare −17 and −22. _____

7. Write two inequalities to compare 16 and −2. _____

Compare. Write < or >.

8. 9 ▢ 2   **9.** 0 ▢ 6   **10.** 3 ▢ −7   **11.** 5 ▢ −10

12. −1 ▢ −3   **13.** -8 ▢ −4   **14.** −4.5 ▢ 1   **15.** −2 ▢ −2.5

16. Which costs more, a fruit cup or veggies and dip? Use the given prices to write an inequality that shows your answer.

_____

Fruit cup	$2.49
Veggies and dip	$2.86
Yogurt	$1.97
Fruit smoothie	$3.83
Pretzels	$1.71

17. Which costs less, pretzels or yogurt? Use the given prices to write an inequality that shows your answer.

_____

18. Error Analysis At 9:00 P.M., the outside temperature was −3 °F. The newscaster says that the temperature will be −12 °F by midnight. Bethany says, "It will be warmer outside by midnight." Why is Bethany incorrect?

_____

Additional Practice

Use the number line to compare each pair of numbers.
Write < or >.

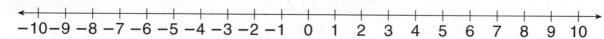

-10 -9 -8 -7 -6 -5 -4 -3 -2 -1 0 1 2 3 4 5 6 7 8 9 10

1. 10 ___ -2

2. $-\dfrac{1}{4}$ ___ $-\dfrac{1}{8}$

3. -5 ___ 0

4. -7 ___ 6

5. 3.2 ___ -2.3

6. -8 ___ -10

Order the numbers in each set from least to greatest.

7. 5, -2, 6

8. 0, 9, -3

9. 2.921, 3.02, 2.901, 2.91

_____

_____

_____

10. -8, -9, 9

11. -5, $-\dfrac{7}{8}$, -4.3, -1

12. -4, -7, -2

_____

_____

_____

Order the numbers in each set from greatest to least.

13. 8, -6, 4

14. -2, 1, 2

15. 7.1, -7, 8

_____

_____

_____

16. $\dfrac{1}{3}, \dfrac{1}{9}, \dfrac{3}{5}, \dfrac{3}{4}$

17. -12, 2, 1

18. -10, -12, -11

_____

_____

_____

19. The lowest point in the Potomac River is 1 foot above sea level.
The lowest point in the Colorado River is 70 feet above sea
level. The lowest point in the Delaware River is sea level. Write
the names of these three rivers in order from the lowest to the
highest elevation.

_____

20. Tina read $\dfrac{2}{3}$ of a book on Monday, $\dfrac{1}{12}$ of the same book on

Tuesday, and $\dfrac{1}{4}$ of the same book on Wednesday. On what day

did Tina read most of the book?

Problem Solving

Use the table below to answer each question.

Continental Elevation Facts

Continent	Highest Point	Elevation (ft) above sea level	Lowest Point	Elevation (ft) below sea level
Africa	Mount Kilimanjaro	19,340	Lake Assal	−512
Antarctica	Vinson Massif	16,066	Bentley Subglacial Trench	−8,327
Asia	Mount Everest	29,035	Dead Sea	−1,349
Australia	Mount Kosciusko	7,310	Lake Eyre	−52
Europe	Mount Elbrus	18,510	Caspian Sea	−92
North America	Mount McKinley	20,320	Death Valley	−282
South America	Mount Aconcagua	22,834	Valdes Peninsula	−131

1. What is the highest point on Earth? What is its elevation?

_____

_____

2. What is the lowest point on Earth? What is its elevation?

_____

_____

3. Which point on Earth is higher, Mount Elbrus or Mount Kilimanjaro?

_____

4. Which point on Earth is lower, the Caspian Sea or Lake Eyre?

_____

Circle the letter of the correct answer.

The table shows the elevations of several locations in a county park. Use the table for 5–6.

Location	Cedar Creek	Buffalo Butte	Yoakum Valley	Holly Field	East Ridge
Elevation (ft)	−6	6.2	−10.3	2	12

5. Which location has a higher elevation than Buffalo Butte?

A Cedar Creek

B East Ridge

C Holly Field

D Yoakum Valley

6. List elevations in order from greatest to least.

F −6, −10.3, 2, 6.2, 12

G −10.3, −6, 2, 6.2, 12

H 12, 6.2, 2, −6, −10.3

J 12, 6.2, 2, −10.3, −6

The Coordinate Plane
Going Deeper

Essential question: *How do you locate and name points in the coordinate plane?*

video tutor

CC.6.NS.6c

1 EXPLORE   Parts of the Coordinate Plane

A Write the definitions of these words from previous lessons in your own words.

coordinate grid _____

_____

_____

point _____

_____

ordered pair _____

_____

_____

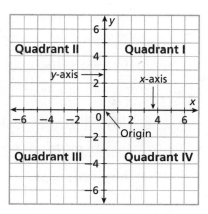

B A **coordinate plane** is formed by two number lines that intersect at right angles. The two number lines are called **axes**.

Use the coordinate plane shown above to write definitions of these words.

x-axis _____

y-axis _____

quadrant _____

origin _____

C The numbers in an ordered pair are called **coordinates.** In the ordered pairs (3, 4), (–2, 5), and (0, –6), the blue numbers are the x-coordinates. Write the definitions of these words in your own words.

x-coordinate _____

y-coordinate _____

The *x*-coordinate tells how far to the right (positive) or left (negative) the point is located from the origin. The *y*-coordinate tells how far up (positive) or down (negative) the point is located from the origin.

CC.6.NS.6b

2 EXAMPLE   Identifying Coordinates and Quadrants

Identify the coordinates of point *D* and name the quadrant where the point is located.

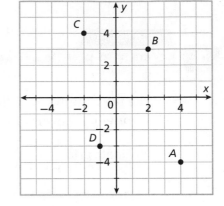

Step 1 Start at the origin. Count horizontally along the *x*-axis until you are directly above point *D*.

How many units did you count? _____

Did you move left (negative) or right (positive) from the origin? _____

The *x*-coordinate of *D* is _____.

Step 2 Now count vertically until you reach point *D*.

How many units did you count? _____

Did you move up (positive) or down (negative)? _____

The *y*-coordinate of *D* is _____.

The coordinates of *D* are (▢ , ▢).

D is in Quadrant ▢ .

TRY THIS!

Identify the coordinates of each point in the coordinate plane and name the quadrant where each point is located.

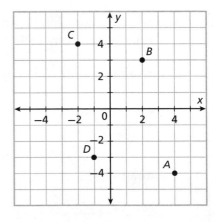

2a. *A* _____

2b. *B* _____

2c. *C* _____

2d. *D* _____

REFLECT

2e. If both coordinates of a point are negative, in which quadrant is the point located? _____

2f. Describe the coordinates of all points in Quadrant I.

_____

Points that are located on the axes are not located in any quadrant. Points on the *x*-axis have a *y*-coordinate of 0, and points on the *y*-axis have an *x*-coordinate of 0.

CC.6.NS.8

3 EXAMPLE   Graphing Points on the Coordinate Plane

Leonardo and Christie walk to school each morning. They pass a post office, a coffee shop, and a church on the way. After school, they often study at the library or meet friends at an arcade before walking home.

The coordinate plane represents a map of Leonardo and Christie's town. The post office is located at (0, 3). Graph and label this location on the coordinate plane.

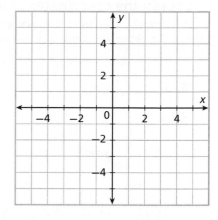

Start at the origin.

The first coordinate of the ordered pair tells how many units to move left or right. How many units will you move?

_____

The second coordinate of the ordered pair tells how many units to move up or down. How many units will you move? _____

Will you move up or down? How do you know? _____

The point that represents the post office is located on the _____.

TRY THIS!

Graph and label each location on the coordinate plane.

3a. Home: $(-4, 2)$ **3b.** Coffee shop: $(3, 2)$ **3c.** Church: $(5, -2)$

3d. School: $(4, -5)$ **3e.** Library: $(-4, -5)$ **3f.** Arcade: $(-2, 0)$

REFLECT

3g. What are the coordinates of the origin? _____

3h. What is true about the *x*-coordinate of any point that lies on the

y-axis? _____

_____

3i. Explain why the ordered pairs (3, 2) and (2, 3) represent different locations on the

coordinate plane. _____

_____

_____

3j. Describe the location of a point that has a negative *x*-coordinate and a positive

y-coordinate. _____

_____

Use the coordinate plane for 1–10.

Identify the coordinates of each point and name the quadrant in which it is located.

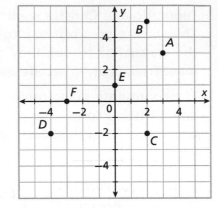

1. A _____

2. B _____

3. C _____

4. D _____

5. E _____

6. F _____

Graph each point on the coordinate plane.

7. $(2, -4)$

8. $(-4, 4)$

9. $(3, 0)$

10. $(0, -5)$

11. Circle the point(s) located in Quadrant III.

$(6, 4)$ $\qquad$ $(-5, -1)$ $\qquad$ $(3.5, -7)$ $\qquad$ $(-1, 0)$ $\qquad$ $(-2, -4)$ $\qquad$ $(-2, 9.1)$

12. a. Choose a point located in Quadrant IV and give its coordinates.

_____

b. Choose a point that is not located in any quadrant and give its coordinates.

_____

13. The September game schedule for Justin's soccer team is shown. The location of each game is graphed on the coordinate plane.

Hawks' Game Schedule
September
Sept 3 – Hawks vs. Jets, Jefferson Field
Sept 10 – Hawks vs. Mustangs, Madison Field
Sept 17 – Hawks vs. Lions, Hamilton Field
Sept 24 – Hawks vs. Arrows, Adams Field

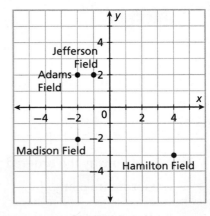

a. Identify the coordinates of each location.

Jefferson Field _____   Madison Field _____

Hamilton Field _____   Adams Field _____

b. On October 1, the team has a game scheduled at Lincoln Field. The coordinates for Lincoln Field are $(4, 4)$. Graph and label this point on the coordinate plane. What quadrant is Lincoln Field located in? _____

Additional Practice

Use the coordinate plane for Exercises 1–12.

Name the quadrant where each point is located.

1. D _____

2. P _____

3. Y _____

4. B _____

5. C _____

6. X _____

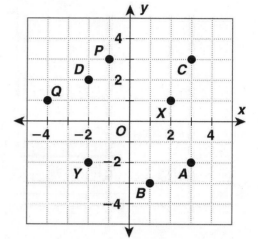

Give the coordinates of each point.

7. X _____

8. A _____

9. P _____

10. Q _____

11. Y _____

12. D _____

Graph each point on the coordinate plane at right.

13. X (3, 1)

14. T (−2, −2)

15. C (1, −2)

16. U (0, −3)

17. P (2, 0)

18. A (−4, −1)

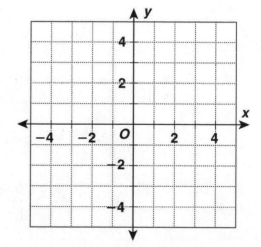

19. Does every point lie in a quadrant? Explain.

_____

_____

20. When a point lies on the x-axis, what do you know about its
y-coordinate? When a point lies on the y-axis, what do you
know about its x-coordinate?

_____

_____

Problem Solving

Use the coordinate plane on the map of Texas below to answer each question.

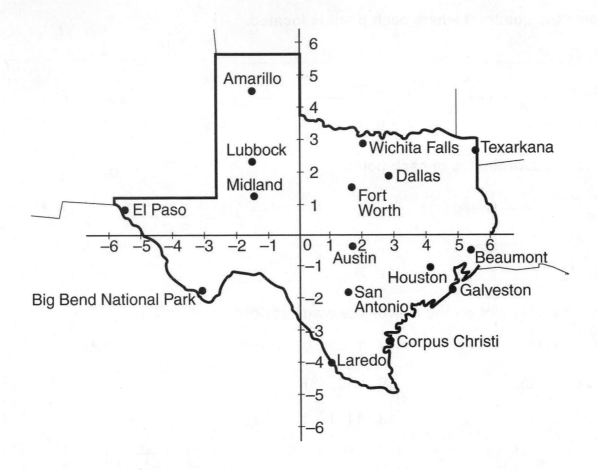

1. Which location in Texas is closest to the ordered pair (5, –2)?

_____

2. What ordered pair best describes the location of Dallas, Texas?

_____

3. Which location in Texas is closest to the ordered pair (–6, 1)?

_____

4. Which location in Texas is located in Quadrant III of this coordinate plane?

_____

5. Which three locations in Texas all have positive y-coordinates and nearly the same x-coordinate?

_____

6. Which cities on this map of Texas have locations with y-coordinates less than –3?

_____

Polygons in the Coordinate Plane

Extension: Finding Area

Essential question: *How can you solve problems by drawing polygons in the coordinate plane?*

CC.6.NS.8

1 EXPLORE **Distance in the Coordinate Plane**

A Graph and label the following points on the coordinate plane.

$A(4, 3)$ $B(-4, 4)$ $C(-4, -2)$ $D(1, -2)$

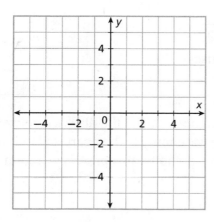

B Count the number of units between B and C.

The distance between B and C is _____ units.

C Count the number of units between C and D.

The distance between C and D is _____ units.

TRY THIS!

Use the coordinate plane to answer the following questions.

1a. What are the coordinates of point P? _____

1b. What are the coordinates of point Q? _____

1c. What is the distance between P and Q? _____ units

1d. What is the distance between $(-4, -4)$ and $(-4, 7)$?

_____ units

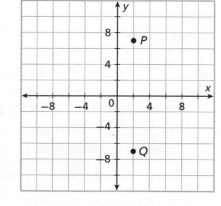

2 EXPLORE Solving Distance Problems

The coordinate plane represents a map. Each grid unit represents one mile.
A retail company has warehouses at $M(-7, 1)$ and $N(5, 1)$. The company
also has two stores along the straight road between the two warehouses.

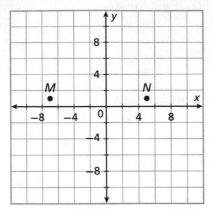

A What is the distance between the warehouses?

_____

Each store is the same distance from a warehouse. Also, the distance between
the stores is half the distance between the warehouses. The nearest warehouse
to store 1 is warehouse M, and the nearest warehouse to store 2 is warehouse N.

B What is the distance between the two stores?

_____

C What are the coordinates of store 1's location? Graph and label this point on the map.
What is the distance from store 1 to the nearest warehouse?

_____

D What are the coordinates of store 2's location? Graph and label this point on the map.
What is the distance from store 2 to the nearest warehouse?

_____

REFLECT

2. Check that your answers match the information given in the problem.

Is each store the same distance from a warehouse?   Yes / No

Is the distance between the stores half the distance
between the warehouses?   Yes / No

Is warehouse M the nearest warehouse to store 1?   Yes / No

Is warehouse N the nearest warehouse to store 2?   Yes / No

A **vertex** is a point common to two sides of an angle, a polygon, or a three-dimensional figure. The *vertices* of a polygon can be represented by ordered pairs, and the polygon can then be drawn in the coordinate plane.

CC.6.G.3

3 **EXPLORE**   **Polygons in the Coordinate Plane**

A clothing designer makes letters for varsity jackets by graphing the letters as polygons on a coordinate plane. One of the letters is polygon *ABCDEF* with the following vertices.

$A(3, -2)$, $B(3, -4)$, $C(-3, -4)$, $D(-3, 4)$,
$E(-1, 4)$, $F(-1, -2)$

Graph the points on the coordinate plane and connect them in order.

What letter is formed? _____

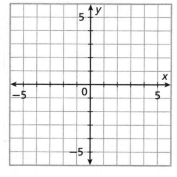

REFLECT

3. What is the distance between vertices *C* and *B*? Explain how you found the distance.

_____

_____

Polygons are named by the number of their sides and angles. A **regular polygon** is a polygon in which all sides have the same length and all angles have the same measure.

Polygon	Sides and Angles	Regular	Not Regular
Triangle	3	△	◸
Quadrilateral	4	▢	⬠
Pentagon	5	⬠	⬠
Hexagon	6	⬡	⬡
Heptagon	7	⬡	⬡
Octagon	8	⯃	⬡

4 EXAMPLE   Finding Perimeter in the Coordinate Plane

This afternoon, Tommy walked from his home to the library. He then walked to the park. From the park, he visited a friend's house, and the two of them walked to a nearby goldfish pond. Tommy left the goldfish pond and stopped at the store before returning home.

A The coordinates of each location are given. Graph and connect the points to show Tommy's path.

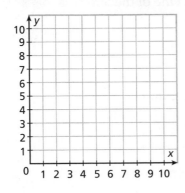

Home (0, 0)

Library (0, 4)

Park (5, 4)

Friend's house (5, 2)

Goldfish pond (7, 2)

Store (7, 0)

B Each grid unit represents one block. What is the distance from Tommy's home to the library?

You can use coordinates to find the distance between two points.

If two points have the same x-coordinate, find the distance by subtracting the y-coordinates.

The distance from Tommy's home at (0, 0) to the library at (0, 4) is $4 - 0 =$ ☐ blocks.

C What is the distance from Tommy's friend's house to the goldfish pond?

If two points have the same y-coordinate, find the distance by subtracting the x-coordinates.

The distance from Tommy's friend's house at (5, 2) to the goldfish pond at (7, 2) is ☐ − ☐ = ☐ blocks.

TRY THIS!

4a. What does the perimeter of the polygon represent?

_____

4b. Calculate the remaining distances. Then find the perimeter.

Library to park _____ blocks   Park to friend's house _____ blocks

Goldfish pond to store _____ blocks   Store to home _____ blocks

Perimeter = _____ blocks

The polygon shown is a regular polygon. Use this polygon to answer the following questions.

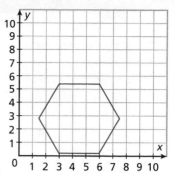

4c. How many sides does the polygon have? _____
This polygon is a regular _____.

4d. What is the length of each side? _____ units. How do you know?

_____

_____

4e. Use your answer to **4d** to find the perimeter.

_____

CC.6.G.3

5 EXAMPLE Finding Area in the Coordinate Plane

John is planning a new deck for his house. He has graphed the deck as polygon *ABCDEF* on a coordinate plane in which each grid unit represents one foot. The vertices of this polygon are *A*(1, 0), *B*(3, 2), *C*(3, 5), *D*(8, 5), *E*(8, 2), and *F*(6, 0). What is the area of John's deck?

Step 1 Graph the vertices and connect them in order.

Draw a horizontal dashed line segment to divide the polygon into two quadrilaterals—a rectangle and a parallelogram.

Step 2 Find the area of the rectangle.

$b =$ _____ feet $h =$ _____ feet

$A = bh =$ ☐ · ☐ = ☐ square feet

Step 3 Find the area of the parallelogram.

$b =$ _____ feet $h =$ _____ feet

$A = bh =$ ☐ · ☐ = ☐ square feet

Step 4 Add the areas from Steps 2 and 3 to find the total area of the deck.

$A =$ ☐ + ☐ = ☐ square feet

TRY THIS!

5. Tabitha is making a wall hanging. She has graphed the wall hanging as polygon *LMNOPQ* on a coordinate plane. The vertices of this polygon are *L*(1, 2), *M*(1, 6), *N*(7, 6), *O*(7, 2), *P*(5, 0), and *Q*(3, 0). Graph the polygon on the coordinate plane. What is the area of Tabitha's wall hanging?

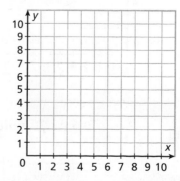

$A =$ _____ square units

Give the name of each polygon.

1.

_____

2.

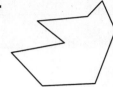

_____

3.

_____

4.

_____

5. A clothing designer makes letters for varsity jackets by graphing the letters as polygons on a coordinate planc. Onc of the letters is polygon *MNOPQRSTUV* with vertices *M*(2, 1), *N*(2, 9), *O*(7, 9), *P*(7, 7), *Q*(4, 7), *R*(4, 6), *S*(6, 6), *T*(6, 4), *U*(4, 4), and *V*(4, 1).

a. Graph the points on the coordinate plane and connect them in order.

b. What letter is formed? _____

c. Find the perimeter and area.

$P =$ _____ units $A =$ _____ square units

Give the name of each polygon. Then find its perimeter and area. Some side lengths are given.

6.

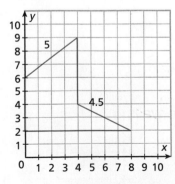

_____

$P =$ _____ units

$A =$ _____ square units

7.

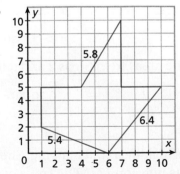

_____

$P =$ _____ units

$A =$ _____ square units

Transformations in the Coordinate Plane
Going Deeper: Reflections

Essential question: *How can you identify the reflection of a point across one or both axes in the coordinate plane?*

video tutor

CC.6.NS.6b

1 EXPLORE   Reflections in the Coordinate Plane

Draw a coordinate plane on graph paper. Label both axes from −10 to 10.

A Graph $(3, -2)$. Then fold your coordinate plane along the y-axis and find the reflection of $(3, -2)$. (Hold the paper up to the light if necessary.)

When $(3, -2)$ is reflected across the y-axis, the coordinates of the new

point are $\left(\boxed{}\,,\,\boxed{}\right)$.

B Unfold your coordinate plane. Then fold it along the x-axis and find the reflection of $(3, -2)$.

When $(3, -2)$ is reflected across the x-axis, the coordinates of the new

point are $\left(\boxed{}\,,\,\boxed{}\right)$.

C Choose four additional points and repeat the steps in **A** and **B**.

Point	Reflected across y-axis	Reflected across x-axis

REFLECT

1a. What is the relationship between the coordinates of a point and the coordinates of its reflection across each axis?

_____

_____

1b. A point in Quadrant II is reflected across the x-axis. The new point is located in Quadrant _____.

1c. A point in Quadrant _____ is reflected across the y-axis. The new point is located in Quadrant II.

1d. **Conjecture** A point is reflected across the *y*-axis. Then the reflected point is reflected across the *x*-axis. How will the coordinates of the final point be related to the coordinates of the original point?

_____

_____

Recall that a figure has *line symmetry* if there is a line that divides the figure into two parts that are mirror images of each other. In the coordinate plane, the *y*-axis is a vertical line of symmetry for the entire plane. The *x*-axis is a horizontal line of symmetry for the entire plane.

CC.6.NS.6b

2 EXPLORE   Relating Reflections Across the Axes

Plot the points B(−4, 3), C(−4, −3), and D(4, −3) on the coordinate plane.

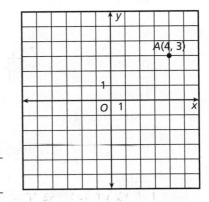

Which point is a reflection of
point *A* across the *y*-axis? _____

How are the coordinates of point *A* and point *B* related?

_____

_____

Which point is a reflection of point *A* across the *x*-axis? _____

How are the coordinates of point *A* and point *D* related?

_____

What two reflections can be used to get from point *A* to point *C*?

_____

_____

How are the coordinates of point *A* and point *C* related?

_____

REFLECT

2a. How are the points (2, −5) and (−2, −5) related by reflection?

_____

2b. How are the points (−1, −6) and (−1, 6) related by reflection?

_____

2c. How are the points (−3, 4) and (3, −4) related by reflection?

_____

CHAPTER 9

Problem Solving Connections

Treasure Hunt Carlos has heard stories about buried treasure near his hometown. According to local legend, a pirate buried his treasure, drew a map, and hid clues at various locations. He planned to reclaim his treasure one day, but never returned, and the map, clues, and treasure have never been found. Recently, Carlos bought an old map at an antique store. Could this be the legendary treasure map?

COMMON
CORE

CC.6.NS.6b,
CC.6.NS .6c,
CC.6.NS.7a,
CC.6.NS.7b,
CC.6.NS.8

1 Locations in a Coordinate Plane

A Carlos copies the old map onto a coordinate plane. Directions on the back of the map describe distances in steps, so Carlos measures the length of his step and sizes his grid so that each unit represents 1 step.

The starting point on the original map corresponds to $(-5, -4)$ on Carlos's copy of the map. Graph this point on the coordinate plane and label it "Start".

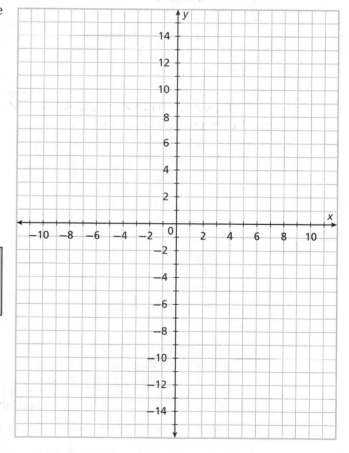

B Carlos reads the back of the original map.

> 1. FROM THE START:
>   15 STEPS NORTH
>   THEN 15 STEPS EAST
>   LARGE CRACK IN NEARBY ROCK

What are the coordinates of Carlos's location after he follows the directions?

_____

Graph this point on the coordinate plane and label it "Rock".

C Carlos finds an old piece of paper inside the rock and follows the directions on it.

> 2. 6 STEPS WEST, THEN 16 SOUTH
>   UNDER THE ROOTS OF AN OLD TREE

What are the coordinates of Carlos's new location? _____

Graph this point on the coordinate plane and label it "Tree".

2 Distance in a Coordinate Plane

A Carlos measured his step length as 3 feet. How many steps has Carlos walked so far? What is this distance in feet?

B Under a tree root, Carlos finds a second map. This map shows a church, a well, and a dry creek bed. Carlos graphs these locations on his copy of the first map as shown.

Give the coordinates of each location.

Church _____

Well _____

Dry creek bed _____

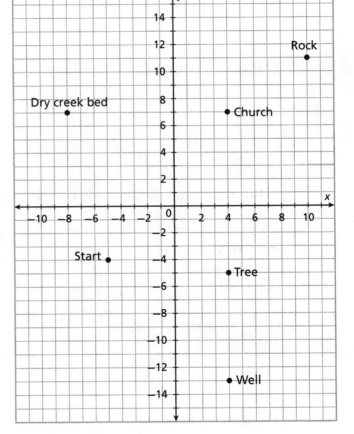

C How far is the dry creek bed from the church?

_____ steps, or _____ feet

How far is the church from the well?

_____ steps, or _____ feet

D Carlos finds these directions written on the back of the second map.

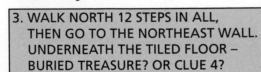

3. WALK NORTH 12 STEPS IN ALL, THEN GO TO THE NORTHEAST WALL. UNDERNEATH THE TILED FLOOR – BURIED TREASURE? OR CLUE 4?

Carlos walks 12 steps north to find the ruins of an old church.

How many steps has Carlos walked from the starting point to the church? What is this distance in feet?

E The crafty old pirate has sent Carlos on a long winding route to the old church. Find a shorter path from Carlos's starting point to the church, assuming that Carlos can walk only north, south, east, or west. Draw your path on the coordinate plane.

Describe how to follow your path from the starting point, and find the distance in steps and in feet.

_____

_____

_____

_____

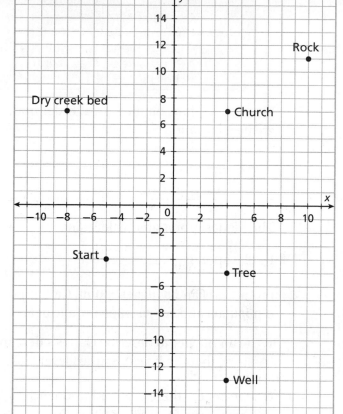

3 Comparing and Ordering

A The church's roof has collapsed and the tile floor is cracked. Carlos locates the northeast wall and begins to dig. Soon he uncovers an old wooden chest. Has he found the treasure?

Carlos opens the chest and finds... several rocks and another piece of paper.

> 4. CASTLE ISLAND'S *EGHHIST INOPT*
>
>   AT THE TOP, USE YER SCOPE.
>   LOOK TO THE SOUTH.
>   GO TO THE PLACE YOU SEE
>   AND FIND ITS MOUTH.

Carlos knows that Castle Island is nearby, but he does not fully understand the clue. Two of the words are scrambled. Carlos turns the paper over and finds a table:

T	O	N	P	T	H	S	I	G	H	E	I
0	5	10	3	12	−9	−1	8	−6	−4	−2	−7

To unscramble the words, first write the numbers in the table in order from least to greatest.

_____

Now replace each number in your list with the corresponding letter from the table.

The scrambled words are _____.

B When Carlos arrives at Castle Island, he sees this sign.

> **WELCOME TO CASTLE ISLAND!**
> Bilge Basin, Elev. −6 ft →
> ← Buccaneer Beach, Elev. 0 ft
> Galley Ridge, Elev. 509 ft ↗
> Pirate's Peak, Elev. 628 ft ↖
> Polly's Park, Elev. 128 ft ↗

List the locations on the sign in order from the least elevation to the greatest elevation.

_____

_____

The highest point on Castle Island is _____.

Its elevation is _____ feet.

C From the island's highest point, Carlos looks south through his binoculars and sees a small remote beach.

Write an integer to describe Carlos's descent to this beach. (Assume that the beach is at sea level.) _____

D On the beach, there is an old wooden sign with faded letters. Carlos can barely read *Captain's Cave, Elev. −3 ft.* He sees the opening of a cave nearby. Could this be the beach's "mouth" described in Clue 4?

Is Captain's Cave above or below sea level? _____

Write an inequality using the elevations to justify your answer.

_____

Is Captain's Cave higher or lower than Bilge Basin? _____

Write an inequality using their elevations to justify your answer.

_____

E At the back of the cave, Carlos moves several large loose rocks to reveal a small recess in the cave wall. He reaches in and pries out another old wooden chest, similar to the one he found at the church. Is this the treasure at last?

Carlos slowly opens the lid and...

IT'S THE TREASURE!!!!

To find the treasure's value, first rearrange the numbers in the table in order from least to greatest. Then replace each number with its corresponding letter.

The treasure has _____ value!

2	−9	5	−6	−1	9	0	−4
U	A	T	B	O	E	L	S

Performance Task

CHAPTER 9

COMMON CORE

CC.6.NS.5
CC.6.NS.6
CC.6.NS.7
CC.6.NS.8
CC.6.G.3

⭐ **1.** The temperature in Cyrus is −7 °F, and the temperature in Smithtown is −15 °C. The expression $(9c \div 5) + 32$, where c is the temperature in Celsius, gives the corresponding temperature in Fahrenheit. Is Cyrus or Smithtown colder? Show your work.

⭐ **2.** Graph the triangle with vertices $A(-4, 4.5)$, $B(4, -1.5)$, and $C(-4, -1\frac{1}{2})$. The length of $\overline{AB}$ is 10. What is the perimeter of the triangle?

⭐⭐ **3.** A parking garage has floors above and below ground level. For a scavenger hunt, Gaia's friends are told objects they need to find are on the fourth level below ground, the first level above ground, the third level below ground, the fourth level above ground, and ground level.

a. If ground level is 0 and the first level above ground is 1, what integers can you use to represent the other levels where objects are hidden? Explain your reasoning.

b. Graph the set of numbers on a number line.

c. Gaia wants to start at the lowest level and work her way up. List the levels in the order that Gaia will search them.

⭐⭐⭐ **4.** Jorge and his friends are setting up a camp. They make the campfire the origin of a coordinate grid. A tree is at (–4, 3) on the coordinate grid, where each grid unit is one yard. A rock is at (3, 3) and a bush is at (3, –2). The camp is the shape of a rectangle, with the tree, rock, and bush as three of the four vertices.

a. Graph and label the campfire, tree, rock, bush, and the fourth vertex on a coordinate grid. Explain how you found the fourth coordinate.

b. Is there a place you could move the rock so that the camp is no longer a quadrilateral? Give coordinates, and explain your reasoning.

Name _____ Class _____ Date _____

SELECTED RESPONSE

1. Which list of numbers is in order from least to greatest?

   A. $-0.8, 1.2, -19, 13, 16, -4, 25$

   B. $-1, -4, -8, 1.1, 1.6, -19, 23$

   C. $-19, -8, -4, -1, 1.1, 1.6, 2.5$

   D. $-1, -4, 1.1, 1.3, 16, -19, 25$

2. Which of the following numbers is the opposite of -37?

   F. -73 **H.** 37

   G. -37 **J.** 73

3. What is the absolute value of 45?

   A. -45 **C.** 0.45

   B. 0 **D.** 45

4. Both coordinates of a point in the coordinate plane are negative. In which quadrant is this point located?

   F. Quadrant I   **H.** Quadrant III

   G. Quadrant II   **J.** Quadrant IV

5. Which of the points on the coordinate plane has coordinates $(-7, 4)$?

   A. A **C.** C

   B. B **D.** D

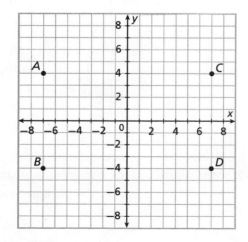

6. Which of the following inequalities is a true statement?

   F. $37 > 73$ **H.** $73 < 37$

   G. $48 > 24$ **J.** $24 > 48$

7. Which of the following numbers is located to the right of -47 on the number line?

   A. -14 **C.** -49

   B. -94 **D.** -57

8. The elevation of the Dead Sea is about 1,310 feet below sea level. Which integer represents this elevation?

   F. $-1,310$ **H.** 131

   G. -131 **J.** $1,310$

9. Which of the following coordinates is farthest to the right of the origin on a coordinate plane?

   A. $(-19, 7)$ **C.** $(4, 15)$

   B. $(0, 12)$ **D.** $(7, 0)$

10. The table shows the low temperature for several days. Which day was the coldest?

Day	Temperature (°F)
Monday	−4
Tuesday	0
Wednesday	−2
Thursday	5
Friday	3

   F. Monday

   G. Tuesday

   H. Wednesday

   J. Thursday

11. Which point is not located in a quadrant?

  A. $(1, -2)$

  B. $(-2.5, 3)$

  C. $(5, 0)$

  D. $(-6, -10)$

12. The point $(-2, -2)$ is reflected across the *x*-axis. What are the coordinates of the new point?

  F. $(-2, -2)$ **H.** $(2, -2)$

  G. $(-2, 2)$ **J.** $(2, 2)$

13. Which statement about negative numbers is **not** true?

  A. Negative numbers are located to the left of 0 on a number line.

  B. The absolute value of a negative number is negative.

  C. Negative numbers are less than positive numbers.

  D. A negative number is less than its opposite.

14. What is the opposite of the opposite of -7?

  F. -7 **H.** $|7|$

  G. 7 **J.** $|-7|$

CONSTRUCTED RESPONSE

Use the number line for 15–17.

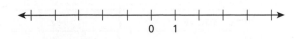

15. The number line has been partially labeled. Label the rest of the number line.

16. Graph the integers -2, 4, 1, and their opposites on the number line.

17. Choose one of the integers from item 16 and show on the number line how to find its absolute value.

Mark drives to work every morning. On the way, he stops for breakfast at a café. His route is mapped on the coordinate plane.

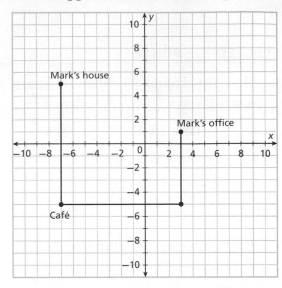

18. Each unit on the coordinate plane represents 1 mile. What is the distance from Mark's house to the café?

_____

19. What is the total distance that Mark drives to work?

_____

20. Will walks his dog at a local park every day after school.

  a. The park is located at $(-4, -3)$ on the map. Graph and label this point.

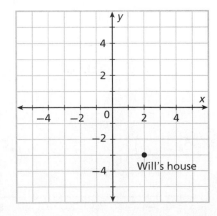

  b. Each unit on the coordinate plane represents 1 block. What is the distance from Will's house to the park in blocks?

_____

Functions

Chapter Focus

You will use equations, tables, and graphs to represent relationships between two variables. You will find solutions to equations with two variables using tables and graphs. Slope will be examined in terms of a unit rate. You will use tables and graphs to find unit rates. Finally, you will write and graph inequalities.

Chapter at a Glance

Lesson	Standards for Mathematical Content
10-1 Tables and Functions	**CC.6.EE.9**
10-2 Graphing Functions	**CC.6.EE.9**
10-3 Slope and Rate of Change	**CC.6.RP.3, CC.6.RP.3a**
10-4 Inequalities	**CC.6.EE.5, CC.6.EE.6, CC.6.EE.8**
Problem Solving Connections	
Performance Task	
Assessment Readiness	

CHAPTER 10

Unpacking the Standards

Understanding the standards and the vocabulary terms in the standards will help you know exactly what you are expected to learn in this chapter.

CHAPTER 10

COMMON CORE **CC.6.RP.3a**

Make tables of equivalent ratios relating quantities with whole number measurements, find missing values in the tables, and plot the pairs of values on the coordinate plane. Use tables to compare ratios.

Key Vocabulary

equivalent ratios *(razones equivalentes)* Ratios that name the same comparison.

coordinate plane *(plano cartesiano)* A plane formed by the intersection of a horizontal number line called the *x*-axis and a vertical number line called the *y*-axis.

What It Means to You

You will make and use tables and graphs that represent ratios.

EXAMPLE

Evan planted some new plants in his garden. He measured the height of the same plant each Wednesday for five weeks. The table shows the measurements Evan recorded.

Week	1	2	3	4	5
Height (cm)	3	6	9	12	15

Determine whether the rates of change are constant or variable.

$$\frac{3}{1} = 3 \qquad \frac{6}{2} = 3 \qquad \frac{9}{3} = 3 \qquad \frac{12}{4} = 3 \qquad \frac{15}{5} = 3$$

The rate of change is constant.

Graph the data and connect the points with line segments. If the rate of change is constant, find and interpret the slope.

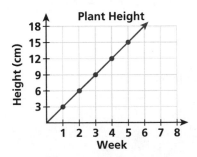

The slope is 3. This means the plant grew 3 cm each week.

COMMON CORE **CC.6.EE.9**

Use variables to represent two quantities in a real-world problem that change in relationship to one another; write an equation to express one quantity, thought of as the dependent variable, in terms of the other quantity, thought of as the independent variable. Analyze the relationship between the dependent and independent variables using graphs and tables, and relate these to the equation.

Key Vocabulary

dependent variable *(variable dependiente)* The output of a function; a variable whose value depends on the value of the input, or independent variable.

independent variable *(variable independiente)* The input of a function; a variable whose value determines the value of the output, or dependent variable.

What It Means to You

You will analyze relationships between two variables and write equations in two variables to represent real-world problems.

EXAMPLE

Car washers tracked the number of cars they washed and the total amount of money they earned. They charged the same price for each car they washed. They earned $60 for 20 cars, $66 for 22 cars, and $81 for 27 cars. Write an equation for the function.

Let c be the number of cars and m be the amount of money earned.

c	20	22	27
m	60	66	81

m is equal to 3 times c.

$m = 3c$

COMMON CORE **CC.6.EE.8**

Write an inequality of the form $x > c$ or $x < c$ to represent a constraint or condition in a real-world or mathematical problem. Recognize that inequalities of the form $x > c$ or $x < c$ have infinitely many solutions; represent solutions of such inequalities on number line diagrams.

Key Vocabulary

inequality *(desigualdad)* A mathematical sentence that shows the relationship between quantities that are not equal.

What It Means to You

You will understand that an inequality has many solutions. You will graph these solutions on a number line and write inequalities to represent real-world situations.

EXAMPLE

Write and graph an inequality for each situation. There are more than 5 students in the auditorium.

$s > 5$

This open circle shows that 5 is not a solution.

The temperature did not get above 3°F.

$t \leq 3$

This closed circle shows that 3 is a solution.

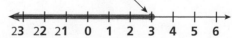

Key Vocabulary

dependent variable *(variable dependiente)* The output of a function; a variable whose value depends on the value of the input, or independent variable.

independent variable *(variable independiente)* The input of a function; a variable whose value determines the value of the output, or dependent variable.

input *(valor de entrada)* The value substituted into an expression or function.

output *(valor de salida)* The value that results from the substitution of a given input into an expression or function.

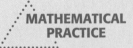

MATHEMATICAL PRACTICE The Common Core Standards for Mathematical Practice describe varieties of expertise that mathematics educators at all levels should seek to develop in their students. Opportunities to develop these practices are integrated throughout this program.

1. Make sense of problems and persevere in solving them.
2. Reason abstractly and quantitatively.
3. Construct viable arguments and critique the reasoning of others.
4. Model with mathematics.
5. Use appropriate tools strategically.
6. Attend to precision.
7. Look for and make use of structure.
8. Look for and express regularity in repeated reasoning.

Tables and Functions
Connection: Dependent and Independent Variables

Essential question: *How do you use equations and tables to represent relationships between two variables?*

The total cost for movie tickets depends on the number of tickets purchased. In an equation representing the relationship between total cost and number of tickets, the total cost is the **dependent variable** and the number of tickets is the **independent variable**.

CC.6.EE.9

1 EXPLORE   **Dependent and Independent Variables**

Maggie and Mykayla rent a double kayak for $15 per hour. Identify the dependent and the independent variables. Then write an equation to represent the relationship between the number of hours and the total cost.

Let *y* represent the total cost and let *x* represent the number of hours that Maggie and Mykayla use the kayak.

The _____ depends on the _____.

_____ is the dependent variable. _____ is the independent variable.

Write an equation.

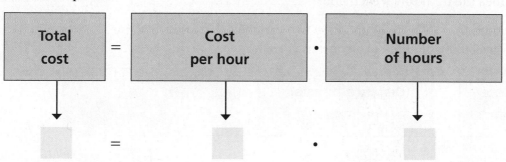

The equation _____ represents the total cost *y* for the number of hours *x*.

REFLECT

1. Explain how you know that the value of *y* is dependent on the value of *x*.

_____

_____

In ❶, to find the cost for x hours, you substituted a value of x into the expression $15x$. The value substituted into the expression is the **input**. You then evaluate the expression to find the value of y, the **output**.

Many real-world situations involve two variable quantities in which one quantity depends on the other. These relationships can be represented by an equation or a table.

CC.6.EE.9

2 EXPLORE Variable Relationships

A freight train is traveling at a constant speed. The distance y in miles that the train has traveled after x hours is shown in the table.

Time x (hours)	0	1	2	3
Distance traveled y (miles)	0	60	120	180

A What are the two quantities in this situation?

_____

Which of these two quantities depends on the other?

_____

What is the independent variable? _____.

What is the dependent variable? _____.

B How far does the train travel each hour? _____.

Use this number to write an equation in two variables that describes the distance traveled by the train at a constant speed.

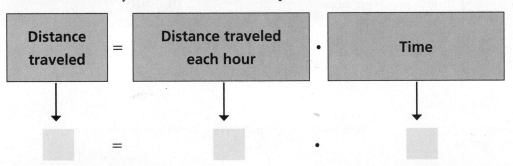

What is the input? _____

What is the output? _____

REFLECT

2. Will the train travel 250 miles in 4 hours? Explain.

_____

_____

Graphing Functions
Going Deeper

Essential question: *How can you use tables and graphs to represent relationships between two variables?*

video tutor

CC.6.EE.9

1 EXPLORE **Finding Solutions of Equations with Two Variables**

Tina is buying DVDs from an online store. Each DVD costs $8, and there is a flat fee of $6 for shipping.

Let *x* represent the number of DVDs that Tina buys. Let *y* represent Tina's total cost. An equation in two variables can represent the relationship between *x* and *y*.

Total cost	=	Cost per DVD	·	Number of DVDs	+	Cost of shipping
y	=	8	·	x	+	6

Complete the table.

DVDs Bought x	$8x + 6$	Total Cost y ($)
1	8(1) + 6	14
2	8( ) + 6	
3	8( ) + 6	
4	8( ) + 6	
5	8( ) + 6	
6	8( ) + 6	
7	8( ) + 6	

REFLECT

1a. Look at the *y*-values in the right column of the table. What pattern do you see? What does this pattern mean in the problem?

_____

_____

1b. A *solution of an equation in two variables* is an ordered pair (x, y) that makes the equation true. The ordered pair (1, 14) is a solution of $y = 8x + 6$. Write the other solutions from the table as ordered pairs.

_____

2 EXAMPLE Graphing Solutions

A car moves at a constant speed of 50 miles per hour. Write an equation in two variables that describes the distance traveled by the car.

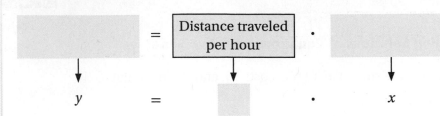

| | = | Distance traveled per hour | · | |

y = ☐ · x

Complete the table to show the distance y in miles that the car will travel after x hours.

Time x (h)	0	1	2	3
Distance y (mi)	0	50		

Write ordered pairs to represent the solutions to this equation that are given in the table.

$(0, 0)$ $\left(1, \right)$ $\left(2, \right)$ $\left(, \right)$

Graph these ordered pairs on the coordinate plane.

Connect the ordered pairs with a line. Extend the line to the right beyond your ordered pairs. Every point on this line is a solution to $y = 50x$. In other words, this line represents all solutions to $y = 50x$.

REFLECT

2a. What are the independent and dependent variables? Explain.

_____

_____

2b. Find three more ordered pair solutions and graph them on the coordinate plane.

_____

2c. What do the points between $(0, 0)$ and $(1, 50)$ represent?

_____

_____

2d. Why is the graph not extended past $(0, 0)$ on the left?

_____

_____

2e. Use the table to record solutions to the equation
$y = x + 2$. Write the solutions as ordered pairs and
graph the ordered pairs. Then graph all of the
solutions to this equation.

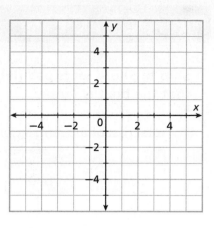

x	-2	-1	0	1	2	3
$y = x + 2$	0	1				

Ordered pairs: $(-2, 0)$, $(-1, 1)$,

CC.6.EE.9

3 EXPLORE Compare Linear Functions

The statements below describe the walking speeds of three friends. Complete the
table for each friend. Then write an equation for each friend's walking speed.

Maddy takes one step per second.	
Seconds, x	Steps, y
0	
2	
3	

Cal takes two steps per second.	
Seconds, x	Steps, y
0	
1	
2	
3	

Brody takes three steps per second.	
Seconds, x	Steps, y
0	
1	
2	
3	

A Use a colored pencil to graph the ordered pairs for
Maddy's walking speed. Draw a line through the points.

B Use a different colored pencil to graph the ordered pairs
for Cal's walking speed. Draw a line through the points.

C Use a different colored pencil to graph the ordered
pairs for Brody's walking speed. Draw a line through the points.

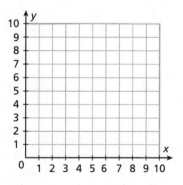

D Which friend's graph is the most steep? Which friends's
graph is the least steep?

E Compare the three equations you wrote. How can you tell from looking at the equations
which of their graphs will be the most steep?

Ship to Shore rents paddleboats for a fee of $10 plus an additional $5 per hour that the boat is rented.

1. Let x represent the number of hours a paddleboat is rented, and let y represent the total cost of the rental. Complete the equation to show the relationship between x and y.

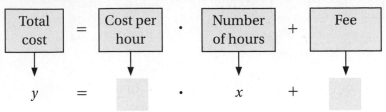

| Total cost | = | Cost per hour | · | Number of hours | + | Fee |

$$y \quad = \quad \boxed{} \quad · \quad x \quad + \quad \boxed{}$$

2a. What are the two quantities in this situation? _____

 b. Which of these quantities depends on the other? _____

 c. What is the independent variable? _____

 d. What is the dependent variable? _____

3. Complete the table.

Time Rented x (h)	1	2	3	4	5	6
Total Cost y ($)						

4. Write the ordered pairs from the table.

 _____

5. Graph the ordered pairs on the coordinate plane. Connect the points and extend the line to the right.

6a. What is the cost to rent a paddleboat for 8 hours?

 _____

 b. The cost to rent a paddleboat for 8 hours is represented on the graph by the point _____ .

7. The cost to rent a paddleboat for _____ hours is $60. This is represented on the graph by the point _____ .

8. Describe two ways to find the cost to rent a paddleboat for 9 hours.

 1. _____

 2. _____

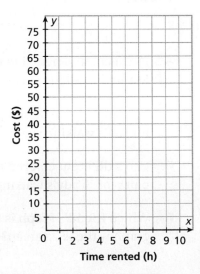

Additional Practice

The table shows the amount Rodrick earns for mowing various numbers of lawns. Use the table for Exercises 1–7.

Money earned ($)		30	45		75
Number of lawns	1	2		4	

1. How much does Rodrick earn for mowing one lawn?

   _____

2. What is the relationship between the amount of money Rodrick earns and the number of lawns?

   _____

   _____

3. Write the relationship described in Exercise 2 as a unit rate.

   _____

4. How much does the amount of money Rodrick earns increase each time the number of lawns increases by 1?

   _____

5. Use the unit rate to complete the table.

6. How many lawns must Rodrick mow to earn $180?

   _____

7. One month, Rodrick mowed 8 lawns. How much did he earn that month?

   _____

Problem Solving

The graph shows the amount of time it took a racecar driver to make several laps around a track at a constant speed. Use the graph for Exercises 1–5.

1. How many seconds does it take the racecar driver to make one lap?

   _____

2. Write the relationship between the number of seconds and the number of laps as a unit rate.

   _____

3. How much does the number of seconds increase each time the number of laps increases by 1?

   _____

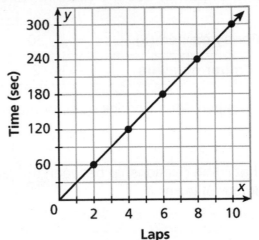

Choose the letter of the best answer.

4. At this rate, how many laps will the racecar driver complete in 6 minutes?

   A   2 laps

   B   10 laps

   C   12 laps

   D   180 laps

5. How long would it take the racecar driver to complete 30 laps at this rate?

   F   1 minute

   G   300 seconds

   H   600 seconds

   J   15 minutes

10-4

Inequalities
Going Deeper

Essential question: *How can you represent solutions of inequalities?*

You have seen the symbols > and < used in inequalities.

- The symbol > means _____.
- The symbol < means _____.

Two additional symbols used in inequalities are ≥ and ≤.

- The symbol ≥ means "is greater than or equal to".
- The symbol ≤ means "is less than or equal to".

CC.6.EE.6
1 EXPLORE **Inequalities with Variables**

A The lowest temperature ever recorded in Florida was −2 °F.
Graph this temperature on the number line.

B The temperatures 0 °F, 3 °F, 6 °F, 5 °F, and −1 °F have also been recorded in Florida.
Graph these temperatures on the number line.

C How do the temperatures in **B** compare to −2?

_____

How can you see this relationship on the number line?

_____

D How many other numbers have the same relationship to −2 as the
temperatures in **B** ? Give some examples.

_____

E Suppose you could graph all of the possible answers to **D** on a number line.
What would the graph look like?

_____

Let the variable x represent any of the possible answers to **D** .

Complete this inequality: x ⬚ -2

When an inequality contains a variable, a solution of that inequality is any
value of the variable that makes the inequality true. For example, 7 is a solution
of $x > -2$, since $7 > -2$ is a true statement. In **1** , the numbers you listed
in **D** are solutions of the inequality $x > -2$.

This number line shows the solutions of $x > -2$:

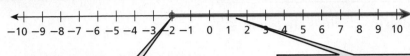

An *empty* circle means the number *is not* included in the solution. -2 is **not** a solution of $x > -2$.

Shade the number line to the right of -2 to indicate all numbers greater than -2. The arrowhead means that the shaded region extends indefinitely.

This number line shows the solutions of $x \geq -2$:

A *solid* circle means the number *is* included in the solution. -2 is a solution of $x \geq -2$.

Shade the number line to the right of -2 to indicate all numbers greater than -2. The arrowhead means that the shaded region extends indefinitely.

CC.6.EE.5

2 EXAMPLE — Graphing Inequalities

Graph the solutions of each inequality.

A $y \leq -3$

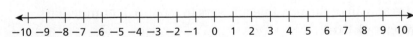

Step 1 Draw a circle at -3.

Is -3 a solution of $y \leq -3$? _____

Will you draw an empty circle or a solid circle? _____

Step 2 Shade the number line.

The variable y represents numbers less than or equal to -3. Where are numbers less than -3 located on the number line?

_____

B $w > 2$

Step 1 Draw a circle at 2.

Is 2 a solution of $w > 2$? _____

Will you draw an empty circle or a solid circle? _____

Step 2 Shade the number line.

The variable w represents numbers greater than 2. Where are these numbers located on the number line?

_____

C $-5 > m$

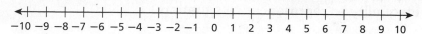

Step 1 Draw a circle at -5.

Is -5 a solution of $-5 > m$? _____

Will you draw an empty circle or a solid circle? _____

Step 2 Shade the number line.

The variable m represents numbers _____ than -5. Where
are these numbers located on the number line? _____

REFLECT

2a. Rewrite the inequality from **C** with m on the left: m ▭ -5

2b. How is $x < 5$ different from $x \leq 5$?

_____

_____

2c. When graphing an inequality that contains $>$ or $<$, use a(n) _____ circle.
When graphing an inequality that contains $\geq$ or $\leq$, use a(n) _____ circle.

TRY THIS!

Graph the solutions of each inequality.

2d. $t \leq -4$
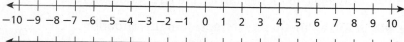

2e. $4 < x$
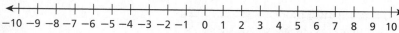

CC.6.EE.8

3 EXAMPLE Representing Real-World Situations with Inequalities

**There are at least 5 gallons of water in an aquarium. Write and graph
an inequality to represent this situation.**

Step 1 Write the inequality.

Let g represent the amount of water in gallons.

Can there be 5 gallons of water in the aquarium? _____

Can there be more than 5 gallons of water in the aquarium? _____

Can there be less than 5 gallons of water in the aquarium? _____

The inequality is g ▭ 5.

Step 2 Graph the inequality.

Draw a(n) _____ circle at _____.

Shade the number line to the _____.

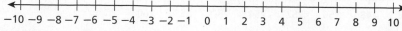

Write and graph an inequality to represent each situation.

3a. Megan must run a mile in 6 minutes or less to beat her best time. _____

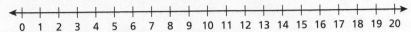

3b. The temperature today will rise above 2 °F. _____

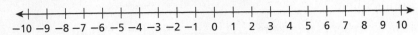

PRACTICE

1. Which numbers in the set $\left\{-5, 0.03, -1, 0, 1.5, -6, \frac{1}{2}\right\}$ are solutions of $x \geq 0$?

_____

Graph each inequality.

2. $t \leq 8$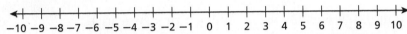

3. $-7 < h$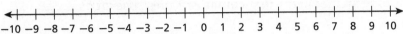

4. $x \geq -9$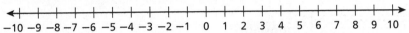

5. A child must be at least 48 inches tall to ride a roller coaster.

    a. Write and graph an inequality to represent this situation. _____

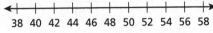

    b. Can a child who is 46 inches tall ride the roller coaster? Explain.

_____

Write and graph an inequality to represent each situation.

6. There are fewer than 15 students in the cafeteria. _____

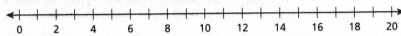

7. No more than 150 people can be seated at the restaurant. _____

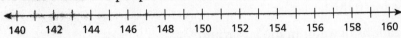

8. At least 20 students must sign up for the field trip. _____

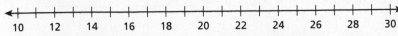

9. Shaun can pay at most $50 to have his computer repaired. _____

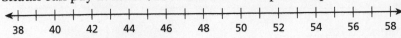

10. The goal of the fundraiser is to raise more than $250. _____

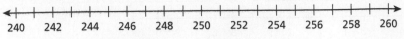

Additional Practice

Write an inequality for each situation.

1. The temperature today will be at most 50 °F. _____

2. The temperature tomorrow will be above 70 °F. _____

3. Yesterday, there was less than 2 inches of rain. _____

4. Last Monday, there was at least 3 inches of rain. _____

Graph each inequality.

5. $t \leq -2$ ←——+——+——+——+——+——+——+——+——+——+——→

6. $j > -5$ ←——+——+——+——+——+——+——+——+——+——+——→

7. $y \leq 0$ ←——+——+——+——+——+——+——+——+——+——+——→

8. $b < \dfrac{1}{2}$ ←——+——+——+——+——+——+——+——+——+——+——→

Graph each compound inequality.

9. $f > 3$ or $f < -2$ ←——+——+——+——+——+——+——+——+——+——+——→

10. $-4 \leq w \leq 4$ ←——+——+——+——+——+——+——+——+——+——+——→

11. $b < 0$ or $b \geq 5$ ←——+——+——+——+——+——+——+——+——+——+——→

12. $y \geq 3$ or $y \leq -1$ ←——+——+——+——+——+——+——+——+——+——+——→

13. $-4 < m < -2$ ←——+——+——+——+——+——+——+——+——+——+——→

Problem Solving

Write the correct answer.

The American College of Sports Medicine recommends exercising at an intensity of 60% to 90% of your maximum heart rate.

1. Mara is 25 years old. Write a compound inequality to represent her target heart rate range while bike riding.

   _____

2. Leia is 38 years old. Write a compound inequality to represent the zone between her maximum heart rate and the upper end of her target range.

   _____

Heart Rates by Age

Age	Maximum Heart Rate	Target Range
20–24	200	120–180
25–29	195	117–176
30–34	190	114–171
35–39	185	111–167
40–44	180	108–162

3. Rudy is 42 years old. Write an inequality to represent at least 70% of his maximum heart rate.

   _____

4. Write a compound inequality to represent 60% to 90% of your maximum heart rate in ten years.

   _____

Choose the letter for the graph that represents each statement.

5. Alena decided to pay not more than $25 to get her old bike repaired.

   A I   C III
   B II   D IV

6. It was so cold last week that the temperature never reached 25 °F.

   F I   H III
   G II   J IV

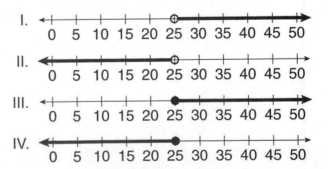

7. There were at least 25 people ahead of Ivan in the cafeteria line.

   A I   C III
   B II   D IV

8. The garden yielded more than 25 pounds of potatoes.

   F I   H III
   G II   J IV

Performance Task

CHAPTER 10

COMMON CORE

CC.6.RP.3
CC.6.EE.8
CC.6.EE.9

⭐ **1.** Jamal bought an automatic watering bowl for his dog. Whenever the bowl has less than 2 cups of water, it automatically refills the dish to a total of 5 cups of water. Write and graph a compound inequality for the possible cups of water, w, in the bowl at any time.

⭐ **2.** The table shows the cost of different numbers of paperback books at a garage sale. Every book costs the same amount. Write an equation to represent the cost, c, of b books.

Books	Cost
2	$5
6	$15
10	$25

⭐ **3.** The table shows how many megabytes of data Helen uploaded over different periods of time.

Seconds	Megabytes Uploaded
2	3
4	6
8	12

a. Graph the points and connect them with a line.

b. What does the slope of the line you graphed in part **a** represent?

c. If Helen upgrades her Internet service to a company that provides a faster upload speed, how might the graph change? Make a sketch of a possible graph, identify the slope, and explain what it means.

4. The graph shows the temperature in degrees Celsius y over time in hours x in Boston, Massachusetts.

a. What is the rate of change of the function shown in the graph?

b. Is the relationship shown in the graph a linear function? Justify your answer.

c. The graph represents the temperature in degrees from 5 pm ($x = 0$) to 1 am ($x = 8$). Would you expect the graph to remain a straight line forever? Why or why not?

Name _____ **Class** _____ **Date** _____

SELECTED RESPONSE

1. Write an equation for the values in the table. Use the equation to find the value of y when $x = 14$.

x	6	8	10	12	14
y	13	19	25	31	?

A. $y = 2x + 1$; 29   **C.** $y = 2x + 3$; 31

B. $y = 3x - 5$; 37   **D.** $y = 4x - 11$; 45

2. Which equation represents the graph in the figure below?

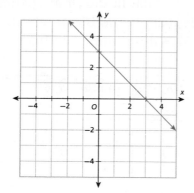

F. $y = 6x + 8$ **H.** $y = -x + 3$

G. $y = \frac{5}{7}x - 3$ **J.** $y = 2x - 1$

3. Tanya walks dogs. She earns $10.50 for each dog she walks. She wants to go to a concert that costs $157.50. Write an equation relating the number of dogs she needs to walk to the amount of money she earns. Find how many dogs Tanya needs to walk to go to the concert. Let n be the number of dogs Tanya walks.

A. $10.5 + n = 157.5$; 147 dogs

B. $10.5n = 157.5$; 15 dogs

C. $10.5n = 157.5$; 1654 dogs

D. $10.5n = 157.5$; 147 dogs

4. A parking garage charges $2.00 for the first hour and $0.50 for each fraction of an hour thereafter. Which statement describes the relationship between the parking fee and the amount of time a person parks in the garage?

F. The parking fee depends on the amount of time a person uses the garage.

G. The amount of time a person uses the garage depends on the parking fee.

H. The parking fee and the amount of time a person uses the garage are independent.

J. The relationship cannot be determined.

5. The data in the table show the relationship between a person's weight on Earth and the person's weight on the Moon. Which equation best represents the person's weight on the Moon, m, as related to the person's weight on Earth, e?

Weight on Earth (lbs)	Weight on the Moon (lbs)
0	0
80	13.60
105	17.85
130	22.10

A. $e = 0.17m$

B. $m = 5.88e$

C. $m = 0.17e$

D. $e = 5.88m$

6. Lei's coach kept track of her time as she ran 12 miles. The results are shown in the table below. What is the rate of change?

Mile	2	4	6	8	10	12
Minute	14	28	42	56	70	84

   F. constant

   G. variable

   H. not defined

   J. all of these

7. Which number would complete the table?

x	3	5	7	9
y	2	6	10	??

   A. 10   **C.** 14

   B. 12   **D.** 16

8. A store charges $1.50 for a 20-oz bottle of sport drink. Which equation best represents the total cost, y, of x bottles?

   F. $y = 20x$ **H.** $x = 1.5y$

   G. $y = 20y$ **J.** $y = 1.5x$

9. Kahlil is recording a beat for a song that he is working on. He wants the length of the beat to be more than 10 seconds long. His friend tells him the beat needs to be 5 seconds longer than that to match the lyrics he has written.

   Write an inequality to represent the beat's length. Give 3 possible beat lengths that satisfy the inequality.

   A. $t > 5$
   16, 21, 22

   B. $t > 15$
   16, 21, 22

   C. $t < 15$
   4, 3, 2

   D. $t < 10$
   4, 3, 2

10 Graph the inequality $w \geq 3.4$.

   F.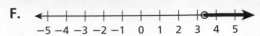

   G.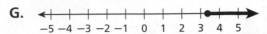

   H.

   J.

11. Yesterday, more than 3 inches of rain fell. Which inequality represents this situation?

   A. $y > 3$ **C.** $y < 3$

   B. $y \leq 3$ **D.** $y \geq 3$

CONSTRUCTED RESPONSE

12. On the first day Corey did 35 sit-ups. On the second day he did 70 sit-ups, and on the third day he did 105 sit-ups. If Corey continues this pattern, how many sit-ups will he do in d days?

Day	Number of Sit-ups
1	35
2	70
3	105
d	

13. Consider the graph of the inequality.

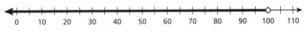

   a. Write the solution set of the inequality in words.

   _____

   _____

   b. write an inequality for the graph.

   _____

   c. Describe a real-world situation that can be represented by the inequality.

   _____

   _____

   _____

Correlation of *Explorations in Core Math Grade 6* to the Common Core State Standards

Ratios and Proportional Relationships	Citations
CC.6.RP.1 Understand the concept of a ratio and use ratio language to describe a ratio relationship between two quantities.	pp. 283–290, 327–330
CC.6.RP.2 Understand the concept of a unit rate *a/b* associated with a ratio *a:b* with *b* ≠ 0, and use rate language in the context of a ratio relationship.	pp. 283–290, 327–330, 331–332
CC.6.RP.3 Use ratio and rate reasoning to solve real-world and mathematical problems, e.g., by reasoning about tables of equivalent ratios, tape diagrams, double number line diagrams, or equations. a. Make tables of equivalent ratios relating quantities with whole number measurements, find missing values in the tables, and plot the pairs of values on the coordinate plane. Use tables to compare ratios. b. Solve unit rate problems including those involving unit pricing and constant speed. c. Find a percent of a quantity as a rate per 100 (e.g., 30% of a quantity means 30/100 times the quantity); solve problems involving finding the whole, given a part and the percent. d. Use ratio reasoning to convert measurement units; manipulate and transform units appropriately when multiplying or dividing quantities.	pp. 283–290, 291–296, 297–300, 301–306, 307–310, 311–316, 317–322, 323–326, 327–330, 331–332, 339–344, 345–350, 387–388, 447–450, 461–462

The Number System	Citations
CC.6.NS.1 Interpret and compute quotients of fractions, and solve word problems involving division of fractions by fractions, e.g., by using visual fraction models and equations to represent the problem.	pp. 139–142, 221–226, 231–234, 235–236
CC.6.NS.2 Fluently divide multi-digit numbers using the standard algorithm.	pp. 5–8, 9–14, 33–36, 37–38, 139–142
CC.6.NS.3 Fluently add, subtract, multiply, and divide multi-digit decimals using the standard algorithm for each operation.	pp. 107–110, 111–116, 117–122, 123–126, 127–130, 131–134, 139–142, 143–144
CC.6.NS.4 Find the greatest common factor of two whole numbers less than or equal to 100 and the least common multiple of two whole numbers less than or equal to 12. Use the distributive property to express a sum of two whole numbers 1–100 with a common factor as a multiple of a sum of two whole numbers with no common factor.	pp. 139–142, 151–154, 155–160, 173–178, 189–192, 193–194, 201–204, 205–208, 231–234, 235–236
CC.6.NS.5 Understand that positive and negative numbers are used together to describe quantities having opposite directions or values (e.g., temperature above/below zero, elevation above/below sea level, credits/debits, positive/negative electric charge); use positive and negative numbers to represent quantities in real-world contexts, explaining the meaning of 0 in each situation.	pp. 395–400, 429–430

CC.6.NS.6 Understand a rational number as a point on the number line. Extend number line diagrams and coordinate axes familiar from previous grades to represent points on the line and in the plane with negative number coordinates. a. Recognize opposite signs of numbers as indicating locations on opposite sides of 0 on the number line; recognize that the opposite of the opposite of a number is the number itself, e.g., $-(-3) = 3$, and that 0 is its own opposite. b. Understand signs of numbers in ordered pairs as indicating locations in quadrants of the coordinate plane; recognize that when two ordered pairs differ only by signs, the locations of the points are related by reflections across one or both axes. c. Find and position integers and other rational numbers on a horizontal or vertical number line diagram; find and position pairs of integers and other rational numbers on a coordinate plane.	**pp. 169–172, 395–400, 407–412, 421–424, 425–428, 429–430**
CC.6.NS.7 Understand ordering and absolute value of rational numbers. a. Interpret statements of inequality as statements about the relative position of two numbers on a number line diagram. b. Write, interpret, and explain statements of order for rational numbers in real-world contexts. c. Understand the absolute value of a rational number as its distance from 0 on the number line; interpret absolute value as magnitude for a positive or negative quantity in a real-world situation. d. Distinguish comparisons of absolute value from statements about order.	**pp. 183–188, 189–192, 193–194, 401–406, 425–428, 429–430**
CC.6.NS.8 Solve real–world and mathematical problems by graphing points in all four quadrants of the coordinate plane. Include use of coordinates and absolute value to find distances between points with the same first coordinate or the same second coordinate.	**pp. 407–412, 413–420, 425–428, 429–430**

Expressions and Equations	Citations
CC.6.EE.1 Write and evaluate numerical expressions involving whole-number exponents.	**pp. 15–20, 33–36, 37–38, 91–94**
CC.6.EE.2 Write, read, and evaluate expressions in which letters stand for numbers. **a.** Write expressions that record operations with numbers and with letters standing for numbers. **b.** Identify parts of an expression using mathematical terms (sum, term, product, factor, quotient, coefficient); view one or more parts of an expression as a single entity. **c.** Evaluate expressions at specific values of their variables. Include expressions that arise from formulas used in real-world problems. Perform arithmetic operations, including those involving whole-number exponents, in the conventional order when there are no parentheses to specify a particular order (Order of Operations).	**pp. 21–26, 33–36, 37–38, 45–50, 51–56, 57–60, 91–94, 95–96, 161–168, 351–356**
CC.6.EE.3 Apply the properties of operations to generate equivalent expressions.	**pp. 27–32, 33–36, 37–38, 91–94, 161–168, 189–192, 193–194**
CC.6.EE.4 Identify when two expressions are equivalent (i.e., when the two expressions name the same number regardless of which value is substituted into them).	**pp. 91–94, 161–168, 189–192, 193–194**
CC.6.EE.5 Understand solving an equation or inequality as a process of answering a question: which values from a specified set, if any, make the equation or inequality true? Use substitution to determine whether a given number in a specified set makes an equation or inequality true.	**pp. 61–66, 95–96, 451–456, 457–460**
CC.6.EE.6 Use variables to represent numbers and write expressions when solving a real-world or mathematical problem; understand that a variable can represent an unknown number, or, depending on the purpose at hand, any number in a specified set.	**pp. 61–66, 67–72, 73–78, 79–84, 85–90, 91–94, 95–96, 143–144, 235–236, 451–456, 457–460**
CC.6.EE.7 Solve real-world and mathematical problems by writing and solving equations of the form $x + p = q$ and $px = q$ for cases in which p, q and x are all nonnegative rational numbers.	**pp. 67–72, 73–78, 79–84, 85–90, 95–96, 135–138, 143–144, 209–212, 213–216, 231-234, 235–236, 457–460**
CC.6.EE.8 Write an inequality of the form $x > c$ or $x < c$ to represent a constraint or condition in a real-world or mathematical problem. Recognize that inequalities of the form $x > c$ or $x < c$ have infinitely many solutions; represent solutions of such inequalities on number line diagrams.	**pp. 451–456, 457–460, 461–462**
CC.6.EE.9 Use variables to represent two quantities in a real-world problem that change in relationship to one another; write an equation to express one quantity, thought of as the dependent variable, in terms of the other quantity, thought of as the independent variable. Analyze the relationship between the dependent and independent variables using graphs and tables, and relate these to the equation.	**pp. 437–440, 441–446, 457–460, 461–462**

© Houghton Mifflin Harcourt Publishing Company

Geometry	Citations
CC.6.G.1 Find the area of right triangles, other triangles, special quadrilaterals, and polygons by composing into rectangles or decomposing into triangles and other shapes; apply these techniques in the context of solving real-world and mathematical problems.	**pp. 351–356, 357–364, 365–370, 383–386, 387–388**
CC.6.G.2 Find the volume of a right rectangular prism with fractional edge lengths by packing it with unit cubes of the appropriate unit fraction edge lengths, and show that the volume is the same as would be found by multiplying the edge lengths of the prism. Apply the formulas $V = l\,w\,h$ and $V = b\,h$ to find volumes of right rectangular prisms with fractional edge lengths in the context of solving real-world and mathematical problems.	**pp. 371–376, 383–386, 387–388**
CC.6.G.3 Draw polygons in the coordinate plane given coordinates for the vertices; use coordinates to find the length of a side joining points with the same first coordinate or the same second coordinate. Apply these techniques in the context of solving real-world and mathematical problems.	**pp. 383–386, 413–420, 429–430**
CC.6.G.4 Represent three-dimensional figures using nets made up of rectangles and triangles, and use the nets to find the surface area of these figures. Apply these techniques in the context of solving real-world and mathematical problems.	**pp. 377–382, 383–386, 387–388**

Statistics and Probability	Citations
CC.6.SP.1 Recognize a statistical question as one that anticipates variability in the data related to the question and accounts for it in the answers.	**pp. 259–264, 271–274**
CC.6.SP.2 Understand that a set of data collected to answer a statistical question has a distribution which can be described by its center, spread, and overall shape.	**pp. 271–274, 275–276**
CC.6.SP.3 Recognize that a measure of center for a numerical data set summarizes all of its values with a single number, while a measure of variation describes how its values vary with a single number.	**pp. 243–248, 271–274**
CC.6.SP.4 Display numerical data in plots on a number line, including dot plots, histograms, and box plots.	**pp. 253–258, 259–264, 271–274, 275–276**
CC.6.SP.5 Summarize numerical data sets in relation to their context, such as by: a. Reporting the number of observations. b. Describing the nature of the attribute under investigation, including how it was measured and its units of measurement. c. Giving quantitative measures of center (median and/or mean) and variability (interquartile range and/or mean absolute deviation), as well as describing any overall pattern and any striking deviations from the overall pattern with reference to the context in which the data were gathered. d. Relating the choice of measures of center and variability to the shape of the data distribution and the context in which the data were gathered.	**pp. 243–248, 249–252, 253–258, 265–270, 271–274, 275–276**